The Last Hurrah
of the James-Younger Gang

The Last Hurrah
of the James-Younger Gang

ROBERT BARR SMITH

UNIVERSITY OF OKLAHOMA PRESS : NORMAN

ALSO BY ROBERT BARR SMITH

Men at War (New York, 1997)
Daltons! The Raid on Coffeyville, Kansas (Norman, Okla., 1996)
To the Last Cartridge (New York, 1994)
Practical Legal Writing for Legal Assistants (Minneapolis/St. Paul, 1996)
The Literate Lawyer (Charlottesville, Va., 1995)

Library of Congress Cataloging-in-Publication Data

Smith, Robert B. (Robert Barr), 1933–
    The last hurrah of the James-Younger gang / Robert Barr Smith.
        p.   cm.
    Includes bibliographical references and index.
    ISBN 0-8061-3353-8 (hc : alk. paper)
    1. Northfield (Minn.)—History—19th century.   2. Outlaws—
Minnesota—Northfield—History—19th century.   3. Gangs—
Minnesota—Northfield—History—19th century.   4. Younger, Cole,
1844–1916.   5. Younger, James, 1848–1902.   6. James, Frank, 1844–1915.
7. James, Jesse, 1847–1882.   I. Title.

F614.N63 S65 2001
977.6'555—dc21

                                                                2001016179

The paper in this book meets the guidelines for permanence and durabil-
ity of the Committee on Production Guidelines for Book Longevity of the
Council on Library Resources, Inc.

1   2   3   4   5   6   7   8   9   10

To the citizens of Northfield, Minnesota, who took on and beat the James-Younger gang, the most famous robbers of all time, and especially to the two citizens killed during the raid.

And to the men of Madelia and other Minnesota towns who pursued the remaining outlaws, drove off the famed James brothers, and killed or captured the rest.

Whoso consents to stand on Duty,
in the army, on the railway train,
in the banking-house or store, must
do it with open eyes, ready to take
the consequences, fully determined,
whatever befall, to play the man

FUNERAL ORATION FOR JOSEPH LEE HEYWOOD

CONTENTS

Illustrations

Bill Caldwell

The Madelia posse that captured the Younger brothers

Transcription of a page from the diary of Newton Persons

MAPS

ACKNOWLEDGMENTS

Nobody writes alone. Every writer has help from many people, and I am no exception. If I have failed to mention anyone here, I apologize.

I am especially indebted to John Lovett, head of the University of Oklahoma Western History Library, who is wonderfully knowledgeable and always ready to help and patiently put up with long afternoons when I monopolized his microfiche machine. Without him and his staff, this book would never have come to pass.

I also owe special thanks to Lisa Bowles of the University of Oklahoma Law Library, who patiently and cheerfully obtained all manner of arcane books for me. If what I needed existed anywhere, Lisa found it for me.

Much help came from the Northfield Historical Society, especially from the very knowledgeable curator of its museum, Sue Garwood-DeLong, and from the personnel of the Northfield Public Library. I owe thanks also to the St. Paul Public Library, especially to reference librarian Brian Karschnia.

In Madelia, the city government offices made calls for me to locate personnel from the Watonwan County Historical Center, and that center kindly opened up on a closed day, in a drenching rain, just so that I could see the exhibits pertaining to the Northfield raid. Subsequently, the museum director, Ruth Anderson, helped me immeasurably in gathering additional materials. Bruce Lindquist, publisher-editor of the Madelia *Times-Messenger*, obliged with an issue that collected considerable information about the raid and the fight at Hanska Slough.

I am grateful to the Rice County Historical Society, Faribault, especially researcher Fran Miller, who went out of his way to collect materials pertaining to the Northfield raid.

The Western History Document Collection at the University of Missouri supplied reams of document copies, and did so with amazing speed. I especially appreciate the assistance of Sharon Brock, who made certain I had what I needed and helped me to determine which of the many documents would be most useful.

The staff of the University of Oklahoma Press, from production personnel to the copyeditor, were without exception highly professional and pleasant to work with, unwilling to settle for anything less than a perfect job. Any claim to excellence this book may have is due in large measure to Jean Hurtado. Any mistakes are mine own.

Last, but surely not least, my thanks to my wife, always supportive and understanding, tolerating my grumbling and profanity and the tapping of my computer keys far into the night.

THE LAST HURRAH
OF THE JAMES-YOUNGER GANG

INTRODUCTION

This is the story of a bandit raid back in 1876. On a pretty autumn day in that far-off year, eight professional outlaws rode into a small town to terrorize and rob its hardworking citizens of their savings. The raid remains the most famous event in western outlaw history, eclipsing its closest rival, the Dalton gang's 1892 disaster at Coffeyville, Kansas. The outlaws were the James-Younger gang, certainly the most celebrated criminals in American history. The place was Northfield, Minnesota.

Northfield seemed the perfect target for the gang. It was a peaceful sort of place, the kind of orderly hamlet where nobody carried a gun. It was a busy mill town, the heart of prosperous farm country, so the outlaws expected there would be lots of money in the bank, ripe for the picking. And the town was small, so they assumed it would be easy to ride clear in a hurry after cleaning out the bank. Moreover, the town had only one bank, which meant all the money was handily collected in one place. All of these factors made Northfield a fine target, a better target, for example, than nearby Mankato, where the citizens' savings were scattered among three banks.

These badmen were bold and confident, with the arrogance of experienced hoodlums who had never known defeat. They were, after all, the James-Younger gang, the much-publicized terrors of

Missouri, Kentucky, Texas, and Kansas. The gang included several of the toughest gunmen in the outlaw world, killers and robbers by trade. What soft-handed townspeople, what peaceful sodbusters, would dare to oppose them? But appearances were deceiving. The outlaws could not know that this raid would be different. They were riding into a hornet's nest.

The James-Younger gang is the most romanticized band of outlaws since Robin Hood and his Merry Men of Sherwood Forest. Even at the time of their depredations, there was much nonsense written about them, most of it glorifying them as champions of the oppressed, generous to the poor and downtrodden, courteous to good women, and nice to children. They were painted as persecuted, honest southern boys, bedeviled by a remorseless society; their Sheriff of Nottingham was the damnyankee government and all its works.

The chief prophet of the noble outlaw faith was one John N. Edwards, a Missouri newspaper editor, who spent years turning these ordinary criminals into paragons of southern manhood. Their criminal deeds were not really their fault, he wrote, for "they were hunted, they were human." Of Jesse James, Edwards wrote,

> We call him outlaw, but Fate made him so. When the war came he was just turned fifteen. The border was all aflame with steel and fire and ambuscade and slaughter. He flung himself into a band which had a black flag for a banner and devils for riders. . . . When the war closed, Jesse James had no home. Proscribed, hunted, shot, driven away from among his people, a price put on his head—what else could he do? . . . He refused to be banished from his birthright, and when he was hunted he turned savagely about and hunted his hunters. Would to God he were alive today to make a righteous butchery of a few more of them.[1]

If Edwards was the longest-winded and most vociferous partisan of the outlaws, he was certainly not alone. Many Missouri people felt as Edwards did, choosing to view the outlaw careers of the Jameses and Youngers as a continuation of the war. The outlaws helped to create their own myth, too, especially Jesse James. Jesse was fond of writing letters to newspapers denying involvement in this or that crime. And one 1872 letter, probably Jesse's work, put the fable exactly: "We rob the rich and give it to the poor."[2] Jesse and his cohorts were well on their way to being folk heroes, long before they decided to rob damnyankees up in Minnesota. When movies came along, filmmakers couldn't wait to get their hands on the James-Younger myth. The silver screen proceeded apace to transmogrify some pretty ordinary hoodlums into down-home boys, not really bad, just misunderstood.

And so, in large measure, treatment of the James-Younger gang in some books and most movies is simply a product of the Robin Hood folklore that has long surrounded the crimes they committed. Consider this verse from a ballad about Jesse:

> Jesse James was one of his names,
> Another it was Howard.
> He robbed the rich of every stitch.
> You bet, he was no coward.
> Jesse stole from the rich
> And he gave to the poor,
> He'd a hand and a heart and a brain.

If Jesse James stole from the rich out of preference, it was only because the rich had more money than poor people did. Edwards and all the others who have likened the James-Younger gang to Robin Hood and his Merry Men have missed at least one simple point: seldom does much of the money in banks belong to the banker. So it was in the Midwest of the 1860s, 1870s, and 1880s, the heyday of the gang. Then and now much of the assets of a bank was made up of the pittances painstakingly saved by a lot of ordinary folks. When a bank was robbed, it was those common people who suffered most, there being no helpful FDIC standing by to protect them from ruin.

Still, the legend of the noble outlaw persisted and grew, long after John Edwards had gone to dust. There were tales of Jesse

James saving the widow's homestead from the heartless banker, an act of largesse that happened all over the west, depending on who told the story. And then there was the transparent nonsense that "them boys was druv to it," good southern kids made outlaws by persecution after the Civil War. There was even the tale about Jesse turning a young man from a life of crime to the straight and narrow path. It's too good not to tell.

It seems a young man stuck up a store, escaping with only three dollars. His horse dead, he was picked up and carried to safety by a mounted stranger. Once clear of pursuit, the stranger questioned the young man and then told him he would take the three dollars back to the store owner. Then came the lecture: "I would like to be where you are, young man, and have the chance that you have to straighten up and go straight; but I am Jesse James and will never be given the chance that you have."[3] After that, the story goes, Jesse found the boy a job, and the young man ultimately succeeded in life. It's a wonderful tale but in sober fact it's probably just another fable. For the teller of the tale learned it only after the Dalton gang had been exterminated at Coffeyville, Kansas. That was 1892, and by then Jesse James had been in his grave for a decade.

Dozens of books and articles have further distorted the history of the James-Younger gang. They range from badly twisted articles in western magazines to dozens of penny dreadfuls like this one from the New York Detective Library: *Frank Reade, The Inventor, Chasing the James Boys with His Steam Team.* Or this one, another penny dreadful from the Log Cabin Library: *Jesse, the Outlaw: A Narrative of the James Boys by Captain Jake Shakelford, the Western Detective.*

Much more appeared in weekly publications such as the *Wide Awake Library*, which did at least one issue on the Northfield raid, filled with invented dialogue, fictitious characters, astonishing events that never happened, and a few more or less real names (Cole Younger was called "Cale"). Even today the James boys ride again in the contemporary comic-book adventures of Lucky Luke. Luke is a laid-back cowboy who rides about on his genius horse,

Jolly Jumper, righting wrongs and protecting the oppressed. He appears all over the world in more than twenty languages, running down all kinds of famous outlaws (he did in the Dalton gang, too, all of whom were drawn to look like Adolf Hitler). At least in the *Lucky Luke* series the bad guys are characterized as buffoons, not heroes. In *Lucky Luke* the James boys—Frank quotes Shakespeare a lot—and a doltish Cole Younger end up being tarred and feathered and run out of town.

Every reader is entitled to know the prejudices and points of view of an author. We all have them, and they color our writing to some degree, no matter how hard we try to be impartial. My view is that the James boys and the Younger brothers were no more than ordinary criminals, bullies who stole the fruits of others' labors because it beat working and did a good deal to inflate their twisted egos. A lot of print and celluloid has been devoted to transforming these men into heroes.

A great deal of time and print has been expended on the thesis that the Jameses and Youngers were driven to a life of crime because they had been on the wrong side in the Civil War and the Yankees would not permit them to live peaceful lives. It is true that both the James boys and Cole and Jim Younger had ridden with the Missouri bushwhackers, specifically, the guerrilla bands of William Clarke Quantrill and "Bloody Bill" Anderson, the worst of a very bad bunch. And it is true that the frontier fighting spilled a lot of blood, much of it innocent, and left an abiding legacy of distrust and downright hatred. That legacy took a very long time to pass away. Before it did, a lot more blood was shed, some of it even after the Confederacy had surrendered.

The guerrilla fighting in Kansas and Missouri was as vicious as war can get, a long and ugly crimson streak of murder, arson, and rape, of midnight burnings and cattle killing, of torture and calculated brutality on both sides. Neither Quantrill nor Bloody Bill survived the war, but many of their followers did. And if there was some paying off of old scores after the war, if it was tough to start over in peaceful pursuits, most of the surviving bushwhackers resumed their lives as law-abiding citizens. They became farmers and merchants, artisans and preachers, lawmen and stockmen, parents and grandparents.

My great-grandfather, an outspoken southern partisan in Platte County, Missouri, was among those who went on with their lives after the guns fell silent. Although he did not ride with the bush-whackers during the war, his views were so well known, so loudly expressed, that in 1864 he was hunted through one long night by vengeful Union supporters intent on killing him. In time, however, along with nearly all the other Missouri rebels, my great-grandfa-ther picked up his life and went on. He died in 1884, a respected member of the community. He and most of the other citizens who had supported the southern cause, Quantrill men or not, returned to the ways of peace.

But not the James and Younger boys.

Whatever moved the brothers to turn their hands to dishonest living, whether it was greed, sadism, love of notoriety, a taste for excitement, or some combination of these potent elixirs, they were not "driven" to make a living robbing and killing people. Nor were they moved by some powerful drive to be avenged on the Yankees, even though they used revenge as a convenient excuse. Most of their crimes touched people from states in which many men had supported the South, especially Kentucky and their home state, Missouri. Whatever compassion they may have felt toward their fellow Missourians, whatever loyalty they felt toward their home state, it did not temper their greed. They may have felt some brief remorse, but they robbed the home folks anyway. And killed.

The history of the American West, especially its badmen, is the province of myth and fable. The history of the James-Younger gang, and their disaster at Northfield, is replete with all sorts of wonderful tales that may or may not be true. I have tried to sort out the fabulous from what is probably the truth, and I have prob-ably guessed wrong more than once. As with all good pieces of western mythology, a good many questions remain unanswered.

In the saga of the Northfield raid, the major riddle is whether the James brothers were present at all. Neither one admitted he was there, nor did any of the Younger boys publicly say Frank and Jesse were part of the gang. The absence of any such evidence has moved some writers to conclude that there is no factual basis on which to conclude that the Jameses were part of the outlaw gang. There *is* some very persuasive evidence, however, and there are some fairly powerful inferences to be drawn from it. It suffices to convince me, at least, that both James brothers were present at Northfield and that one of them, probably Frank, cold-bloodedly murdered the assistant cashier of the First National Bank of Northfield.

So this is the story of a bandit raid, of the citizens of a stout, brave little town, and of a posse of ordinary men who weren't afraid to take on a gang of famous criminals. The raid ended in disaster for the outlaws and triumph for the people of Northfield. The raid was the trademark shoot-and-hurrah James-Younger attack, a botched raid by a collection of arrogant hoodlums who thought they could push peaceful citizens around and take what these citizens had saved. To some degree this is the story of an outlaw gang, but, more important, it is the story of the ordinary citizens of Northfield and Madelia and other quiet southern Minnesota townspeople who refused to be buffaloed by a band of lawless ruffians.

Southern Minnesota was, and is, the heart of the heart of America, industrious, law-abiding, warm, and welcoming. It is a fine area, a pleasure to visit, and its people are pleasant and friendly. You have the feeling, though, that if another band of outlaws showed up to hurrah one of its towns today, the citizens would reach for their rifles again, just as they did in 1876.

CHAPTER ONE

THE DESPERADOES

This book is not primarily about the hoodlums who made up the James-Younger gang, but the gang members are nevertheless major players in the Northfield drama and thus require some space. In the first place, it is important to remember that in one way or another all of these men were products of the vicious Civil War guerrilla struggle along the Kansas border, or of the chaos of postwar Missouri, or of both. Although this does not begin to excuse their behavior—always lawless, sometimes downright sadistic— it goes far to explain their indifference to human life and property. As I commented in the introduction, the James brothers and the Youngers were no more "driven" to a postwar life of crime than any other Missouri guerrilla was. What the border war *did* do, however, was give the brothers a chance to taste the intoxicating delights of licence and violence and easy money. The boys' natural proclivities did the rest.

The James brothers were veterans of the bushwhackers, the Civil War guerrilla bands of Quantrill and George Todd and Bloody Bill Anderson. So were Cole Younger and his brother Jim. Bob and John Younger were too young for the war but turned outlaw after the fighting had ended. There is a striking similarity between the two sets of brothers. The James boys hailed from a farm in Clay County, in western Missouri; the Youngers were born in Lee's

Summit, just to the south in adjoining Jackson County. Both families were solid, honest, respectable and, by the standards of the time, well-to-do. Both families suffered terribly during the war, but so did most families in the region.

It is said that the Youngers and Jameses were related, but this is just one of the many myths that have grown up around American outlaws. The Youngers *were* related to the Oklahoma outlaws Grat, Bob, and Emmett Dalton, who were shot down in 1892 by angry citizens in Coffeyville, Kansas. Adeline Dalton, the mother of Grat, Bob, and Emmett (and of Bill, killed later as part of the Doolin gang), was a Younger, the aunt of Cole and the rest of the boys. Oddly, there was a remote connection by marriage: a niece of the second husband of the James boys' mother married Cole Younger's uncle.[1] However, there was no blood connection between the Younger brothers and the James boys, except for the spilled blood of other people.

The James boys' father, Robert, became a minister and settled in Clay County with his wife, Zerelda Cole. They worked a 275-acre farm near Kearney (then called Centerville), and Robert still found time to found three Baptist churches and help to establish William Jewell College in Liberty. Of their four children, three lived to adulthood, a daughter and two sons. The boys were Alexander Franklin James, called Frank, and Jesse Woodson James.

There's a certain amount of mythology surrounding even the early days of the James brothers' life in Missouri. For example, one source says that the boys were actually half brothers, Jesse having been sired by "a Clay County Physician." The same source also maintains that Bob Ford didn't kill Jesse, who lived on for many years under another name. A similar story is told by a superannuated impostor, one J. Frank Dalton—that he was in fact Jesse James, having lived for a century or so and used "72 identities" while gadding about the country on the business of the "Knights of the Golden Circle." The Knights were supposed to be a group of unreconstructed rebels who maintained huge repositories of weapons for a second civil war and even furnished Gatling guns to the Sioux who killed Custer. There were *two* Jesse Jameses, according to this tale, the outlaw Jesse and his cousin, "Dingus." Conveniently for outlaw history, this Jesse also had a brother named Frank, a doctor, and they happened to have a brother-in-law named Cole Younger, a "civil engineer." And so on, curiouser and curiouser.[2]

There's a whole book about this, including the story that Jesse James actually killed Wild Bill Hickok in Deadwood and was once married to Myra Maybelle Shirley, better known to history as Belle Starr.[3] As if that weren't enough, it asserts that Jesse became one of Henry Ford's original backers and a financial supporter of Thomas Edison. The book is a delight to read but about as reliable as Mother Goose. Sadly for those who believed claptrap like this, the exhumation and DNA testing of the body in Jesse James's grave proved conclusively that Jesse was indeed murdered in St. Joseph back in 1882 and had been underground ever since.

In fact, both Jesse and Frank were full brothers and grew up on their parents' farm in Clay County. What little education the boys had, they received at rural Pleasant Grove School. Reverend Robert James's busy, respectable life changed abruptly in 1850, when he went west to the California gold fields. In those days many men left their families for the California diggin's simply to escape the routine of married life, but Robert seems to have had loftier motives. For all Reverend James's good works would not provide what he wanted most for his growing family—education.

The accepted reason for his going is that he thought he might turn California paydirt into more Missouri churches and education for his children. Reverend James never returned. He died in Marysville not long after he got to the gold country, probably of cholera, and the family was left on its own. Zerelda was a widow at twenty-six.

Zerelda Cole James was made of stern stuff, a formidable lady almost six feet tall. She was determined to hold on to the farm and raise her children. And so in 1855, after a short-lived, unhappy marriage to a farmer named Simms, she married Dr. Reuben Samuel. By all accounts, the doctor was a gentle, kind man who treated Zerelda's boys and their sister, Susan, as his own. The children called him Pappy. Life on the Samuel-James farm flowed on in its peaceful, busy way, and the family seems to have been happy and close. In time Dr. Samuel and Zerelda produced four more children.

The James brothers grew up as ordinary Missouri farm kids accustomed to the outdoors and to hard work. Religion played a substantial part in the life of the family, and one story says it was a lasting one. Years after Jesse had taken the outlaw trail, he met a Baptist minister who had known him before the war. Even then, the minister said, even after all the blood, Jesse still carried his New Testament, tattered and much thumbed. And so the James boys grew up, used to the good things of Missouri farm life: lots of hard work, a close family, and church on Sundays.

Until the war. The trouble had been coming for a long time, and there had been rumblings and mutterings long before the first cannon spat its venom at Fort Sumter. The James family's Clay County was in the eye of the storm. The boys and their neighbors grew up in a world permeated by the violence and hatred and passionate rhetoric of the death struggle between free soil and slavery. There was venom even in the children's play, where the enemy was always old John Brown and the Kansas Redleg leader Jim Lane.

The roots of the bitter struggle along the Kansas-Missouri border had been growing deep for twenty years and more. Back in 1820 the Missouri Compromise established that all of what was called the Unorganized Territory—the Louisiana Purchase less Missouri—should be free soil. In 1854 two new territories were created, Kansas and Nebraska. The residents of each were to decide whether slavery would be permitted in their territory. The pro-slavery party was convinced that Nebraska would vote free-soil and became determined to bring Kansas into the Union as a slave state. If Kansas entered the Union on the free-soil side, the South would lose its critical free soil/slave state equilibrium in the United States Senate.

Such a loss of power was unthinkable, and to prevent it the pro-slavery men were determined to fight. The anti-slavery settlers were equally dedicated. Colonies of New England immigrants appeared in Kansas, and their settlements began to grow and multiply. Money poured in from the East to support them, and so did crates of Sharps rifles, affectionately known as "Beecher's Bibles" after the abolitionist clergyman. Some called these free-soil colonists "rifle Christians."[4] A good many Union men lumped all southern sympathizers together as poor white trash, vulgar thugs the free-soil men collectively and contemptuously called "pukes." Not to be outdone, southern colonists appeared as well, and men began to openly take sides. And as people became angrier, they became less particular about how they advanced their political and moral aims.

As one Kansas newspaper bitterly editorialized, "I have seen thousands of armed Missourians cross the river . . . to vote in an election, and return home the next day." And, indeed, when Kansas elected a pro-slavery legislature in 1855, 6,307 votes were cast by only 2,905 lawful voters. The surplus ballots came from a mob of invaders from Missouri, with "guns on their shoulders, revolvers stuffing their belts, bowie knives protruding from their boot-tops, and generous rations of whiskey in their wagons."[5]

"Bleeding Kansas," the eastern papers called it, and the name stuck. There was much raiding, stock killing, and barn burning certainly, but how much actual human bleeding there was will never be known. One source estimates that no more than fifty-five men died in factional strife during the 1850s.[6] Another account, however, puts the death toll at about two hundred for a single thirteen-month period in 1855–56.[7] As the years went by the hatred mounted, even among the majority of Kansas men who only wanted a new life and a place to call their own.

Some of the Missouri "border ruffians" were indeed the scum of the earth. For example, there are few nastier pieces of work in history than William Clarke Quantrill, leader of the bushwhacker band with which Frank James rode during much of the war. In later days southern sympathizers frequently portrayed Quantrill as a dashing cavalier, ever merciless to the detested Redlegs and Jayhawkers, unfailingly courteous and deferential to the ladies.

Quantrill, always conscious of his concocted image, seems to have cultivated a reputation for gallantry, writing four poorly rhymed poetic verses in the autograph album of a Wakefield, Kentucky, lass, Miss Nannie Dawson. One of them went like this:

> My horse is at the door
> And the enemy I soon may see
> But before I go, Miss Nannie,
> Here's a double health to thee.[8]

Thus the southern sympathizers, who for their part cordially detested Union partisans of the same stripe, men such as Doc Jennison and Jim Lane, the "Grim Chieftan," who killed, robbed, and generally terrorized anybody who seemed to show a preference for the South.

Somewhere in between each side's characterization of the other as the Antichrist, somewhere in the middle, lay the truth, not that many people cared much about that any longer. By the time fighting broke out between the United States and the new Confederacy, both sides in Missouri and Kansas had gone far beyond reason or toleration or even a little mercy.

Things had gotten so bad that in May 1856, in the chamber of the United States Senate, a South Carolina firebrand very nearly killed abolitionist Massachusetts senator Charles Sumner. Representative Preston Brooks, the attacker, beat the older man terribly with a heavy cane after Sumner had spent two days fulminating against "the harlot slavery" and castigating one of its staunch partisans, Brooks's kinsman Andrew Butler, the senator from South Carolina.[9] Brooks did not even let Sumner rise from his seat before he attacked: chivalry was one of the first casualties of this bitter dispute. After the assault southerners sent Brooks dozens of canes in congratulation, another sign of the depth and bitterness of the division over slavery.

The day before Brooks's cane splashed blood across the benches of the Senate, a mob of pro-slavery border ruffians, many of them from nearby Missouri, had descended on the staunchly free-state town of Lawrence, Kansas. Lawrence was named for a Massachusetts mill owner whose fortune helped to support anti-slavery causes, and its streets bore names like New Hampshire and Vermont. The border ruffians said they were a lawfully appointed posse, but they sure didn't act like one. Out in front of the ruffians was a former United States senator, David Atchison, who made sure the mob went about its duty in the proper spirit: "Be brave, be orderly, and if one man or woman dare stand in your way, blow them to hell with a chunk of cold lead."[10]

That edifying exhortation pretty well set the tone for the day, and the ruffians, brim-full of righteousness and booze, lived up to their names, burning, brutalizing, looting, and even killing a couple of Lawrence's residents. Abolitionist papers all over the country cried out at the Lawrence "massacre" and free-soil immigrants poured into the territory in great numbers. And if what happened at Lawrence was bad, there was much worse to come.

In the same week of the Lawrence raid and Brooks's battering of Sumner, an aging fanatic, a perpetual drifter who had failed repeatedly at everything but fathering children, set out to avenge both of these events in the holy name of abolition. Skulking through the warm May night at a place called Dutch Henry's Crossing, grim old John Brown and his dutiful sons slashed unarmed Pottawatomie Creek farmers to bloody death with surplus artillery swords. The victims were said to be "pro-slavery men," although none of them owned slaves. Afterward Brown asked God's blessing on this ugly slaughter, confident that the Almighty somehow rejoiced at murder in the dark. Old Brown had already traveled well down the long, dreary road to Harper's Ferry, slaughtering men who had not harmed him and delighting in the blood.

It is one of the enduring paradoxes of American history that this seedy old man, drenched in the blood of other people, would become a rallying point for a good cause, subject of a song that would become the anthem of abolition. A Kansas farmer, writing in his diary, saw the future clearly and scribbled out this doggerel:

Old Brown
John Brown
Osawatomie Brown
He'll trouble them more when his Coffin's
nailed down![11]

Later on, on the quiet Marais des Cygnes River, pro-slavery marauders murdered free-soil settlers, an event that horrified eastern abolitionists and even moved John Greenleaf Whittier to write a poem about the event. Other pro-slavery men burned Brown's home at Osawatomie and killed one of his sons. In Easton, Kansas, border ruffians murdered a free-soil man, butchering him with hatchets until he was "literally chopped to pieces . . . and his bleeding corpse flung before his young wife."[12] A free-soil settler named Buffum pleaded with southern partisans to be allowed to keep his team of horses; he was, he said, crippled, and the support of his old father, two sisters, and his deaf-mute brother. For answer he got a bullet in the belly as a "God-damned abolitionist."

And so long before the cannons roared at Sumter, Kansas had known a thousand angry days and fear-haunted nights, and nothing would ever be quite the same again. As a result, the border war would reach heights of ferocity unsurpassed anyplace else in America. Both Jayhawkers and Ruffians believed passionately in the righteousness of their cause, so passionately that the Ten Commandments ceased to apply to anybody who disagreed with them.

This was the angry, bitter, passionate world in which the James brothers grew to manhood. In their part of western Missouri, in Clay and Jackson and Platte Counties, a great many people favored the South, and as the violence grew in intensity men were increasingly forced to take sides.

In late April of 1861 the war came to Missouri. Frank James enlisted at Centerville on May 4, when the Confederate general Sterling Price came recruiting. Frank was eighteen then, tall, skinny, and hawk nosed. He was well educated for his time as well, an avid reader of the classics and fond of quoting from Shakespeare. Popular history says he was able to read German, French, and Spanish, although it is not clear where he would have acquired these skills in rural Missouri.

Sterling Price's expedition ran head-on into Nathaniel Lyon's small Union force at Wilson's Creek, Missouri, on August 10, 1861. Wilson's Creek was probably young Frank's first experience of real action. As Civil War battles went it was small, but it was a serious fight, and a good many men died in it. Wilson's Creek could fairly be called a rebel victory, even though the Union force withdrew in reasonably good order. Even so, the Confederate forces were driven out of Missouri into Arkansas by early 1862. Along the way, a different sort of enemy attacked Frank James: ordinary measles. Left behind when Price fell back from Springfield in February 1862, Frank was captured, somewhat ignominiously lying in a hospital bed. He was paroled and returned to his mother's farm.

One story has Frank arrested by local Union officials and released on bond, apparently after signing the customary oath of allegiance to the United States. Still, he was suspect, suspect in a highly suspicious land. Another version says that in spring 1863 he was again jailed in Liberty, Missouri, and at last he had enough. Frank broke jail, and after that he could only "go to the brush," as the saying went.

Frank now entered the world of the guerrilla, a dreary, twilight world of ambush, murder, and betrayal. In the *Annals of Platte County*, the county historian bewailed the anarchy and brutality of western Missouri in 1863:

> Prowling murderers, by day, dressed in Federal uniform and bearing forged military orders, searched houses, barns, and stables for arms; and at night returned as "Red-legs" to rob and hang the people. The militia were active in suppressing "bushwhackers," but gave themselves no concern about thieves and murderers. I administered [the wills] on three persons who were murdered by "Red-legs."[13]

Roving bands of guerrillas were much given to hanging to make men divulge where they had hidden their valuables, if they had any. The idea was to hoist a man off the ground, let him strangle and struggle a while, then let him down and ask him where his treasures were. If his replies were displeasing to his tormentors, the process was repeated. And sometimes, by neglect or design, even men who were willing to hand over everything were let down too late.

Brutality and arson and murder by one side inevitably provoked retaliation by the other. In response to the ravages of Quantrill's band, the Union command ordered that captured guerrillas should "be hung as robbers and murderers" rather than treated as prisoners of war. Quantrill's brutality to prisoners, only occasional before, became a regular practice. Other bushwhacker leaders like Bloody Bill Anderson had always delighted in killing their enemies. The federals responded in kind.

Much of the killing done by Anderson and men like him—on both sides—was not directed at armed men in enemy uniform. In the autumn of 1864 a guerrilla band that included both James boys rode up to the home of a Mr. Baynes in Chariton County, Missouri. The band, dressed in Union uniform, called Baynes outside to ask directions, pretending to have lost their way. When they rode off, they left Baynes dead in his own doorway, five bullets in his body. His crime was apparently no more than having Union sympathies.

The worst of the guerrilla bands on both sides paid little attention to wearing uniform or to any of the other customs of war. Bushwhackers often dressed in Union blue, and federal militia frequently rode in civilian clothing. Many bands simply used the excuse of war to prey on anybody they met. One southerner summed up the situation pretty well: "Low lived men who claim to be Union or Rebel as occasion requires, [ride] the country destroying life and property, regardless of law and usages of regular warfare."[14]

Many regular soldiers despised all guerrillas, no matter which side they fought on. Tough rebel brigadier Tom Rosser spoke for all real soldiers on both sides. Guerrillas were, he said, a "nuisance and an evil to the service, . . . a terror to the citizens and an injury to the cause, . . . a band of thieves, stealing, pillaging, plundering and doing every manner of mischief and crime."[15]

On a single night in Platte County, next door to Clay County on the west, marauders hanged two citizens and robbed a third after strangling him almost to death. They were in the process of committing still a fourth outrage, hanging an eighty-year-old man, when local miltia jumped them. The criminals were Red-legs—at least that's what they said they were. In any case, they galloped off with one man wounded, leaving behind all manner of loot, including a stolen burial suit. A Platte County newspaper, the Weston *Sentinel*, sneered, "There were no marble yards on their route, or doubtless each of them would have stolen himself a tombstone."[16]

Much verdant farm country turned to wasteland as farmers packed up what they had left and sought safety from the depredations of the guerrillas on both sides. Many citizens moved west to California and Oregon; others fled to Iowa and Illinois, or to towns held securely by regular Union garrisons. Protected by dependable troops, they felt reasonably safe, able, as one said, to walk the streets "in broad open daylight." Behind them the refugees left a "once pleasant country" in ugly emptiness, "forsaken and desolated, ruined, and only fit to bats, owls, and cockralls to inhabit. . . . Everywhere the country was ravaged and burned-out, dotted with . . . the ruins of buildings, despoiled of doors, sashes, and everything movable."[17]

All of western Missouri was scarred by stone chimneys standing alone and forlorn, like headstones, above the charred ruins of burned-out homes. For years after the war these lonely chimneys were called "Jennison Monuments," after ferocious Doc Jennison, whose Seventh Kansas Volunteer Cavalry burned and killed just as enthusiastically as the guerrillas of Quantrill and Anderson.

Things really went to hell in a handbasket in the summer of 1863. First, in August, came the collapse of a makeshift Kansas City jail, in which a number of the guerrillas' womenfolk were confined, including three of the Younger women. Five women were fatally injured, and others were badly hurt. Among the victims were several sisters and cousins of some of Quantrill's men, and one of the dead was a sister to the bushwhacker leader Bloody Bill Anderson. The notion quickly spread that the Union command had deliberately weakened the structure to cause the accident. Although the idea was pretty clearly wrong, many of the guerrillas jumped at the chance to believe it. On the heels of the jail's collapse the Union commander, Gen. Thomas Ewing, promulgated General Order No. 10, which laid on the machinery to banish from Missouri the families of guerrillas and their sympathizers.

Order No. 11 was shocking even for those dreadful days. The residents of three and a half Missouri counties, including Jackson, were abruptly given just fifteen days to evacuate. For many of the miserable evacuees, these farms were the only homes they had ever known, the place where they had begun married life, the birthplace of their children, the burial ground of their parents and other kin. For most people, Order No. 11 meant the end of everything they had worked for, the destruction of their small corner of the earth. It was Exodus.[18] And it was in this ugly world that Jesse and his brother Frank grew to manhood.

Epics like the *Life, Times and Treacherous Death of Jesse James* accurately reflected the beliefs of many partisans of the South in the border wars. To a great many people, the Missouri bushwhackers were unqualified heroes, forever unvanquished, performers of all kinds of prodigious deeds. A fine example is the story of Cole Younger executing fifteen opponents at once, lining them up so exactly that they all died from a single bullet penetrating their skulls at the same place.[19] There was even a song, set to the tune of "Roving Gambler," in which a good southern girl sings,

> I'll bundle up my clothing
> With my true love by my side,
> And I'll rove this wide world over,
> And be a guerrilla's bride.[20]

Quantrill ranks with the most cold-blooded killers of this or any other war, but even he was uncritically admired by many southern sympathizers. A somewhat clumsy ditty of the time went like this:

> Come all you bold robbers and open your ears
> Of Quantrell [sic] the lion heart you quickly
> shall hear; He'd take from the wealthy and give to the poor
> For brave men there's never a bolt to his door.[21]

Still, for all his ugly, undistinguished past, Quantrill seems to have been an able guerrilla leader. He had a certain panache, and he managed to stay at large and do substantial damage to the Union until his luck ran out in the fading days of the war. His premier feat was a second raid on Lawrence, Kansas. The details of the raid, like much of the border war, are shrouded in uncertainty, and one of the long-debated mysteries is whether both James brothers were at Lawrence. It is not clear when Frank James joined Quantrill, but it is probable that he was following Quantrill as early as the autumn of 1862, in plenty of time to ride along on the Lawrence raid.

Quantrill led about four hundred fifty men into Lawrence on a pleasant morning in August 1863, and this time the raiders came to kill. Nobody knows exactly how many Lawrence men died that grim day, but the death toll is at least one hundred fifty. The raiders came prepared: they carried death lists of known pro-Union men, and many of the male residents of Lawrence were simply collected and shot down in the streets. Some were gut-shot and left to suffer; at least two were bound and thrown into a burning building.

One of the male survivors of the raid watched the raiders burn and loot and "saw that every man was shot down at sight." As he hid in the cellar of his home and his wife pleaded vainly with the marauders, Quantrill's men tore up books, broke up chairs, and started a fire that destroyed his house. "Now father," the survivor wrote afterward, "why have we been so terribly punished. . . . Quantrill said here, after he had satiated his hate and revenge, that he was now 'ready to die.'"[22]

Well over one hundred of the town's best buildings were burned out, and property loss reached one and a half million dollars, an immense sum at that time. All that night dogs howled mournfully in the smoke of burning Lawrence. Frank James and Cole Younger were certainly present at Lawrence that terrible morning. Some of the wilder tales of the border war place Jesse there, too, shooting down Union men wholesale.

Such exciting mythology notwithstanding, Jesse was not present at Lawrence. Nor did he serve under Quantrill, in spite of much legend to the contrary. Even so, the egregious *Life and Times* calls the Jameses and Youngers "leaders" at Lawrence. It says Jesse killed thirty men, "running his score up to this time about one hundred," and Frank shot thirty-five.[23] That improbable body count leaves precious few of the hapless Lawrence men for anybody else to kill. As to Jesse at least, the tale is pure moonshine, for at the time of Quantrill's attack on Lawrence Jesse was still on his parents' Clay County farm.

For all the nonsense written about them, the bushwhackers were a formidable bunch. Many of them had grown up on horseback, and all of them were comfortable with weapons. They usually operated in small groups, often in country they knew intimately. They were armed to the teeth, each carrying a rifle or shotgun and at least two pistols. One account says incredibly that Bloody Bill Anderson, Jesse's longtime leader, carried eight Colts in his belt and another four in his saddlebags.

Even after Frank left for the brush, young Jesse stayed at home behind his mother's plow. His stepfather could not run the farm alone, and family allegiance ran very deep in those days. Jesse was still quite young, slight, baby-faced, and blue-eyed. Any urge Jesse had to join his brother took second place to family loyalty.

Until the spring of 1863, or so the classic story runs. It is an oral tradition only. However, considering some of the things that happened to hundreds of other families on both sides, it has the ring of truth. The story goes like this: Before Frank broke parole and joined the bushwhackers, the James family was not molested by

Union forces. However, in May 1863 the James place was visited by local militia searching for Frank. Frustrated, the militia turned on anybody they could reach. Young Jesse, only sixteen, got off comparatively lightly. Caught plowing, he was terribly flogged, but the men who abused him learned nothing from him about his brother's whereabouts. Mrs. James, pregnant, was pushed around and her dress torn but otherwise escaped unhurt.

Jesse's stepfather was treated far more brutally. The militiamen hanged him four times, waiting until he writhed and gagged, letting up on the rope a little to demand he tell them where Frank was, then hauling him up again to slowly strangle. The doctor never told them what they wanted to know, or perhaps he couldn't because he didn't know. At last they left him dangling, but Mrs. James quickly cut him down. The old man lived but only barely. He carried the rope scars to his grave and was never quite himself again, for he had been without oxygen too long. Young Jesse never forgot.

There was more. A week later both his parents were arrested and jailed in St. Joseph. The charge was "feeding and harboring bushwhackers." At least that was the charge against Jesse's mother. Dr. Samuel was never charged with anything, nor was Jesse's sister Susie (or maybe she was, and Dr. Samuel was not, depending on what version of the legend you read).

To deepen the scars Jesse already carried, Zerelda was six months' pregnant when she went to jail. Not only did she care for her two youngest children behind bars, but she was still there when she gave birth. She and her husband were released a short time later but only after taking the prescribed oath of allegiance to the Union. Neither was ever tried.

In spite of the hardships of his parents—or maybe because of them—Jesse stuck it out on the farm for at least most of 1863, but by late 1863 or early 1864 he was gone to join a bushwhacker band, a subunit of the men commanded by Bloody Bill Anderson and George Todd.

Once young Jesse hit the outlaw trail, he quickly acquired a reputation among the guerrillas. "For a beardless boy," said Bloody

Bill, "he is the best fighter in the command."[24] This was no small praise, considering the ferocity and fighting ability of the experienced guerrillas who followed Anderson. Jesse was slim, smooth-skinned, and relatively small, with tiny feet and something of a baby face with a little turned-up nose. One account says Jesse sometimes even dressed as a girl to scout Union troop dispositions.

Jesse followed Bloody Bill into Ray County, Missouri, in summer 1864. And there, at Heisinger's Lake, he and four other guerrillas ran afoul of the ancient German patriarch who owned the house they were looting. Heisinger was a man of many summers, but he turned out to be young of both heart and eye and a staunch Union man withal.

As Jesse and his four cohorts rummaged through Heisinger's possessions, the old man drilled a bullet through Jesse's right lung. Jesse's companions were routed, and Jesse was out of the war. He very nearly died, and it was the middle of September before he could ride with the bushwhackers again.

In that month Jesse was present at the tragedy at Centralia, Missouri, next to Lawrence perhaps the nastiest event of the ugly border war. Even in a time in which bushwhackers often sported enemy ears and scalps hanging from their horse harnesses, even in a war in which prisoners were often hung, the Centralia incident is particularly ugly.

Todd, Anderson, and several hundred of their men camped about four miles from Centralia, and the next morning Anderson took about thirty men and rode in to hurrah the town. They looted industriously and set fire to the train depot. As was their custom, the bushwhackers also partook copiously of the town's whiskey supply, knocking back straight shots out of women's slippers stolen from a neighboring store.

They were well oiled and ready for further sport when a train pulled into the town's station. Among the occupants were a couple of dozen Union soldiers, some wounded or sick, all apparently unarmed and going home on leave. Anderson and Todd's men pulled the bluecoats from the train, lined them up, and murdered them. One account says that Anderson shot all the helpless Union soldiers himself, his men handing him loaded pistols as he emptied the one he held.

Jesse was present at Centralia, but there is no evidence that Jesse participated in the murders. Frank later denied that either he or his brother had anything to do with them, but said both took part in the fight that followed.

Centralia was as cold-blooded a killing as any in the history of the Civil War. There is no evidence—as at least one apologist for the Jameses alleges—that the handful of Union soldiers ever fired a shot.[25] The sole northern survivor later plainly called Centralia what it was—murder.[26] Leaving Centralia, Anderson, Todd, and their men turned on a pursuing Union force of green Missouri Volunteers. It was a classic ambush, and the inexperienced Volunteers were soon surrounded on a little hill.

Most of them died there, many after they had surrendered, some of them scalped. Their commander, Maj. H. J. Johnson, apparently made the mistake of dismounting his inexperienced men. The rebels promptly swamped them in a howling mounted charge. Only a few Union soldiers were able to mount and escape. Major Johnson died with his men, and tradition tells us that Jesse personally shot him down. Frank James is said to have boasted about the Centralia fight in later years, announcing pompously that "the only battles in the world's history to surpass Centralia are Thermopylae and the Alamo."[27]

Newspaperman Edwards exulted that Jesse killed seven of the Union men, and Frank, "on excellent authority, is reported to have killed eight also."[28] The dime novel writers inflated the James brothers' part beyond all believing—anything for a sensational story. Some versions of their exploits placed them at the trainside massacre and credited Jesse with killing all twenty-six of the luckless Union soldiers. Others said Cole Younger did the deed, lining the unfortunate twenty-six up in a row and killing them all with a single bullet.[29]

Two weeks later Anderson's men surrounded another group of captured Union militiamen, again ready to kill in cold blood. "We better shoot the sons of bitches," they shouted. On this occasion the federal men were lucky: Confederate general Sterling Price was present to intervene and order the prisoners paroled.

Not long after the Centralia bloodbath, the furies finally caught up with both George Todd and Bloody Bill Anderson. On September 23 Todd took a Spencer rifle ball in the neck near Sugar Creek, Missouri. He lasted only a few hours, and one of the mourners at his grave in the town's cemetery was young Jesse James. Toward the end of October, Bloody Bill rode into a Union ambush a half mile north of the hamlet of Orrick, Missouri, and was filled with bullets before he could fire a shot of his own.

On New Year's Day 1865 Quantrill crossed the Mississippi north of Memphis. He did not last long. Run down by a Union guerrilla band led by a nineteen-year-old captain, Quantrill was shot and paralyzed from the waist down. He lasted twenty-seven days in a Louisville hospital. True to form to the end, he made a will excluding his mother and sister, leaving his money instead to Kate King, the Missouri girl who had followed him into the brush in 1864. It is said she invested wisely and prospered, running a St. Louis bordello of efficiency and some fame for many years.[30] The brothel was probably a better memorial than Quantrill deserved.

Frank James surrendered at Samuel's Depot, Kentucky, on July 26, 1865, and was promptly paroled. According to legend, Jesse was not so lucky. Coming in to surrender at Lexington, Missouri, he rode into a picket of the Second Wisconsin Cavalry who shot him in spite of the white flag he and his companions carried.

The wound was very nearly fatal, and Jesse would not return to the war. Jesse was hurt so badly that he apparently was not required to take the oath of allegiance administered to all surrendered Confederates. Union Major Rogers, commanding at Lexington, thought the oath superfluous in Jesse's case, since it seemed obvious that the youngster "would soon be surrendering to a higher authority than his." And so the major waived the oath-taking requirement for Jesse. Nevertheless, Jesse was included in a formal surrender.

Mythology transmogrified Frank and Jesse from ordinary guerrilla fighters into southern heroes of almost Wagnerian proportions, unconquered and unconquerable, especially when they turned to outlawry after the war. Take this sample, a paean of praise to Jesse:

> Foremost in every battle . . . riding like a
> centaur, a dead shot with either hand. . . .
> Always singling out the most prominent enemy,
> he rode against him like an avenging Nemesis.[31]

This dreadful purple prose, besides ignoring the fact that centaurs don't ride, being half horse themselves, did not mention the seamier side of the dirty frontier war.

Nobody will ever sort out fact from fancy in the mass of fable that surrounds the bushwhacker days. Writers on both sides inflated the deeds of their partisans, or invented them entirely if the real thing were not thrilling enough. In the forefront of southern apologists stood newspaperman John Edwards. His accounts of the fabulous deeds of the James and Younger brothers strained credulity at every turn. Over the years Edwards, who finally lost a long battle with the bottle, never wavered in his defense of the brothers.

Take, for example, a variation on the story of Cole Younger killing the fifteen Union prisoners. Cole, the story goes, wanted to test the power of an Enfield rifle, so he ordered the fifteen Jayhawkers tied in a row and drove a bullet into the line of men. Cole expected to drop ten men with a single round and was upset when only three prisoners fell. "Cut the dead men loose," Edwards has him saying. "The new Enfield shoots like a pop-gun!" And then Cole continued to shoot, seven times altogether, until all fifteen men lay dead. Edwards finished with a flourish: "[S]even times had the avenging son feasted his eyes on the agonies of those who had been foremost in the murder of his father."[32]

All of which is bit much, especially for Cole Younger. He was a hard-core guerrilla, but what we know of his behavior on other occasions during the war suggests that he would not amuse himself of an afternoon wantonly murdering more than a dozen men, a few at a time. To the contrary, Cole had been known to restrain other bushwhackers from gratuitous murder on more than one occasion. And the Enfield was hardly "new." It was the 1853 pattern standard British military rifle, an excellent weapon, and some nine hundred thousand of them were imported into the United States by both North and South from 1861 on. And it was hardly a "pop-gun," being chambered in a robust .577 caliber. The story sounds very much like more of Edwards's grandiose moonshine, but the legend refuses to die a natural death.

The Younger boys' grandfather, Charles Lee Younger, was a substantial citizen in western Missouri. A vigorous man in other ways as well, Charles fathered nineteen children, eleven of them illegitimate. Among them was Adeline, who would be the mother of the notorious Dalton boys. One of Charles's sons was Henry Washington Younger, who became a prosperous farmer in Jackson and Cass Counties in western Missouri. Henry was a slaveholder, but he was also profoundly opposed to secession.

Thomas Coleman Younger—called Cole—was Henry Washington's seventh child. Cole was a tall, big-boned man, running to fat in his middle years and after. Cole's father was affluent according to the standards of the times, running a dry goods store and several farms. Although he did not favor secession, he tried very hard to remain neutral; for a while he kept on with business as usual, selling dry goods and fine horses in the midst of chaos and destruction.

And then, in July 1862, Henry Younger made the long ride home from Kansas City, carrying a considerable amount of cash in a money belt. He never arrived. He was found, foully murdered, lying dead on a lonely road with three bullets in his back, by a Mrs. Washington Wells and her son—or maybe her hired hand—Sam, who is described as a "hairy, crude, semiliterate farm boy." We'll meet young Sam Wells again a little later as a full-grown bandit, only then he'll be called Charlie Pitts. Cole always believed, perhaps correctly, that the elder Younger had been murdered because "I had joined to fight for the Confederacy."[33]

The killers were probably a band of federal militia led by Captain Walley, who had quarreled with Cole at a dance sometime before. And in early 1863 federal brigadier general Benjamin Loan wrote to another Union general, "[I] arrested a Captain Walley, who had murdered one Harry Younger in Jackson County, for his money. The evidence of his guilt was so clear and conclusive that he confessed it."[34] Loan added that he had convened a court-martial to deal with Walley but that his witnesses, all Missouri militia, had been ambushed on the way to court by guerrillas "under Bird Younger, a son of the murdered man." And so nothing ever happened to Walley, then or after. And that is remarkable in itself if Cole Younger was convinced that Walley had killed his father.

And so Cole joined the bushwhackers. And to his father's murder Cole later added another reason for hating the Union enemy. His sister, he said, was "criminally assaulted" by a Union captain. Cole did not spell out what "criminally assaulted" meant, only that the officer's "brutal treatment" of his sister inspired him—with other bushwhackers—to ambush and kill the officer and several of his men, lying in wait for their prey behind a clothesline they had fabricated out of rope and a collection of "blankets, quilts, sheets and small pieces." When Cole told the story to his friend Harry Hoffman long years after, he added that he stood beside the captain's corpse and cried out, somewhat melodramatically, "Sister, I have kept my word!" Maybe so, but then, Cole was never opposed to making a good story even better.

Henry's widow, Bursheba, was later burned out of one of their farms, and the family suffered under the heavy hand of Missouri and Kansas guerrillas. For a while Jim Younger obeyed his elder brother and stayed home, although he wanted to follow Cole and join Quantrill. While Cole was away with the bushwhackers, fourteen-year-old Jim became head of the household and guardian of his two younger brothers. These youngsters, John and Bob Younger, were only eleven and nine, but eager to take part in the war.

And so Cole plunged into the twilight world of the guerrilla war. While he had the reputation for being a fine horseman and a crack shot, Cole was not the bloodthirsty fanatic many of his fellow guerrillas were. In fact, it is documented that he saved the life of a Union colonel who had been wounded and threatened with death by a guerrilla chief.

Although Cole was present at the Lawrence massacre, he later said that he was unprepared for the savagery and wanton murder there, and he denied taking part in the murders at Centralia. Later, a captain, Cole served in Louisiana and Arkansas. He served in Texas, too, and there, near the hamlet of Scyene, where his mother had settled after Order No. 11 drove her from her home, Cole met a Missouri acquaintance named John Shirley. He also met Shirley's feisty daughter, Myra Maybelle, then sixteen or so, an encounter which would give birth to a number of abiding legends.

Jim Younger, chafing at being left out of the action, finally joined Quantrill in the spring of 1864. At first the youngster rode as a scout, but he became a full-fledged fighting member of the band just in time to be present at the bitter end. That end came in a muddy farmyard near Louisville, Kentucky, in May 1865. There Quantrill got his death wound, and Jim was led off to end his brief guerrilla career in a federal jail in Illinois.

Now, with the fighting over, the Younger family returned to Jackson County. There they faced the dismal task of rebuilding. No southern sympathizer could hold office in postwar Missouri or practice any profession, including being a preacher or lawyer. He could not even vote. And he was liable to stand trial for any wartime act now considered criminal. Carpetbaggers swarmed into Missouri to dominate commerce and government.

Still, most pro-slavery Missourians sighed and made the best of a bad time. Most took the loyalty oath, which carried with it conditional amnesty. Neither Cole nor Jim had much confidence in the protection of the amnesty, but both finally decided to return to their family. It was a time to try to pick up the pieces and above all to live quietly and avoid trouble. But avoiding trouble was the one thing the Younger family could not do.

In January 1866 John Younger killed a man. He and Bob had driven their mother to Independence for supplies, and there one Gilcreas had made some remarks about Cole and Jim in her presence. When John, only fifteen, took umbrage, Gilcreas swatted him in the face with, of all things, a frozen mackerel. When Gilcreas moved his hand toward his hip, John shot him between the eyes with one of Cole's pistols. Because Gilcreas carried a heavy slungshot, a coroner's jury decided John fired in self-defense, but John had provided still another reason for the family to continue to feel uneasy.

Writer Homer Croy says that in January 1866 Cole rode over to Kearney to visit "his old friend and saddle companion, Frank James." Croy even produced some dialogue, supposedly uttered when Cole first met the ailing Jesse James. "'I want you to meet my brother Jesse,' said Frank. 'He's kind of poorly. He picked up a couple of lungshots at the end of the war when he was coming into the Burns school-house to surrender.'" Thus spake Frank, or at least that's what Croy says he said. And there, Croy tells us, the great scheme was born. Why not rob a bank? "The idea was breathtaking. Everybody hated banks. They charged usury; they cheated farmers."[35]

Whether or not the grand plan actually started that way, a large band of men rode into the square in Liberty on a Tuesday afternoon in February 1866. Two of them entered the bank. One shoved a pistol into the face of the bank's cashier, a Mr. Bird. "All birds should be caged," said the grinning bandit. "Get inside the vault, Mr. Bird, and step lively." Whoever the robbers were, the two inside men forced the banker to fill a large grain sack with nearly $60,000 worth of bonds and paper money. Hearing the excitement, two William Jewell College students moved toward the bank. As they did, one robber opened fire. Young George Wymore, called "Jolly," went down with a mortal wound.

The killing of Jolly Wymore was an ugly harbinger of much worse things to come. It was also wholly unnecessary, for the youth was unarmed. Which bandit shot Wymore has never been established. The murder infuriated peaceful people in Clay County, for the youngster was considered one of the most peaceable and promising young men in the county, . . . shot and killed while standing on the opposite side of the street. [It was] a deliberate murder without any provocation whatever. . . . [T]he murderers and robbers are believed by many citizens . . . to be a gang of old bushwhacking desperadoes who stay mostly in Jackson County.[36]

One or both of the James boys could have been part of the gang that stuck up the Clay County Savings Bank. This daring holdup was the first peacetime daylight bank robbery on record, and the loss was so great that it forced the bank to settle with its depositors for sixty cents on the dollar. To this day it is not certain who all the bandits were. While Cole Younger and Frank James may have been part of the gang, it is probable that Jesse was nowhere near Liberty at the time. Jesse was still an invalid, his painful chest wound healing slowly. Jim Younger has been named as part of the gang, but his participation is unlikely.

Cole Younger was almost surely part of the gang, for over the next few years he cashed a number of the bonds stolen from the bank. As usual, though, Cole had a glib explanation. "I was happy to cash bonds given to me by friends," he said much later. "I never knew where the bonds came from as I never asked it of the friends who had given them to me to cash."[37] It may well be significant that in the summer of 1866, having cashed some bonds back East, Cole met Frank James in Independence and Jesse at the family farm in Kearney.

Altogether, over the next decade, the James-Younger gang is supposed to have stopped and looted four trains and a couple of stagecoaches, robbed at least eleven banks, and made off with the cash box from the Kansas City Fair. Along the way they left some twelve or fifteen dead men behind them. The exact total of their criminal escapades will never be known. When a gaggle of outlaws attains a certain notoriety, some crimes committed by other people will inevitably be laid at their door. The crimes described in the next few pages are only those in which the gang was probably involved.

Whether the Jameses and Youngers were part of the next bank attack is uncertain. This was a strike at the Hughes and Wasson Bank in Richmond, Missouri, carried out by a gang that may have been as large as a dozen men. On May 22, 1867, four outlaws entered the bank and came away with some $4,000, but only after a shootout with the townspeople. Richmond mayor John B. Shaw, running toward the outlaws with his revolver in his hand, went down, dying, with a ball in the chest.

The raiders then attacked the local jail, in what may have been an attempt to break out some diehard Confederate agitators imprisoned for continuing to advocate secession. Young Frank Griffin, son of the jailer, opened up on the raiders with a rifle but took a round in the forehead from one of them. When Griffin's father ran to his son, one of the raiders shoved a pistol against the old man's head and pulled the trigger, then shot him again as he lay across his son's body. The gang galloped out of town, unscathed, but the countryside was aroused. If any of the James or Younger boys were involved, they got away clean. "But," one source said, "at least three of their comrades were caught and lynched."[38]

From this point on, the new pastime of bank robbing became quite the vogue in Missouri, though which crimes can accurately be laid to the James-Younger gang is not at all clear. In March 1868 robbers stuck up the Long Banking Company in Russellville, Kentucky, rode off with about $14,000, and left the bank president, Nimrod Long, and another man slightly wounded. Cole Younger and both James boys were probably part of this raid.

It may have been part of the Russellville loot that financed the Younger family's move to Texas in the autumn of 1868. Long-suffering Bursheba traveled with Cole, John, Bob, and Jim to Scyene, a small town in Dallas County. Which brings us to the abiding legend of Belle Starr, later famous as the Bandit Queen, the center of endless fables, including an astonishing piece of silliness that has her riding with Quantrill and killing four men before she saw her eighteenth birthday.

In fact, Belle was neither bandit nor queen but a small-time horse thief. She was also one of the ugliest women in all of Indian Territory, as years and hard living erased what beauty she may have started out with. Belle loved to flaunt a revolver or two and have her picture taken on big horses. She spent a lot of her time with criminals, too, and even married two, both of whom expired of lead poisoning.

Born Myra Maybelle Shirley in Missouri, daughter of a fairly well-to-do family, she had some education, certainly, and perhaps that is what gave rise to the later wonderful tales about her erudition:

> [She was] a worshipper of Verdi, Gottshaulk, Rubenstein and Wagner[;] . . . a devotee of Pliny, and the naturalists; Socrates and the philosophers; Voltaire and the satirists; Homer and the epics; Moore and the lyrics.[39]

She was, moreover, "an accomplished musician," a "Diana in the chase, a Venus in beauty, a Minerva in wisdom," and more. On no particular evidence, predictably, an enterprising reporter for the *St. Paul Globe* even told his readers that the fabulous Belle rode with the raiders at Northfield.

By 1864 the Shirleys had fallen on evil days, for Mr. Shirley's businesses had become almost worthless in the maelstrom of war. They moved south to safer, more agreeable climes. The family settled in Scyene, about ten miles from Dallas, in those days a wild-and-woolly cowtown, its streets either choking red dust or glutinous red mud, depending on the season.

In Scyene Belle grew toward womanhood. And in Scyene, legend tells us, she met the James boys and Cole Younger, whose mother now lived nearby. Belle fell hard for the dashing Cole, the story goes, and when Cole rode north again, he left young Maybelle pregnant. At least Maybelle said so later on, although to his dying day Cole staunchly denied paternity of Maybelle's daughter, Pearl. Homer Croy, ever alert for a good story, has Cole riding back and forth between Texas and Missouri, cavorting with Belle between robberies. After Pearl's birth, he says, Cole came back to Texas "now and then" to see little Pearl. When he was away he pined for Belle, "the only woman who had come into his life. . . . As soon as he made a big haul he would go down to Texas, get Belle and baby Pearl and go the Pacific Northwest."[40] This tale is about as likely as snow in June. Many years later Cole's friend Harry Hoffman wrote that Belle "was Cole's best girl friend. He told me of her, but never said anything about Pearl Younger."[41]

Meanwhile, back in Missouri, the James boys were busy. In December they struck a bank in Gallatin, in the process wantonly shooting down both a clerk and Capt. John Sheets, the bank's president, and wounding a local attorney. According to one account, Jesse shot Sheets because he was "irritated by the cashier's slowness in handing over the cash."[42] Three days later Sheets died from his wounds, and the notion then spread that he had been murdered in revenge for the wartime death of Bloody Bill Anderson. As the story went, the robbers thought that Sheets was in fact Major Cox, who had led the troops who killed Bloody Bill and who also lived in Gallatin. The Platte County history reported that as early as January 1870 the James boys were "producing consternation throughout the State" and that a militia company was being raised to combat them.[43]

In Texas, sometime in the winter of 1870–71, John Younger got into trouble in a Scyene saloon. It seems he tried to shoot a pipe from the mouth of a man best described as the village idiot. The terrified man sought out the Dallas sheriff's office, and a warrant was issued for John's arrest. The deputy sent to arrest John kindly told him that he could finish his breakfast and meet the deputy at the local dry goods store afterward. What happened after that is lost in the mists of time, for there are several versions. What is certain is that a shooting scrape erupted between John and a friend and the deputy, who also had a friend with him. When the smoke cleared John was shot in the arm, the deputy was mortally wounded, and the deputy's friend was dead. John left Texas at the high lope. He spent some time in Arkansas, but by spring he was back in Kansas City.

Meanwhile, in June 1871, four men rode into Corydon, Iowa, where much of the town was gathered to hear a speech by one Henry Clay Dean, who had considerable fame as an orator. While the populace hung on Dean's golden words, four men raided the Corydon bank, tied up the cashier, and made off with several thousand dollars. On the way out of town, according to one possibly apocryphal tale, the bandits stopped long enough for one of them to ask Dean for recognition. The orator graciously obliged. "I yield to the man on horseback," he said, and the rider announced that the bank had been robbed and maybe somebody ought to turn the cashier loose.

The robbers were almost certainly Jesse and Frank James, Cole Younger, and a new man named Clelland Miller. Clel (or Clell) Miller was Missouri born. He had joined Bloody Bill Anderson's guerrillas sometime in 1864. Chances are he met Jesse James during his brief time as a guerrilla, if he did not know him before.

After the Corydon raid, Jesse wrote a letter to the Kansas City *Times* vehemently denying that either he or Frank were involved in the robbery, but then, Jesse made a practice of writing letters denying he was involved in much of anything. It is hard to have much faith in his denials. Still, the only gang member arrested for the Corydon holdup was Miller, although he produced some alibi witnesses and was acquitted.

All four Younger boys now gathered in St. Clair County. There Cole had apparently invited Jim and John to join him on the owlhoot trail. Jim at least did not approve of Cole running with the James brothers, but Cole paid no attention. Laughing, he only said, "We are rough men used to rough ways."[44] He could not know that those very words would return to haunt him just five years later.

In April 1872 the gang hit a bank in Columbia, Kentucky. The cashier, R. A. C. Martin, tried to shout an alarm, and one of the bandits shot him down simply because he yelled. As frantic customers bailed out the doors and windows, the gang hastily grabbed a paltry $600 and ran for it. As in so many robberies in those days, the identity of the outlaws is not certain. But Pinkerton detective

Yankee Bligh named Cole, Jesse, and Frank as three of the robbers. If so, the chances are that Clel Miller was the fourth.

In fall 1872 three men stuck up the ticket sales office at the Kansas City Exposition. One robber seized the money box from the cashier and stuffed the money into his pockets. When the cashier bravely tried to recover the money, one of the bandits fired at him. Although he missed, the bullet badly wounded a little girl attending the fair with her mother. The robbers got away, but the man who snatched the box identified himself as Jesse James.

Jesse later wrote his usual letter denying involvement, incidentally mentioning that Cole and John Younger were also innocent, a bit of notoriety that irritated Cole Younger, up to that time not a suspect. Newspaperman John Newman Edwards, always Jesse James's chief apologist and admirer, published a letter purporting to come from the fairground robbers, offering to pay the girl's medical bills and talking about how innocent they were compared to the evil profiteers of the U. S. Grant administration. The ever-faithful Edwards rhapsodized about how the raid was so daring "that we are bound to admire it."[45] But then, Edwards could never see anything much wrong with Jesse's exploits, no matter who got killed along the way.

Edwards was not the only shameless apologist for the gang. The Osceola *Democrat* ran a series of articles in praise of the Younger boys, a marvelous collection of nonsense that was later assembled into an entire book. A good many other writers pitched in, too, among them Augustus Appler, who reproduced a speech by Bob Younger to a posse captured in the act of pursuing the Youngers. "Now gentlemen," Bob says, "we have you in our power." And he goes on for two single-spaced pages in small type before releasing the posse as an act of mercy. It is impossible to believe anybody making such an enormous oration to his would-be enemies, unless he was trying to talk them to death.

Jim Younger had also returned to Texas in winter 1872, apparently upset about a plan Cole had laid out to rob another bank, this time in eastern Missouri. In Dallas Jim signed on as a member of the city police force (there were only nine officers in all). The job didn't last long, for in February 1873 Jim and another Dallas cop were indicted for robbery. Sensibly leaving Texas before trial, Jim returned to St. Clair County.

Back in Missouri, John Younger had agreed to ride with Cole on the bank raid. And in May 1873 two men pushed into the Ste. Genevieve Savings Bank, stuck up cashier O. D. Harris, purloined his watch, and snatched some $4,000. Using Harris as a shield against the aroused townspeople, the robbers made for their horses—held by two other gang members—and galloped out of town. The usual uncertainty surrounds the identity of the Ste. Genevieve robbers, but it is probable that they were the James boys, Cole Younger, and John Younger, on his first job. As they fled, curiously, they were shouting "Hurrah for Hildebrand!"—apparently a reference to a well-known local bushwhacker, Sam Hildebrand. Hildebrand was a killer, felled by a policeman he tried to stab just the week before.

Bob's introduction to outlawry was to be a different sort of operation. Train robbery was in its infancy in the early 1870s, but it already showed promise. As early as the fall of 1862 the Reno brothers had successfully robbed two trains, and everybody knew express cars often carried large sums of money. Why not try one?

So the gang gathered. This time Jesse James brought in a friend, Bill Chadwell and Cole added Charlie Pitts, another Jackson County man. Charlie, it seems, was none other than Sam Wells, whom we last met next to the corpse of Henry Younger. With Frank James, Cole, John, and Bob Younger, and probably Jim as well, the outlaw contingent numbered eight. And so, in July of 1873, the gang moved against the Chicago, Rock Island and Pacific near Adair, Iowa.

First they broke into a railroad shack and stole a hammer and a prybar used to pull railroad spikes. And then, on a curve near a place called Turkey Creek, the robbers, masked like Ku Klux Klansmen, pulled some spikes from the railroad ties. They then knocked loose the fishplate that connected two sections of rail, tied a rope to the loose rail, and took cover in a railroad cut. As the train rumbled toward them, they yanked the rail out of line.

The locomotive hurtled from the tracks and crashed into a ditch, fatally crushing or scalding the engineer, John Rafferty, and smashing up the fireman badly. The gang invaded the express car and were disappointed to find only $2,000, instead of the bonanza they had expected. To this comparatively paltry sum they added another thousand or so stolen from the passengers and galloped off into the gloom. Lawmen followed the gang's trail into Missouri, where it disappeared.

Jim Younger, upset by the death of the engineer, declined his share of the loot and swore he'd never take part in a train robbery again. The rest of the gang went along with Jesse, who typically classified the dead men as fair game simply because they worked for the railroad. Both Jesse and Cole later wrote letters denying any part in the robbery.

Indeed, at times it is difficult to be sure where all the Youngers and Jameses were during the years after the Civil War. In addition to the stories told about their whereabouts by the various brothers, there are dozens of tales told by others, and now it is too late to sort out fact and legend. According to one story, Frank James worked "for two years in the early '70s" for a man named Maupin, on the Red River near Colbert's Ferry, where the Texas Road crossed into Indian Territory. Frank allegedly called himself "Frank Rapp" in those days. If the story is true, no doubt he felt safe and comfortable with Maupin, himself once a rider with Quantrill's guerrillas.[46]

In January 1874 the gang rode out to rob again. Once more the James boys brought Clel Miller, and three of the Youngers joined them. Jim, still upset by the murder at Turkey Creek, opted out. The job was another train, this time the Iron Mountain road at a tiny Missouri town called Gad's Hill, some hundred miles south of St. Louis. This time the robbery was bloodless, for the gang simply held up the train as it stopped at Gad's Hill station.

They started with the express car safe, then worked their way through the train robbing passengers of their watches and money, making something of a show of looking at the male passengers' hands and looting only those who were not "working men." Two particularly well-dressed passengers were forced out into the cold and made to strip to their underwear. Another man, whom the bandits apparently thought was a detective, was strip searched. As a final grand gesture, one of them handed a note to the train engineer describing the robbery and the brilliance of the robbers, conveniently leaving a blank in which the nearest newspaper could fill in the amount they carried off. The gang then rode off into the late afternoon and got away clean, retreating westward and stopping for meals at farmhouses, where they were said to have conducted themselves as gentlemen, paying for everything they got. Which is not hard when you pay your bills with somebody else's money.

The same robbers may also have held up a stagecoach between Malvern and Hot Springs, Arkansas, two weeks before. On that occasion the robbers made a great show of announcing they would not rob Confederate soldiers. They even returned a watch taken from a man who said he had served the southern cause, and they made a speech about being driven to outlawry by the damn Yankees.

Both the stagecoach robbery and the Gad's Hill holdup were blamed on the James-Younger gang. Even the St. Louis *Dispatch* announced that the brothers were the perpetrators, no doubt to the horror of the editor, none other than John Edwards who was out of town at the time. There was so much well-publicized lawlessness in Missouri that the eastern newspapers had taken to calling Missouri "the robber state." And there was worse to come.

This time, it would be deliberate kidnapping and murder in cold blood. As the gang scattered, the Pinkerton agency set out in pursuit. One of Pinkerton's operatives, an experienced officer named Whicher, rode into Clay County, Missouri, posing as a farm laborer and trying to hire on to work at the James place. The next time anybody saw him he was dead on a Jackson County road, riddled with bullets. The murderers were almost surely the James boys, and the killing was not over yet.

In March 1874 John and Jim Younger mortally wounded a Pinkerton agent and a Missouri peace officer, but not before the

Pinkerton fatally shot John. For reasons that are still unclear, Jim did not manage to notify his brothers of John's death, although he started out to find and tell them. Cole and Bob were in Arkansas and learned of their brother's death only from a newspaper they read over the breakfast table. Stricken, Bob stayed in Arkansas while Cole searched for Jim. The brothers held counsel together and finally split up. Cole departed for Florida, hoping to get into the cattle business, and Jim headed for California and safety with his uncle Coleman. Only Bob returned to Missouri. One of the more peculiar Jesse James books asserts that John Younger was not killed after all but showed up in Fort Smith as none other than "hanging judge" Isaac Parker.[47] An extraordinary feat, that, considering that Judge Parker was well known in politics as early as 1864 and was elected to Congress ten years later.

Jim was soon working on the California ranch of Drury James, the James boys' uncle. Bob, restless and uncertain, left Missouri quickly and by the end of April was visiting his sisters in Denison, Texas. In that same month, up in Kearney, Missouri, Jesse James was marrying his love of many years, his first cousin Zerelda Mimms, called Zee. The couple honeymooned in Texas. Jesse and Bob spent some time together there, too, and a friendship ripened.

During the spring and summer of 1874, somebody held up several stages around Austin and San Antonio. Predictably, Jesse was identified as one of the robbers, but there is no solid evidence to connect him with these crimes. On somewhat more tangible evidence, he was named one of three men who held up an omnibus across the Missouri River from Lexington, Missouri. People on the Lexington side watched helplessly as three gunmen held up the passengers. One woman, strolling nearby, identified the robbers as the James brothers and "Will" Younger. She had known the Younger and James families, she said, and even spoke to two of the outlaws, who heeded her plea to return two stolen watches and to leave the single female passenger alone. This apparently solid identification came unstuck when Zerelda Samuel wrote the witness a letter, at which the witness decided she "was prepared to doubt the accuracy of my recognition" and declined to sign a formal statement.[48]

In December four men robbed a bank in Corinth, Mississippi, of several thousand dollars' worth of cash and jewelry. The inside men carried "ugly looking knives" this time, and one of them slashed the bank's cashier across the forehead. The James and Younger boys were suspected, and Cole Younger was identified from a picture as the leader. The use of knives was at that time uncharacteristic of the James-Younger gang, and it cast some doubt on the identification. An incident the following day made it even more unlikely that the brothers were to blame for the Corinth raid.

On December 8 the gang, or maybe a different gang, struck once more. It was a train again, the Kansas Pacific, this time at Muncie, Kansas, and the haul was a big one, some $30,000. At Muncie the gang drove a party of section hands to pile ties on the track, then locked up the hands and settled down to wait. The rest was easy, and nobody got hurt in the process. The robbers were probably Jesse and Frank James, Cole and Bob Younger, and Clel Miller, although there are other candidates, depending on whose account you read. Bob used his share of the loot to lease a farm in Jackson County and moved there with his girlfriend.

It is about six hundred miles between Muncie and Corinth and therefore highly unlikely that the same people struck in Corinth on one day and in Muncie the next afternoon, although there is an outside chance that part of the gang was in Mississippi and part in Kansas. It is more than likely that the gang in fact robbed the train at Muncie. Shortly after that raid the James boys' friend Bud McDaniel was arrested for drunkenness in Kansas City. When the law nabbed him, Bud was carrying more than $1,000 in cash. Still worse—for him—he also carried items of jewelry identified as part of the loot from the express car. Bud would not incriminate his friends, however, and shortly afterward he broke jail in Lawrence, Kansas, and was killed in the pursuit.[49]

The legend persists that the outlaw brothers could take shelter, among other places, down in Indian Territory, deep in the great bend of the Canadian River, at that mysterious, forbidding lair called Younger's Bend. The place was named, so the story goes, by old Tom Starr, patriarch of the clan, who was proud of the visits Cole Younger and one or more of his brothers made to this rugged, hostile stronghold. And there, according to legend, a whole generation of other outlaws took refuge, hard cases from Oklahoma, Missouri, and Arkansas, including the James boys: "Belle and uncle Tom Starr would protect them and feed them and it was difficult for the officers of the law to find them."[50]

The James brothers were indeed hard to find. Some Pinkerton detectives, frustrated, concentrated their efforts on them. The Pinkertons took a special train into Clay County and then walked several miles through the night to the James farm at Kearney. And there, at the end of January 1875, occurred one of the most famous incidents in American outlaw history. Thinking Jesse and Frank were at the farmhouse, the Pinkerton agents surrounded the place. And in an attempt to drive out their quarry, they threw into the house what the newspapers called a "bomb," followed quickly by a second one.

These devices may well have been only flares or smoke bombs, intended only to smoke out the occupants of the house. Or they may have been intended to set fire to the James home. Letters from Pinkerton surfaced in the last decade, indicating that Pinkerton intended to destroy the house, and the James boys too, if possible.[51] And there is other evidence that the "bomb" may have been an incendiary device called a Birney shell, produced by the United States arsenal at Rock Island and filled with a mixture of gunpowder and coal tar. It may have been furnished to the Pinkertons by order of Gen. Phil Sheridan.[52] On the other hand, a newsman named Lewis, said to be a friend of Frank James, said flatly in a 1925 article that "[t]here was no bomb" and also asserted that Frank James believed the same thing. The devices were, said Lewis, only a sort of oil lamp made of iron and brass, with a couple of wicks sticking out the top. They were "flares," he said, and only detonated when Dr. Samuel shoved them into the fireplace.[53]

According to Dr. Samuel, he used a shovel to push the flare toward the fireplace, where it exploded. Whatever the object was, flare or grenade, it tore off Mrs. Samuel's right arm at the elbow and mortally wounded eight-year-old Archie Samuel.

Many years later William Pinkerton, son of the agency's founder, denied that the device was anything like a bomb. It was, he said, "a metallic case or shell stuffed with lampwick and soaked in coal oil." "While these torches burned, those persons on the outside could see all that was going on within." Nobody, said Pinkerton, expected Dr. Samuel to do what he did. Of course the device exploded, Pinkerton said, just as a kerosene lamp would do if you threw it into a fireplace. The other devices, he added, were kicked out through the door and burned out harmlessly in the yard.[54]

The pro-James partisans were furious at the attack on the Samuel farm, and they blamed the Pinkerton agency. Edwards, led the charge with a rabid editorial:

> Men of Missouri, you who fought under Anderson, Quantrell [sic], Todd, . . . recall your woodscraft and give up these scoundrels to the Henry rifle and Colt's revolver. It is because like you they were at Lawrence, and Centralia . . . and wherever else the black flag floated.[55]

If Edwards and other fervent James supporters cried out loudly for blood, so also did a number of ordinary people who thought the Pinkertons had overdone it. For the moment the attack on the James house seemed to dwarf the robberies and murders laid to the James brothers. In March a Clay County grand jury returned several indictments, including one against Allan Pinkerton himself, but nothing ever came of the accusations except more anger.

And then one night in April a Kearney man named Daniel Askew was called out of his house and shot down on his own doorstep. Askew lived near the James place, and one of the men indicted for the bombing had worked for Askew as a hired hand. No evidence connects any James or Younger with the killing, but the act would not be out of character for, in particular, Jesse. A Liberty lawyer named Samuel Hardwick (or Hardwicke) first moved from his farm into town, then fled to St. Paul, Minnesota, and did not return for years. Hardwick's only offense, according to Pinkerton, was his concern that the continuing lawlessness in Missouri was creating an atmosphere in which new people were afraid to settle; the lawyer had done no more than talk with Alan Pinkerton.[56] Other sources involve Hardwick more deeply, one alleging that he "sent a wire to Chicago stating that the whole gang would be at the James farm . . . on a certain day and night."[57] How Hardwick would know such critical details was not explained.

In the spring of 1875 an attempt was made in the Missouri legislature to obtain amnesty for the James brothers and for Cole and Jim Younger. It failed to get the required two-thirds vote, however, although it had considerable support. Meanwhile, the robberies continued, first a store in Clinton, Missouri, in May and then a bank in Huntington, West Virginia, in September. The raiders in the first crime may well have been a gaggle of amateurs imitating the James-Younger gang. The second robbery was almost surely committed by Cole Younger, Frank James, and two henchmen, Thompson McDaniel and Tom Webb.

Webb was captured in Tennessee and sent to prison. McDaniel was mortally wounded during the escape into Kentucky. Dying, he asked, "Did they get Bud?" "Bud" might have been McDaniel's brother, killed during a jailbreak after he was arrested for his part in the Muncie robbery. But "Bud" also could have been Cole Younger, whom his friends sometimes called by the same name. The physical description of one of the robbers fit Cole very closely. As usual, Jesse weighed in with one of his standard letters proclaiming that "since the amnesty bill was introduced in the Missouri legislature last March," he had never been out of Missouri. There were, he added, also as usual, "hundreds of persons in Missouri" who would swear to that.

In the spring of 1876, however, Jesse James had a new strike in mind, and the first person he enlisted was Bob, who called Jesse his friend. They got together at a Kansas City hotel, and there Jesse laid out his plan to strike a rich bank someplace in far-off Minnesota, perhaps at Mankato, in the rich black-earth farming country.

One tale says the gang picked Minnesota because the Liberty lawyer, Hardwick, had moved to St. Paul; the gang still nursed a grudge against this man, whom they thought had been "involved with the bomb-throwing detectives" at the James farm.[58] There is no evidence for this theory, which is even more far-fetched than Cole Younger's later claim that the gang rode north to get revenge on ex-Union general Ben Butler.

Whatever the motivation to strike a bank in Minnesota, Jesse had already done some thinking. He would include Bill Chadwell in the band, he said, because Chadwell came from Minnesota and knew the terrain. Old reliable Clel Miller would go along, too. Bob apparently liked the idea of ready cash for his new farm and agreed to talk to Cole. On the other hand, writer Homer Croy tells us that Jesse opposed the idea of a raid so far from home. "But Bill painted such a land of milk and honey—with not a single bee— that the others persuaded Jesse to fall in with the idea."[59] However Jesse may have felt, Cole was not enthusiastic. In the last years of his life, he told a Missouri friend that "it was as if a voice had come from heaven that said to him 'don't make that trip to Minnesota.'"[60]

Cole did not like the idea of operating so far from home. He was also dubious about Chadwell, a small, buck-toothed man who ran off at the mouth almost incessantly. One inventive writer says Cole argued hard that the gang should instead raid "some rich town in Canada," where the outlaws could pick up "a big booty, and retire to some foreign country, since he could have no peace in this." Instead of protecting his brother, Cole cabled Jim in California: "Come home. Bob needs you." So Jim left his placid, honest life at La Panza, California, thinking his kid brother might be in trouble.

Cole's involvement of Jim got Bob's back up, especially when he found out that Jim had been lured back to Missouri. And Jim was angry, too, feeling with some justification that he had been lured East on false pretenses. But because Bob was determined to ride with Jesse, both Cole and Jim agreed that if Bob went, they must go as well.

Now for the planning. The operation would be expensive. There would be train fare north, plus money for good hotels and meals and entertainment. They would need first-class horses once they got to Minnesota, horse furniture, and sober suits for camouflage, and there might be unforeseen expenses. And frugal living did not appeal to the outlaw brothers; it surely was not part of their mystique. The boys liked to live as high on the hog as possible when they could. As one Oklahoma old-timer put it,

> The outlaws would sometimes pay as high as twenty-five dollars for one meal. Money was no object. . . . The small boys would feed the outlaw's horses. They would sometimes pay a dollar an ear for every ear of corn that was fed to their horses.[61]

All of these requirements cost money, and that called for a robbery. Jim Younger, still upset about the whole scheme, refused to take part, so the rest of the gang recruited a stand-in, Hobbs Kerry, to fill the ranks. On July 7 they flagged down a Missouri Pacific train at a place called Rocky Cut, a bottleneck in the midst of a railroad construction site near Otterville, Missouri. This one went smoothly. The gang captured a railroad flagman and used his red lantern to stop the train. Without a shot fired, the robbers milked two safes to the tune of some $15,000 while the terrified passengers sang hymns.

Chadwell at least was well satisfied with the haul at Rocky Cut. He wrote his brother-in-law in Minneapolis, promising him a share of the golden horde waiting for the gang in Minnesota banks:

> I've made a good haul, and if you want $100 or $200 say so. I will be coming up into the Northwestern country, in a few weeks, and I know where we can make another good haul, and will give you some more.[62]

Now the bandits had their bankroll, and nothing remained but to travel north to their bonanza. Thousands of words have been spent on why the outlaws planned a strike so far from home, for the northland was terra incognito to Jameses and Youngers alike. The probability is that the gang was beginning to feel the heat of pursuit by the Pinkertons and local lawmen. Cole Younger had another explanation.

In his autobiography, *The Story of Cole Younger, by Himself*, Cole later included a whiny passage complaining that the brothers were unjustly blamed for every robbery committed by anybody. "[We] could not," he wrote, "go out without a pair of pistols to protect ourselves." They would therefore make one last payday, he said, and "start life anew in Cuba, South America or Australia."[63] Cole's words are an eerie echo of the ambitions of his distant cousins, the Daltons, sixteen years later. The Daltons also wanted to make a big strike and flee the country, but the good citizens of Coffeyville, Kansas, shot them to pieces before they could leave for greener pastures.

Hobbs Kerry incautiously flashed his share of the loot around southern Missouri and got himself arrested. He promptly told his captors that the James and Younger boys, Chadwell, and Miller had also been involved in the Rocky Cut raid. Jesse wrote his usual "Who me?" letter to the Kansas City *Times*. He also reviled Hobbs Kerry as a "notorious liar and poltroon" and offered alibi witnesses (also as usual). And then he said why, he didn't even *know* those people Charlie Pitts and Bill Chadwell. Jesse outdid himself this time, going so far as to blame the Rocky Cut raid on one Bacon Montgomery, who had led a Sedalia posse that pursued the robbers. Montgomery responded by offering to make himself available for questioning if Jesse would do the same, but Jesse would have none of that very reasonable offer.

Instead, he and the gang would travel north, away from pursuit and notoriety, to find a fat bank in unwary, peaceful Minnesota. Jesse and his brother Frank, Cole, Jim, and Bob Younger, Charlie Pitts, Minnesota native Bill Chadwell, and the ubiquitous Clel Miller made eight experienced hard cases, surely more than enough talent to cow a whole town full of Yankee sodbusters and shopkeepers.

Bill Chadwell, dark haired, clean shaven, and husky, was the key man on the raid, for he had local knowledge. He was in fact William Stiles, probably born in Monticello, Minnesota (though author Homer Croy says he was born in Missouri and migrated north later). Arrested in St. Paul, he had done some time for horse theft and later drifted south to Missouri, now calling himself Chadwell. According to one Minnesota historian, he had been the surveyor for Dodge County. According to this source, Chadwell left a wife in Minnesota, a woman who received public assistance at times after the raid, including "beer for medicinal use."[64]

Chadwell may have had a half sister or stepsister living at Cannon Falls, a hamlet some sixteen miles east of Northfield. She was Minnie Merrill, adopted daughter of a minister and a student at Carleton College along with Alonzo Bunker, teller at the Northfield bank in the year of the raid.[65] Chadwell may also have lived near Cannon Falls in days gone by. If he had, he would have been intimately familiar with the countryside, the perfect guide during the gang's escape.

Clel Miller was born in Holt in Clay County in 1850. If he did not know Jesse and Frank James before the war, he surely met Jesse during his service with Bloody Bill Anderson. Miller was present in the fight in Ray County, Missouri, in which Bloody Bill was killed by Union forces. Miller was captured there and confined until the spring of 1865. Short, husky, and comical, he was an experienced bandit, for he had ridden with the gang at least since the Corydon robbery back in the spring of 1872.

Charlie Pitts, as Sam Wells now called himself, had been with the gang at least since the Turkey Creek derailment near Adair, Iowa. Born in Indian Territory, he was a Jackson County man, a friend of Cole Younger's. Thirty-two years old, he was a big, surly man with bushy black hair, a mustache and goatee, and a loud, profane mouth. He was surely part of the gang during the Rocky Cut robbery because, the story goes, he thereafter jilted his light-'o-love, a lady called Lillian Beamer, and married somebody else.

Beamer, understandably irritated by his false heart, promptly told law officers how her erstwhile sweetheart made his living.

Another tantalizing story makes Sam a Shawnee Indian who married a neighbor of the Youngers, started a family near Kansas City, and later worked on the railroad building south from Parsons, Kansas. His wife, a stout pioneer lady born Jennie Fisher, told an interviewer much later that Sam left her at Choteau, in Indian Territory, and went, or so she thought, "to the Kansas wheat fields," returning with a wagon load of flour. The couple and their children moved on to rent a farm near Chetopa, Kansas, where Sam left Jennie alone again. This time he would not return. As Jennie said, "While gone he met the Younger brothers and joined them. I think he thought he would avenge the killing of his father as they knew who had killed him. He was killed in Minnesota with them."[66] Maybe so. Jennie never gave dates when she told her tale. It is therefore possible that from time to time Sam was absent long enough to join the gang for a raid and then ride back to his trusting wife.

So the gang was gathered. There seems little question that these eight were the whole outlaw complement, although one entertaining story of the raid asserts that there were "14 white men, three Negroes and an Indian guide."[67] The eight men who would strike Minnesota were tough and experienced. As Cole Younger said more than once, they were "rough men and used to rough ways." They were indeed. They were accustomed to hard riding and hard living on the back roads and in the thickets of half a dozen states. They were used to fatigue and pain, their own and other people's. And they were well accustomed to killing.

A sodbuster bank in yankee Minnesota ought to be easy pickin's.

CHAPTER TWO

THE GANG MOVES NORTH

In August, 1892, Jesse and Frank James began the journey to Minnesota cautiously enough, hidden under a tarp in the bed of a wagon. Taking no chances, they were already lying down beneath the canvas when the wagon left the James barn in the dusk of a summer evening, the barn door opened and quickly closed by a young black boy who worked for the James family.[1]

The ride lasted from the time the boys got clear of Clay County until they reached a rendezvous where the rest of the raiders waited with horses for everybody. When the gang got to Council Bluffs, Iowa, they sold their horses; nobody knows to whom. An alternative story is that the gang got started north from Belle Starr's place at Younger's Bend, in Indian Territory. According to this story, it was here that Chadwell spun a tale of gold just waiting to be stolen way up there in Minnesota. Everybody liked the idea, except, perhaps, Jim Younger and Jesse James. But "knowing full well of his greatest weakness, the others roused Jesse's Confederate sympathies."[2]

From Council Bluffs (one book says from Fort Osage), the bandits traveled by train to Minneapolis, where they took counsel together about the next move. Some versions of the story have the gang riding horseback all the way north. "The Missourians rode splendid horses into Minnesota,"[3] wrote Robertus Love. More recent researchers have opted for travel by train, which makes a good deal more sense in any case. It is unlikely that these experienced campaigners would choose to wear out their crucial horseflesh on the long ride to Minnesota. We know that they bought horses once they had arrived, and there is no record that they sold any horses in Minnesota. After the raid, in captivity, Cole Younger told an interviewer that he did not ride his mount but bought the one he rode from a man named French of St. Peter, Minnesota.

Harry Hoffman, Cole Younger's longtime friend, wrote many years later that the gang rode north in the wagon together, creaking along through Missouri, across Iowa, and into southern Minnesota. There, according to Hoffman, "two of them went into a town and bought eight saddle horses."[4] Hoffman's narrative directly contradicts other accounts, however, which pinpoint the places in Minnesota where various gang members bought horses and horse furniture. Had the bandits wanted only to substitute new horses for old, they surely would not have bought new saddles and bridles as well.

One fascinating tale of the raid, told much later by a Rice County doctor, related that four of the gang traveled north a month before the Northfield attack. They came "at the instigation of one Kit Rose, who was born in Steele County near the Rice County line, and thought the gang should cool off here." Something went wrong with their plans, however, and the gang members became suspicious of Rose. And so, said the doctor, who was only eight years old at the time of the raid, the outlaws shot Rose and planted him in a "local pasture."[5] There is no factual support for this fable, save one other writer's vague reference to the gang contacting a "friend of Bill Chadwell" in Minnesota.

In Minneapolis, Pitts and Bob Younger indulged in some poker their first night in town and came away nearly $200 poorer. The next day all the gang members moved on to St. Paul. There Cole and Chadwell registered at the Merchant Hotel and that night had a fling of their own at Salisbury's poker emporium, where they did very well. When Bob showed up with Pitts, Cole quit, refusing for some reason to play with his brother. Croy says that on the last day of August they found time to go to a baseball game, a contest between the Winona Clippers and the St. Paul Red Caps.

Meanwhile, the James brothers, Clel Miller, and Jim Younger traveled to Mollie Ellsworth's house outside St. Paul, a place said to be a brothel of some fame and reputation. Chadwell showed up a little later in the evening and spent some time chatting with one of the working girls, Kitty Traverse, whom he apparently knew. The five bandits decided to stay on with Mollie, for here they could gamble and pursue other forms of felicitous entertainment and talk to other denizens about the lay of the land, especially its banks. Cole ultimately joined them at Mollie's place.

One reliable source calls Mollie's place Nicollette House,[6] but that statement is probably inaccurate. Nicolette House was not a bordello; then and afterward it had the reputation of being the finest hotel in the twin cities, over the years host to several United States presidents. Another writer has the manager of Nicolette House so suspicious of them that he had the house detective guard their room, a tale far more consistent with the staid atmosphere of a good hotel. Two nights later the manager was relieved to find that the men—six of them—had simply played cards all night.[7]

A persistent tale has it that during the outlaws' stay at Mollie's popular bagnio, Mollie recognized one of her guests as Jesse James. Nothing daunted, Mollie asked the famous outlaw what he was up to in Minnesota. "Oh, nothing," said Jesse. "I am going out into the country for a few days and will be back soon; then you and I will go to the centennial."[8] Mollie said later that she had indeed known Jesse in Minnesota, and for years before that, in St. Louis. There is no confirmation of Mollie's boast, but previous acquaintance may be the very reason the gang stopped at her house.

This is an engaging tale, but if it happened, it's probably a variation on a story about a meeting between Bill Chadwell, the Minnesotan, and Kitty Traverse, one of Mollie's whores. Chadwell and Miss Kitty were apparently already acquainted, but whether the relationship was purely professional or based on friendship is not known. Dallas Cantrell attributes the same conversation to Chadwell and Kitty. And he adds that Kitty, somewhat alarmed to see that Chadwell is clanking with weaponry, warns him that he risks arrest. At which Chadwell somewhat ominously replies, "I shall die like a dog or eat the hatchet," whatever that mysterious statement may have meant.[9]

The robbers' leisurely sojourn at Nicolette House—or at Mollie's, or both—is typical of their whole Minnesota expedition. Throughout there seems to have been no sense of urgency shown by any of the raiders. Instead, they behaved as if this trip were some sort of Grand Tour. They stopped a good deal here and there to gamble, whore, and generally live the good life. Not only were they in no hurry, they made no attempt to remain inconspicuous. To the contrary, they dressed well, ate well, stayed in good hotels, and talked to everybody they met. The only measure they took to remain anonymous was to adopt aliases, but otherwise they seemed oblivious to the risk that anybody would recognize them.

Which is precisely what happened. For when the six men left Nicolette House and went out on the streets of St. Paul, Chadwell met Patrick Kenny, a local policeman who knew him. Worse, Officer Kenny had once arrested Chadwell for horse theft. How are you, asked the officer, and what are you doing? I'm doing well, thanks, said Chadwell; and I'm planning to travel to the Black Hills in the near future (which may even have been the truth).[10]

On August 26, perhaps inspired by Chadwell's unhappy meeting with Officer Kenny, Jim Younger, Miller, and the James brothers went across the Mississippi to Red Wing. There they stayed at the National Hotel, posing as cattle buyers and using various aliases, and there they bought four horses, including a buckskin and a "splendid bay," and horse furniture to match.[11] Meanwhile, Charlie Pitts and Cole Younger had taken a train to St. Peter, where they assumed false names and checked in at the American House. They shopped around town for gear and also found a couple of horses, a bay and a horse with white socks. Chadwell and Bob Younger stayed on in St. Paul.

In one version of the Northfield story, the Red Wing bandit contingent split up almost immediately. The James brothers went down to Brush Prairie—near Northfield—where they arrived by the twenty-eighth. There they announced that they were interested in buying farmland from John Mulligan. When they reached an agreement with Mulligan, the Jameses said their money was in a Red Wing bank. During the bargaining, they would have had at least some opportunity to learn a good deal about the Northfield area, and they asked a lot of questions about the character of the town and its people. They asked Mulligan a series of questions about the country to the west of town, "how far the woods extended, and all about the roads," studying a map as they talked.

On the twenty-ninth the James boys rode on to Northfield and spent part of a day in the little town on the Cannon River. There they talked to townspeople—still representing themselves as the buyers of Mulligan's farm—and learned what they could. It may have been then, according to the Rice County *Journal*, that the bandits "visited all our hardware stores before the raid to see if they could find any rifles or good arms of any kind."[12] Also according to the *Journal*, the bandits said to Mulligan, "Why, according to your statement of the Northfield people a very few men so inclined could capture the town, couldn't they?" or something very like that. And Mulligan agreed that was probably so. Although the *Journal* solemnly reported this conversation as fact, it sounds like mythology. It's hard to imagine any outlaw making a statement like that anywhere near his intended target.

In St. Peter, Pitts and Cole Younger had been awaiting Chadwell and Bob Younger, but when the latter two failed to appear, on the thirtieth Cole and Pitts traveled on to Madelia, southwest of Northfield. There they stayed at Col. Thomas Vought's Flanders House hotel, where Cole struck up a friendship with Vought. As Cole talked cattle driving with his genial host, Chadwell and Bob Younger were registering in a St. Peter hotel as Messrs Cooper and King of Illinois.

Cole Younger's friend Harry Hoffman told the story of the gang meeting a farmer named Joe Brown on an "obscure road" in southern Minnesota. The farmer noted the "thoroughbreds" the eight men were riding but was entirely taken in by their story that they were from Tennessee, traveling about looking for "timber claims." Brown invited them to stay at his farm, and on the way there the eight produced what Hoffman called a covered wagon. This conveyance, they explained, was their "camp and supply wagon." Mrs. Brown, the story goes, was suspicious, and even berated her husband for "taking up with no-account strangers" but was charmed and mollified by Frank James's quotation of Scripture: "I was a stranger, and you took me in."

Mrs. Brown now content, the outlaws stayed on with the farmer for several days, riding off in the morning and returning at the end of the day. What they were doing, says Hoffman, was training their horses to do extraordinary things, including these:

> They familiarized them with the explosion of six-guns; taught them to swim easily without lunging and with confidence. They taught them to stop instantly if the rider fell from the saddle and to return to the fallen man. If the reins fell from the hand of the rider to the ground, they stopped and stood still until they received further orders. . . . In this manner a horse became a super-horse—they loved their masters and in turn were given as much care and attention as humanly possible.[13]

All of which prompted one perceptive amateur historian to comment ,"Oh, if they could but cook!"[14] And indeed all this training seems a bit much for the very limited time the gang members had and their traveling here and there between Minnesota towns. In any case, Hoffman tells us that the bandits rode away on September 1, leaving behind them their wagon and the team that pulled it.

On September 1 the gang finally came together in Mankato, a pleasant town near the confluence of the Minnesota, Blue Earth, and Le Sueur Rivers. A couple of gang members got a $50 bill changed at the First National Bank, no doubt to get a look at the inside. One source says the gang had decided to strike the Mankato bank, or that they were actually riding into town to rob it, when they came upon a large group of citizens gathered near the bank. Some of the citizens pointed toward the band of robbers, who immediately aborted the raid. One account says they tried again later in the day but encountered another collection of citizens and called the Mankato raid off entirely.

Their alarm had been both premature and unnecessary as it turned out, for the the crowd was no more than a bunch of side-walk superintendents gathered to observe a construction site, and the pointing citizens were only drawing attention to the gang's fine horses. Another tale says that Jesse met a Missouri acquaintance—maybe Charles Robinson—in Mankato. "Hallo, Jesse," said the man. "What brings you up this way?" Jesse managed a smile in return. "Hell, man, I don't know you," he replied, or "I guess you have mistaken your man."[15] Whether or not Jesse thought he had fooled his acquaintance, Mankato had become a bad bet for the outlaws. There is a story that the acquaintance notified local lawmen; if they reacted, there is no official history of it.

One source has the sheriff announcing, "By God, there'll be no robberies in this town—let's go to the bank." According to this tale, the bank's employees were alerted and armed, but nothing happened until the next night, when two of the visitors went to "a local saloon, described as 'a rendezvous for the lowest criminals.'" The next day the same book has the bandits visiting the bank again, and again being frightened off by the crowd of gawkers watching other men work.[16]

By contrast, Cole Younger wrote that the gang had decided against Mankato before they arrived in Minnesota. Instead, he said, Northfield became the target because they "had been informed that ex-Governor Ames of Mississippi and Gen. Benjaman [sic] Butler of Mass had deposited $75,000 in the national bank of that place." His account has the self-serving, whiny tone Cole so often took when he tried to justify the gang's enormities and glorify their character:

[W]e came to the conclusion that they [the people around Mankato] had enough to do to care for the farmers who had already suffered too much from the grasshoppers to be troubled by us; therefore we went to Northfield in expectation of getting the $75,000 belonging to ex-Governor Ames and General Butler.[17]

In fact, if Cole really heard about Butler and Ames having money in the Northfield bank, there was no truth to it. Both men were shareholders, but neither had any money on deposit.[18] It is also permissible to doubt the purity of Cole's concern for the locust-plagued farmers of Rice County. We know that the gang had reconnoitered the Mankato bank before coming to Northfield, and it is a fact that grasshoppers were not an unusual pest anyplace in the Midwest. They had devoured everything in sight in various parts of Minnesota from 1873 through 1876.[19] In James-Younger country, Clay County had been invaded by hordes of the voracious insects just the summer before the raid.[20] Care for the hard-earned savings of struggling farmers had never been high on the gang's list, with or without grasshoppers. It seems unlikely that the outlaws began to care about farmers, particularly Yankee farmers, for the first time in Minnesota.

About six o'clock in the morning on September 7, a farmer walked out into his yard at Cannon City, a few miles south of Northfield. He headed for his well, which lay between the Gordon Inn next door and the inn's barn. As he drew his water, he looked over at the open double doorway of the barn and must have been surprised to see a group of strangers squatting on their heels in the doorway playing cards. Nevertheless, the farmer walked over to the strangers and said good morning. "Morning, Boss," said one, in what the farmer, a Civil War veteran, thought was a southern accent. Were they having a good game? the farmer asked, and the same man replied that they were "playing to see who would have to pay the hotel bill."

The farmer was alarmed by the men, who were armed and dressed to travel. He noticed, too, that the men watched him

suspiciously and that "the horses' bridles were supplied with cartridges held in looped straps and that the horses were eating with
bits in their mouths." Returning home, he told his wife that he was
worried about a "bad-looking gang of men in Gordon's barn." He
was afraid they were criminals, "highwaymen," and was so worried that he could not eat breakfast. Instead, the farmer went back
to his front gate, from which he could see the owner of the Gordon
Inn sitting on the front porch of his hostel.

About that time a "large, good-looking, well-dressed man" came
out of the hotel and stopped to ask the farmer if there was a store
nearby where he could buy "cee-gahs." The farmer directed him
to a shop a block away. Returning, the stranger offered the farmer
a cigar and pressed more on him when he took only one. "Have some
moah," said the stranger, and the two men smoked and chatted
together until the big stranger went back inside the inn. Worried,
the farmer walked over to the inn and sat down with the owner,
who told the farmer he'd be glad when that bunch were gone. The
cigar smoker and another man had slept in the inn, Gordon said,
but the others spent the night in the barn and came in singly to have
breakfast after the ones in the inn had eaten. Gordon was afraid to
ask his mysterious guests to pay their bill.

Now the two men inside the inn walked down to the barn, and
the whole group rode out, the "cee-gah" man in front, and headed
down the path that led to the inn fence. Gordon started to open the
four-bar gate, but the leader waved him away. "Nevah mind, Grandpop," he yelled, and jumped his horse cleanly over the gate. All the
men behind him did the same, and the last one threw Gordon a red
bandanna tied in a knot. "There you are, Grandpop," he cried, and
then the whole band was gone, clattering off down the road from
Cannon City to Northfield. The bandanna contained a handful of
bills, much more than enough to pay the hotel bill.[21]

The story persisted long afterward that the affable man who
bought the cigars was Cole Younger. More likely it was Frank
James, for it is reasonably certain that Cole did not travel by way
of Cannon City. Another source says that the James brothers, Pitts,

and Bob Younger stayed the night before the raid at the Stetson farm on the old Faribault road, some five miles from Northfield, although Cole puts the other party at Cannon Falls at that time. Another version of the bandits' progress has the James boys, Chadwell, and Bob Younger staying at a Cannon City hotel.

Just where all the bandits spent the night before the raid is not entirely clear, nor is it particularly important. Intertown rivalry accounts for some of the uncertainty. At the time, both Mankato and Elysian claimed to be preraid stopovers, and St. Peter chimed in that the bandits spent that night in caves on the edge of the Minnesota River. Cole, who may be accepted as the authority on this, traced the bandits' approach to Northfield as follows.

The bandits headed for Northfield over two routes. Cole and one party spent the night of September 4 at Le Sueur Center, where court was in session. The town was full of lawyers, Cole remembered, and so the outlaws slept on the floor, their night made noisy by the judge and lawyers having, as Cole put it, "a high old time." On this point, Cole's memory may have been playing tricks on him, for Le Sueur Center was not the county seat, where court sessions were generally held. The county seat was a town called Cleveland, and that is probably where the party stayed.

That same day the James brothers, Pitts, and Bob Younger made it as far as Janesville. Marley Brant's *The Outlaw Youngers* tells us,

> Cole was perturbed with Jesse once again, claiming that Jesse's vanity was at fault for their having to forgo the Mankato plan. He and Frank decided on their own that Frank would travel with Jesse and Bob so that he could keep an eye on them lest they try to cook up something other than the agreed-upon plan to go to Northfield.[22]

Maybe so, but it's worth noting that no special arrangement should have been required. Frank had probably ridden with Jesse every day thus far. Moreover, if Cole was indeed angry because the Mankato bank had been left unrobbed, that certainly gives the lie to Cole's later crocodile tears over the poor farmers afflicted with hordes of grasshoppers.

In any case, on the night of September 5, according to Cole, Jesse's party arrived in Waterville. Cole and the others spent that same night in the little hamlet of Cordova at the Dampier House hotel, and at Millersburg's Cushman Hotel on Wednesday the sixth.

Northfield historians have suggested a slightly different route than the one laid out by Cole. In this version, the gang did not split up until it reached Cordova, southwest of Northfield. One contingent went almost due east, past Faribault to Cannon City (not to be confused with Cannon Falls), then north toward their target. This group included, according to Northfield lore, the James brothers, Jim Younger, and Clel Miller. The other group of outlaws—Bob and Cole Younger, Pitts, and Stiles—headed for Millersburg (Millers-*burgh* in some versions), some eleven miles west of Northfield.

Stories of happenings on the bandits' ride to Northfield abound. One intriguing tale fits with the story that part of the outlaw gang spent one night near Cannon Falls. It goes like this. At about sundown on September 6, six horsemen, riding in pairs, dismounted in the yard of a country schoolhouse near Henry German's farm, about nine miles from Red Wing and some three miles from Hay Creek. One of the riders—or perhaps a seventh man—came over to the German farm and "demanded a ham and two pounds of butter." Mrs. German "was only too glad to comply in order to get rid of him, for she didn't think he was of good character." The rider did not offer to pay but returned to the schoolhouse.

Members of the German family stayed awake all through the night, for nobody trusted the six riders. Nobody from the house could get to the barn to get a horse, so the presence of the strangers went unreported to authorities. At about 3:00 A.M., the mysterious horsemen were gone, leaving the top of the schoolhouse stove covered with grease where they had fried Mrs. German's ham in Mrs. German's butter. The story was handed down in the German family that names were left scrawled on the school's blackboard. Two of them were Frank James and Jesse James.[23]

This story is probably not accurate, at least not entirely. First, it is reasonably clear that by the sixth—the night before the raid—the bandits were traveling in two groups of four. Second, Cannon Falls is a considerable distance from Northfield, perhaps twelve or thirteen miles, maybe more on the roads of the day. And according to the German family story, the farm lay only seven miles from Red Wing, which puts it east of Cannon Falls, farther still from Northfield.

Cole's version, that Jesse and his companions stayed the night of the sixth no more than five miles from their target, makes a good deal more sense. However botched the raid itself would turn out to be, veteran outlaws in no hurry would not put their precious horses, their means of escape, through a long day's ride the day before the strike at the bank. If the story is true that Jesse, Bob, and Frank ate their lunch in a Northfield restaurant at about 1:00 P.M. the next day, they surely did not spend the night before close to Red Wing, and probably not in Cannon Falls either.

Traditional stories of the raid tell us that one or more of the gang entered Northfield's hardware stores, ostensibly to price weapons but in fact to see how well the town was armed. The Northfield *News* later reported that Jim Younger had come into Manning's, just two doors from the bank, asking the price of various firearms and asking whether they were loaded. Although Manning offered to sell his visitor a weapon "at a reduced price," Younger replied that he "could get them cheaper in Faribault." The Rice County *Journal* told its readers that some of the bandits "visited all our hardware stores before the raid. . . . [T]hey inquired of several if there were any gun stores in town."[24]

Northfield tradition has the outlaws making their final plans in a grove of trees above the Cannon River, today a public park called the Oddfellows' Grove. It is not certain whether this meeting was before or after they ate—and drank—in Northfield, if they did, but they would have gotten together just before riding into town to strike the bank. Cole Younger later wrote that they did just that, riding "back on the Janesville road two or three miles to consult and arrange our plans."[25]

These plans, according to Cole's account, called for three bandits to enter the bank. They would go into town across the Cannon River bridge and wait until they saw Cole and Clel Miller, a quarter mile behind, ride into town. Cole and Clel would wait outside to provide support if somebody gave the alarm. If that happened, Cole was to get the inside men out of the bank. Whether the raid succeeded or not, he said, the whole gang would then leave town the way they had approached, by the road to Janesville.

The other three outlaws were to wait near the bridge, a covering force in case the raid went sour and fighting began. If something went wrong at the bank, their function would be to hurrah the town and overawe its citizens, firing their pistols and giving the rebel yell. If there were too many people around the bank, the raid was to be canceled and the leading trio of outlaws was to ride on through town, down the road to the neighboring mill town of Dundas. Much later Cole wrote piously that the gang intended to "make our retreat before the alarm was given, if possible, but if we failed and an alarm was given, what shooting was to be done should be for the purpose of frightening the people from the street, and in no case were there to be an attempt to kill."[26]

This description of the gang's pure motives may be taken with several grains of salt. Cole was hoping for parole or pardon when he wrote this, so he surely put his best foot forward. And considering the trail of dead men the gang had left behind in some of its earlier robberies, it's highly unlikely the outlaws did not intend to shoot to kill if they met any real resistance. Setting aside the fact that these men were all experienced professional outlaws, many of them ex-bushwhackers, it is plain nonsense for Cole to suggest that he and his comrades would not shoot down anybody who was trying to shoot them.

And so the most famous outlaw gang America ever saw mounted up and rode down into Northfield, across the Cannon River bridge, into history.

CHAPTER THREE

COWS, COLLEGES, AND CONTENTMENT

At the city limits of Northfield there stands a big sign that no visitor can miss. Northfield, it says, Cows, Colleges and Contentment, which pretty well sums up the temperament of the town. This is the black-earth country of Minnesota, an enormously productive land of spotless farms, hardworking people, bursting corn cribs, fat cattle, and bumper crops. People here are justly proud of their land and their industry: the call sign of the radio station in Waseca, a similar small town south of Northfield, is KOWZ.

And that pride in hard work and achievement characterized Northfield back in 1876, too. People were very busy minding their children, milking their cows, sacking flour at the mills, and measuring yard goods at the store. Work and family were the foundation of their placid world, with church and education not far behind. Their lives were busy and peaceful, and the brawling, untamed west was so far away that nobody in Northfield carried a gun anymore. Both men and women hunted with firearms, of course, and they shot at targets for fun, but gunfights were something that happened someplace else, not in Northfield.

Northfield was a long way from what most people considered the frontier. Rice County, in which Northfield lay, was as remote from the Wild West as the moon. Part of that Wild West was far to the south, in the dangerous hills and draws and thickets of Indian

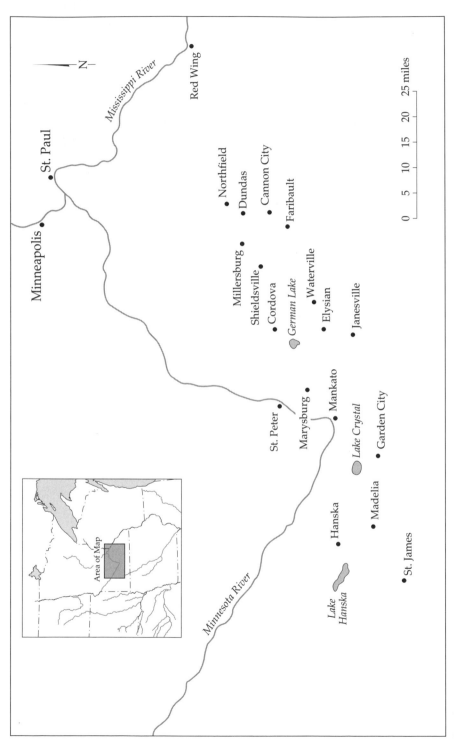

Southwestern Minnesota, 1876

Territory. It was down in feuding Texas as well, where men killed each other over ancient, half-forgotten wrongs or shot people they didn't know because of some imagined insult to their kin. And it was over in the wild-and-woolly cow towns along the Kansas railheads, raw, rough places like Wichita and Newton and Abilene and Ellsworth. It lay farther west, too, in Montana, where three columns of the tiny United States Army were trying to run down a large force of hostile Sioux and Cheyenne.

Down in Missouri and Kentucky there was always trouble, too. Lawless men killed and robbed, especially the famous James brothers and the Younger boys. Everybody had heard of them and their depredations, but things like that didn't happen in Northfield or in Minnesota generally. The telegraph carried word of all kinds of bandit crimes across the country in a flash, and the newspapers passed on the gruesome details. Thank God people like the Jamese and Youngers didn't come up to peaceful Minnesota. They were a long way away, and good riddance.

The raids of bandits like the Jameses and Youngers were exciting to read about, of course, but there was much else to interest the people of Northfield in summer 1876. Out in the Dakotas the tiny United States Army was trying to do something about the refusal of the northern Sioux to return to the reservations assigned them by the government. It was not an easy task, for the Sioux were out in great numbers. In early March Brigadier George Crook tangled with a large force under Crazy Horse at a place called Twin Buttes, and in June, outnumbered at least five to one, the army fought the Indians to a bitter draw on the Rosebud River. Excitement over the Sioux campaign rivaled interest in the great Centennial Exposition of the same year, to be held in Philadelphia. After all, there were lots of people in and around Northfield who vividly remembered the bloody days of the great Sioux war in 1862.

Excitement peaked toward the end of June, when Lt. Col. George Armstrong Custer made the imbecilic decision to divide his small regiment into three elements in the face of an enormous encampment of horse Indians. These Sioux and Cheyenne were the finest light cavalry in the world, in the words of American cavalry officers, and they proceeded to demonstrate their excellence by killing Custer and more than two hundred of his men. The crisis would not pass until November, when Col. Ranald McKenzie's cavalrymen swept out of a bitter night to destroy a major Indian encampment.

Still, all of these exciting things were reasonably far away, and daily life was placid and comforting. The countryside around Northfield was lush and fertile, with black-earth prairie and hardwood forest. There were scattered marshes and lakes as well. In the summer the prairie was a mass of wildflowers in riotous bloom. It was full of game, too, this bounteous land, elk and deer, prairie chickens and pigeons, ducks and geese. Beaver dammed the creeks and streams, and the lakes were full of northern pike and smallmouth bass.

The first white man to see the Cannon River valley may have been a French priest named Menard, who disappeared in this area in 1660 while on his way to minister to the Huron. Other explorers followed. There were other adventuresome Frenchmen in the days before 1759, that momentous year in which two murderous British volleys put an end to the vast, trackless empire called New France. More men followed after that, enchanted by the lush beauty of southern Minnesota. And some of them stayed.

The most memorable of these was Alexander Faribault, who traded in the Cannon River country as early as 1827. In time he ran six trading posts and won the trust of the Dakota Indians with whom he bartered. He repaid that trust by sheltering surviving members of the Wahpekute band of the Dakotas from white vengeance after the Sioux uprising of 1862. No bird of passage, Faribault built his home at the confluence of the Cannon and Straight Rivers, and there he lived and died.

In 1854 the town of Faribault was started there, on the road up from Iowa to St. Anthony. Named for Jean Baptiste Faribault, son of the trader, it was platted in 1855 and by 1876 was a thriving community, upstream of Northfield to the southwest. To the eager white immigrants, the whole country was a garden just waiting to be tilled. They ran their fingers through the rich black soil and sensed what the Indians had known for long years: the Indian name for the area was Waseca, "rich and fertile."

Joseph Nicollet, a Frenchman, also traveled this virgin land in the late 1830s. Nicollet was in the region on a War Department scientific survey, and his report waxed warm in praise of the valley of the Cannon. He called it the Undine region, after the legendary German water spirits who dwelled in its lakes and streams. More explorers followed Nicollet, and they also returned singing the praises of the lovely virgin land. Young, brawny America was moving west to claim its destiny, and so it was only a matter of time before the settlers came to put down roots and turn the prairie into farmland. With settlement came peace and stability.

Nobody in 1876 Northfield could have dreamed that their town was about to be invaded by outlaws, let alone the worst criminal gang of the day. That sort of thing happened elsewhere, not in Northfield, where crime meant minor pilfering or a Saturday-night drunk disturbing the peace. The men of Northfield were industrious and law-abiding, the sort of solid citizens who rose with the sun and worked until dark, good family men who attended church on Sunday. Most had a sense of humor, for all their industry, like the Rice County farmer who attended a neighbor's funeral. He listened intently as the preacher intoned, "The Lord giveth and the Lord taketh away." The farmer agreed: "What," he murmured, "could be fairer than that?"[1]

Northfield's men were peaceful, too, for there was nothing for them to fear. They carried guns only for hunting or target shooting, and there was no local law enforcement to speak of, certainly no hard-case lawdogs like the men who kept some sort of order down in the Kansas cow towns. But if the citizens were peaceable, they weren't shrinking violets either. Plenty of the local men had served in the federal army during the Civil War, for Minnesota had enthusiastically answered the Union's call for volunteers. The village of Morristown, with only one hundred legal voters, sent seventy men off to fight for the Union. The Cannon River country did the same. In addition to local militia outfits such as the Rice County Guards and the Cannon River Guards, local men served in at least the Second ("the Bloody Second"), Fourth, Sixth, and Eighth Minnesota Volunteer Infantry and in the Mounted Rangers, who operated against the Sioux. Altogether, at least eight hundred Rice County men had followed the flag during the Civil War.[2]

Some had served in one of the most illustrious of all the Union regiments, the First Minnesota Volunteers. G Company of that famous outfit had started life as a local unit, the Faribault Volunteers. In fact, G Company's flag, lovingly presented by the ladies of Faribault, eventually became the regimental colors. The First Minnesota's wild bayonet charge saved the federal left flank—and maybe the war—on the second day of Gettysburg. That bloody, roaring, hell-for-leather rush had cost the regiment more than 80 percent of the men present on the field, the highest casualty rate any unit suffered during the war. And the remains of the First Minnesota fought again the next day, helping to break Pickett's charge and end southern hopes forever. If the men of Northfield and the nearby towns had put weapons and killing aside for industry and family, they remained very tough cookies indeed, and they were about to prove just how tough they were.

And so, in autumn 1876 Northfield was a peaceful village. Crime consisted of minor pilfering or a Saturday night drunk disturbing the peace. Even a few years after the raid, the Rice County *Journal* reported on twelve days' worth of local malefactors: six of these were up for being drunk and disorderly; one was fined $10 for shooting inside the city limits, and two got small fines for unnamed offenses. One of these, doubtless the most irritating of the lot, was discharged by the justice of the peace on his promise to leave town.

The pages of the *Rice County Journal* are a mirror of the thriving Northfield of the 1870s. The undertaker, Theodore Miller, reassuringly offered his "largest and finest stock of coffins" on the front page. His ad ran next to one for Dr. S. D. Howe of New York, who boasted that his Arabian Tonic had cured ten thousand cases of consumption. If you missed out on having consumption, the resourceful doctor made Arabian Liver Pills, too, by which "the liver is aroused into healthy action, the stomach cleansed, and the bowels regulated."

The carpet dealer, J. Matheis, assured everybody that he had prime goose feathers "constantly on hand," F. V. Bingham offered Artistic Photography, and the haberdasher, S. Hanauer, was "Not to Be Undersold." You could find out where to look for real estate, who could sell you a stove, and when Urbana College started its term in Ohio. You could learn that a farmer "who has recently left the grasshopper district" was looking for a farm near Northfield or Dundas, or that Mr. E. B. Brockman was calling in his debts. You could subscribe to the *Journal* for only $2 a year and learn anything you needed to know.

The heart of Northfield was the Cannon River and the busy mills along its banks. At the zenith of the milling business, there were seventeen mills scattered along the river between Northfield and Faribault. Upstream, to the south, was the nearby hamlet of Dundas. Dundas was first settled in 1857 by a couple of Canadians named Archibald, who named their new hamlet for either a Canadian county or a British statesman. The Archibalds built a mill on the Cannon, a big one, probably the first stone mill anyplace in Minnesota. By 1858 it was producing Archibald's Extra Flour, known and prized all over the United States and as far away as Great Britain. Dundas's great days are long gone now, for the mill is only a ruin, burned out in 1892. The Archibalds' precious flour patents were sold to another milling company; today it's called General Mills. In 1876, however, Dundas was a thriving little town.

Farther upriver, some fourteen miles to the south southwest, the town of Faribault flourished. Downstream was the village of Cannon City, and farther to the southwest, on the great bend of the Minnesota River, lay the substantial community of Mankato. Established in 1858, it took its name from Mahkato, a word Nicollet used to describe the Blue Earth River, which meanders up from the south to join the Minnesota at Mankato. The town was a natural site for

a landing to handle steamboat traffic on the Minnesota, both passengers and freight. Because of its location at the confluence of the
two rivers, it had been an Indian camping-place time out of mind.

Farther upstream from Northfield lay the town of Madelia, organized in the same year that Mankato was born. Madelia was named
for a daughter of one General Hartshorn, a founder of the town; it
was somewhat obscurely explained that Madelia was "an elision and
reconstruction of Madeline." At the time of the raid, Madelia was a
bustling country town, the county seat of Rice County.

West of Northfield lay the large, heavily timbered expanse of
the Big Woods, a forest that extended from the Cannon River to the
Minnesota, some forty miles east and west, and about sixty miles
south from St. Cloud to Mankato. East of Northfield, however, the
terrain changed abruptly. Where the country out west was swamp,
lake, and hardwood forest, most of the land east of the town was
prairie.

In territorial days a United States Army major named Dodd
built a military road from St. Peter, on the Minnesota, to tiny St.
Paul, about forty miles north of Northfield, on the east side of the
Mississippi. St. Paul—which had begun life with the somewhat
undistinguished name Pig's Eye—was located near the army's Fort
Snelling, which held the strategic forks of the Mississippi and the
Minnesota. Nearby, on the east bank, was St. Anthony's Falls, a
prime source of water power for milling. A little settlement put
down roots there and joined with another village across the river.
In time, the two became one town, Minneapolis, a combination of
the Greek *polis*, city, and *minne*, the Dakota word for "water." In
time a bridge linked the two tiny settlements, and both began to
grow.

The hand-hewn Dodd Road wound through the primeval
woods west of the town site and remained a landmark as Northfield grew through the years. Settlers who lived west of Northfield
told you where they lived by reference to how far their home was
from the Dodd Road. Major Dodd had built well, for parts of his
road were still visible as late as 1947. The James-Younger gang

would use the Dodd Road, both in their deliberate approach to the town and in their desperate flight from the pursuing furies of the local populace.

Just how Northfield got its own name is lost in the mists of time. One theory is that its founder, John North, joined his own name to that of another early settler, Ira Stratton Field, a farmer and black-smith. Field was originally an abolitionist legislator who hailed from Jamaica, Vermont, and had known North before either man came west. It would be logical for North to combine his name with Field's, since the men were not only acquaintances but fellow New Englanders and dedicated abolitionists.

Or maybe the town was named for one of the New England Northfields, towns in Massachusetts and Vermont. It seems most likely, however, that it was simply named for New York–born John Wesley North, a New England lawyer who saw the Cannon valley in early 1855 and realized its potential. North had come to Faribault from Minneapolis (called St. Anthony in those far-off days). He already owned a quarter interest in the town site of Faribault, fourteen miles upstream, but he was much taken with the valley of the Cannon, with its fertility and the potential of its unlimited water power. "The whole valley of this River is beautiful and very fertile," he wrote. And in that lovely valley he remained.[3]

It was indeed beautiful and fertile. Oak trees and black walnuts were thick up and down the valley, and the rich black earth would grow almost anything. North, ambitious and energetic, bought 320 acres from the original owners of the site, and in the autumn of 1855 he laid out his new town. As he sold off lots and watched the settlement grow, North kept a careful eye on the morality of his new town. Each deed carried a stern covenant, a warning that no liquor could be sold on the premises.

In 1858 an enterprising man named Kimball built the Mansion House hotel across the Cannon River from North's burgeoning new town and promptly equipped it with a bar and plenty of whiskey. Within weeks three local men appeared with axes and smashed up Kimball's "barrels and bottles," and his new saloon. They did such a thorough job that the Mansion House never reopened. Nevertheless, neither North's careful covenants nor sharp citizen axes would delay for more than a few years the arrival of saloons for thirsty residents.

The town site was perfect. There was water in plenty, for people and animals and crops, and wild plum and crab apple flourished. Hardy and courageous men and women were already farming along the Cannon, and these people put down deep roots. These stout folks were hardy and enterprising, builders and stayers, so much so that they helped out when John North asked them to volunteer their own sweat and timber for his first mills and for a bridge spanning the Cannon. North connected his new town with the road head at Waterford, three miles away.

In the beginning North's motive was entirely commercial. "I did not at first contemplate starting a town," he wrote in 1880, "much less a city. I only thought of a mill." And sure enough, by the end of 1855 North had a sawmill built and cutting lumber, and in the next year he completed his grist mill, "three run of stones" driven by the waters of the Cannon, "one of the best in the Territory" in those days. In January 1856 North built a house and moved his family in.

Several other enterprising merchants set up for business in the same year, including two men who built a novel sawmill in which the saw was driven by a steam engine of an impressive forty horsepower. A man called Jenkins opened a tent-top "hotel" before 1856 was out. His roof lasted until the night a monstrous rain tore it to shreds with twenty-five men sleeping under it. The next day innkeeper Jenkins "posted off to Hastings for shingles." Civilization was coming to Northfield.

In March 1856 the Coulson brothers opened Northfield's first store and almost immediately sold out to Hiram Scriver, who put the very respectable sum of $10,000 into his new dry goods enterprise. Scriver was a Canadian immigrant, a shrewd businessman who would be the first mayor of Northfield and would serve in the Minnesota legislature in 1877 and again in 1879.

His mills built and operating, North seems to have warmed to the idea of fathering a new and thriving town. He took on the role of the new town's cheerleader and deluged eastern acquaintances and papers with enthusiastic letters about this promised land of Minnesota. The flow of immigrants increased and continued, farmers took up land all around Northfield, and the little town thrived. If at first North had been interested only in the abundant water power of the Cannon and in developing the settlement on its banks, he put down his own roots in the town he had built from nothing.

He was a man ahead of his time, was John North, not only an ardent abolitionist and a staunch foe of John Barleycorn but also a tireless champion of women's suffrage. The village he founded grew and prospered, and showed signs of permanence by the time Minnesota became a state in 1858. North himself acquired a statewide reputation as a delegate to the state constitutional convention of 1857 and as head of the Minnesota Republican delegation to the 1860 convention that nominated Abraham Lincoln.

In those days the town center of Northfield was close to the river, as it is today. When the town was originally surveyed and laid out in about 1855, the streets were planned in an orderly grid, and from the beginning the plan called for civilized amenities and some green and peaceful parks. The town's first homes were frame structures that would have been right at home in Vermont. Down by the Cannon River bridge lay a pleasant plaza flanked by busy streets on both sides. In the center of the square today stands a monument to the townsmen who served the Union in the Civil War. It wasn't there in 1876 to exasperate the Missouri outlaws; the townspeople didn't erect it until 1921, presumably on the thesis that it doesn't pay to rush these things.

If the early settlers in Northfield were a snapshot of New England, other immigrants soon appeared to leaven the mix. As a Minnesota newspaper chuckled, "We are American, Canadian, Irish, German, Norwegian and Indian, besides being considerably mixed up ourselves. We ain't very particular, we ain't. Some how, the races have got into hotchpotch here."[4] Sure enough, everybody got along at least reasonably well. Northfield's best-known barber was Italian, and the leading butcher was Jewish. The stores were run by Yankees, Norwegians, and Germans. Life was full, busy, peaceful, ared abundant.

> Every substantial citizen kept a cow and a horse. He raised a large garden. Wages were low and men would work 10 hours for one dollar; prices of food stuffs were also low. Nobody got rich, but everybody was comfortable.[5]

And the country grew. West of Northfield a French colony of some two hundred families appeared, together with small enclaves of Germans, Norwegians, and Swedes.

By 1860 Rice County boasted 800 farms. A great many farmers raised wheat as their main crop, and that wheat needed to be turned into flour. When the Civil War ended, John North's original flour mill was producing some seventy-five barrels a day. By this time North had sold out to a man named Wheaton and moved on, to become surveyor-general for the new territory of Nevada and in time a justice of its supreme court. And then, still following his dream of city building, North moved on again, to help in founding the California cities of Riverside and Pasadena and to become a federal judge in blooming, booming California.

Wheaton sold North's mill to Jesse Ames, a onetime sea captain turned mill owner and entrepreneur. By 1869 Ames had turned the old North sawmill into a second flour mill, a bigger plant that could produce 150 barrels of flour in twenty-four hours. By 1875 the mill would handle 175 barrels, and in time, with improvements, it reached the prodigious production of 400 barrels per day.

Ames developed a special process that produced superb flour for bread, and by the 1870s Northfield flour was famous. It fetched premium prices well above those for flour from other parts of Minnesota, and in 1876, the year of the James-Younger raid, Northfield flour won a prize for excellence at the Centennial Exposition in Philadelphia. That long-awaited celebration of American independence and success was attended by, among other people, both president J. C. Nutting and cashier G. M. Phillips of the First National Bank of Northfield. Their eagerness to attend the great centennial event may well have saved their lives, for they were not in the bank when eight hard-eyed men in long dusters rode into town. In that boom year Jesse Ames was vice president of the First National Bank of Northfield.

Jesse Ames's son, Adelbert, had risen to become a Union major general during the Civil War and was a division commander at Gettysburg. While still an artillery lieutenant, he had won the Medal of Honor on the bloody field of First Manassas, staying in command of a section of Regular Army artillery in spite of the pain of a terrible wound. Son-in-law of the detested Benjamin "Beast" Butler, Ames served a while as Reconstruction governor of Union-occupied Mississippi, then as regularly elected senator and again as governor. In 1876, the year of the raid, he retired to Northfield, where he held stock in both his father's mill and the bank.

And in that bank, grumbled Cole Younger later, both Adelbert and Butler kept misgotten "southern money." Inevitably Cole, with his usual effrontery and "poor me" attitude, offered Adelbert Ames's retention of this mythical Civil War booty as some sort of justification for the attempt on the Northfield bank. Cole offered no evidence that Ames looted Mississippi, although he darkly referred to Butler as "Silver Spoons," presumably a reference to Butler's supposed pillage in the South.[6]

Cole's vengeful mutterings against Ames and Butler smack of after-the-fact justification. Even if Ames did ride back north with some southern loot, "southern money" was not much of a catch if it was in Confederate States currency, and even Cole did not allege that Ames made off with a wagonload of gold. Moreover, it is a matter of record that neither Butler nor Ames, though they owned stock in the bank, had money on deposit there at the time of the raid.[7]

More industry followed the mills and the farms. The town supported a plow factory, a tannery, a foundry, at least three shoemakers, and the usual blacksmiths and tinsmiths and wagon menders.

Several cooperage shops labored to produce the barrels for North-field's premium flour. In time Northfield factories would also pro-duce cigars, flax, and bricks that were famous all over the Midwest, and in time a fire department was founded to protect the growing city.

By 1865 the town had its own private banks. The Northfield Improvement Association busied itself planting trees, and schools appeared. So did churches, including All Saints Episcopal, conse-crated in spring 1867. With additions, All Saints still holds services today. A city hall was built in 1875, complete with cupola, just three years after Northfield proudly opened its opera house.

And so the town grew and prospered. In 1867 a Northfield res-ident, Horace Goodhue, wrote excitedly to his bride-to-be:

> There are heavy forests only half a mile to the west and rolling prairies to the east and south. The bluffs are almost hills and Northfield is more like a New England village than any other which I have seen in the west. We have four churches, a bank, a weekly paper, three lawyers, five or six doctors, a dozen or more stores and from twelve to fifteen hundred inhabitants, and this is where only thirteen years ago the Indians had a scalp dance and land was selling for $1.25 an acre.[8]

By this time Northfield was shipping thousands of barrels of flour every month, plus many thousands of bushels of unprocessed wheat. The flour, Gopher State and Northfield XXX, was well known even beyond Minnesota. In the year in which Goodhue wrote hap-pily to his fiancée, the iron foundry and the tannery were already in operation.

In those days you rode into Northfield across the Cannon River bridge, the wooden span that carried the road from the west. If you dismounted and walked across into the town you found yourself in Bridge Square (Mill Square in those days, and later Horsecollar Park). And if you walked farther east across Bridge Square, you were on Fourth Street and quickly came to Division Street. Division ran roughly north and south, generally parallel to the Cannon

River. Division Street was the center of town, lined with businesses in both directions from the square.

As you walked through the square toward Division Street you came to two hardware stores on your right, run by A. R. Manning and J. S. Allen. Next to them to the east, separated from them only by a narrow alley, was a solid business building called the Scriver Block. The building was built by Hiram Scriver, the early visionary merchant and first mayor of the town. The Scriver Block was a fine stone structure, which in 1868 cost its owner some $15,000, a substantial sum for the time. On the corner of the square and Division Street was Lee and Hitchcock's dry goods emporium. Upstairs, above the businesses, there were offices, which you reached by an outside stairway around the corner, on Division Street. The northern front of the building, facing the square, held not only Lee and Hitchcock's but also Scriver's own dry goods business.

On the east side of the Scriver building, fronting on Division Street, stood the First National Bank. Across the square to the north and overlooking it were the offices of the *Rice County Journal*. The *Journal* was a weekly paper then, published every Thursday. The *Journal* offices were on the second floor, above the Harvey Allen Store and next to the post office (still only a lean-to in those days). From the *Journal*'s windows its publisher, C. A. Wheaton, would have a ringside seat for the James-Younger gang's strike at his city's bank.

If you crossed the square and turned to the right down Division Street you were walking south, and the first business you came to on the right was the bank. Although it was housed in the Scriver Block on the southeast corner of Bridge Square, it fronted on Division Street. Across from the bank, facing it across Division, were the Wheeler Drugstore, several other shops, and the Dampier Hotel. The hotel was the second building from the corner, about opposite the Scriver building; Wheeler's drugstore was three doors farther south. Both businesses would play a vital part in the ferocious fight that pleasant September afternoon in 1876.

Although it wasn't very big, Northfield knew the value of culture and education. Along with several churches, the town prided itself on having not one but two colleges. One was Carleton, a Congregational school. Its treasurer was Joseph Lee Heywood, a quiet, highly respected citizen who also served as bookkeeper of the First National Bank of Northfield. Carleton, established in 1866 as Northfield College, emphasized the value of both religion and education, reflecting Northfield's abiding New England heritage. It opened modestly in 1866, with just twenty-three students and only one professor, a young Dartmouth graduate named Horace Goodhue.

The other college was St. Olaf's, like Carleton a small, excellent liberal arts college (both schools are still small and excellent). St. Olaf's was founded in 1874, and for a while it taught all its classes in two well-used wooden buildings outgrown by the public schools. But the little college was confident and successful, and three years later it began building up above the town on Manitou Hill, which would be its permanent home. It built in brick, to last, and its ambitious curriculum included religion, Norwegian, Greek, Latin, German, science, and mathematics. Northfield's colleges would produce a number of famous scholars, among these were philosopher-economist Thorstein Veblen, a Carleton graduate, and St. Olaf's Ole Rolvaag, whose *Giants in the Earth* became the defining novel of Norwegian prairie migration.

The town's dedication to culture did not stop with its colleges and churches. Early on, in 1857, led by John North, the citizenry set up the Northfield Lyceum Society and gave it its own building. The Lyceum provided both meeting space and a lecture hall, where the society offered debates on the burning issues of the day, such as women's suffrage and temperance. Not surprising, the Lyceum Society's first president was John North. Hiram Scriver was also a member, as was Thomas Buckham, who spent twenty-eight years as a judge of Rice County.

The society also sponsored the town's first lending library. It had willing allies in the Odd Fellows, the Masonic Lodge, and the Northfield Improvement Association, all of which public-spirited guilds worked mightily for the elevation and success of their thriving little town. By the end of 1865 a handsome two-story YMCA building was completed on Division Street, complete to the large *Welcome* carved in the stone above the front door.

North himself built the first house in Northfield, donated land for a public park, and constructed American House, a hotel of three stories. The building was later occupied by the infant Northfield College, before it became Carleton College in 1877. Not all the town's activities were devoted to the pursuit of knowledge and culture. There were dances, church socials, picnics, amateur theatricals, and rowing parties on the Cannon River.

The town took its civic responsibility seriously in politics as well. North was called the father of the Republican party in Minnesota. Traditionally, Northfield has ever after been a staunchly Republican town. Indeed, after the smashing 1936 Franklin Roosevelt victory, the local paper quipped that only "Maine, Vermont and Northfield gave majorities to the Republican candidate."[9]

In 1876 the First National Bank of Northfield was a new creation, the offspring of the recent union of two private banks. Its small offices in the Scriver Block shared walls with the businesses of Scriver and Lee and Hitchcock, both opening onto Bridge Square, and with Miller's, south of the bank and opening onto Division Street, like the bank. The bank's quarters were temporary, the same space that had housed one of its small parent banks. They were to serve only until the bank could move into a larger, permanent place. Since the bank's digs were only temporary, the arrangement of the counters and furniture had not been changed from the private bank days.

Because the bank's counters dated from the early days of private banking in Northfield, they had been built "after the style of store counters," in the words of Alonzo Bunker, the teller at the time of the raid. Banks of later vintage had counters of fine wood, well defended by wrought-iron grills and bars, but the antique design of the Northfield bank meant that at one point—close to the Division Street door—the working area was entirely open save for the low counter, easy enough for an active man to climb over. The rest of the counter was screened by a tall railing, which had glass panels set into it.

The heart of the bank was its modern vault. It was the best that money could buy, a product of the Detroit Safe Company. Inside that vault was a first-class safe, made by Evans and Watson of Philadelphia and inscribed "First National Bank." It was 6,500 pounds of formidable iron, and it boasted a newfangled, state-of-the-art Yale time lock, called a "chronometer lock" in those days. It was an impressive testament to the bank's determination to protect its depositors. It is still in Northfield, still glaring at intruders in the beautifully reconstructed bank, a part of the Northfield Historical Society's excellent museum.

The bank had every reason to be proud of its fine safe; just getting it to Northfield had been an achievement. It had made its way to the bank by way of Pittsburgh, and from there had travelled down the Ohio, to Cairo, Illinois. From Cairo the safe had been shipped up the Mississippi to Stillwater, Minnesota, and then had come to Northfield over the uncertain roads of the day, hauled by a sturdy four-horse team.

Ironically, just a few days before the raid the president of Carleton College had come to the bank to see the wonderful new time lock. He had asked Joseph Lee Heywood, the quiet assistant cashier, "Now if robbers should come in here and order you to open this vault, would you do it?" And Heywood smiled and answered simply, "I think not."[10] Heywood's words were prophetic.

The bank's front door and two windows opened east, onto busy Division Street. The bank also had another window and a back door, both of which gave to the west, opening onto the eight-foot alley between the back door of the First National and the side of Manning's Hardware, whose side door also opened onto the same alley. On the day of the raid the afternoon weather was warm, so both the front and back doors of the bank were open. The back door was covered with what Bunker called a "double-blind," a screen device that would block out the afternoon sun but allow the circulation of air. The blind was fastened on the inside. In the warmth of the afternoon a calendar clock ticked lazily behind the counter on the bank wall (it is still there today, keeping perfect time).[11]

September 7, 1876, began like any ordinary day in Northfield. The bank's ledger, still in existence, shows a number of routine transactions. There were dealings with Carleton College, the Grange Mill, John Ames, and a number of other citizens and businesses. Lying in the cash drawers and the safe were $15,455 and a few cents, a fine haul for bandits. Inside the bank were three men, going industriously about the business of their employer. With both the president and the cashier away at the Centennial Exhibition in Philadelphia, the senior man in the bank was thirty-nine-year-old Joseph Lee Heywood. Heywood came of New Hampshire farm stock, both abolitionist and Republican. Leaving home when he was about twenty, he had worked at a variety of jobs in Massachusetts, Michigan, and Illinois.

In Chicago in the summer of 1862, Heywood enlisted in the 127th Illinois Volunteer Infantry, serving at, among other places, Vicksburg and Arkansas Post. Although his health broke down, he returned to the army after some rest at home and finished his service in Nashville as a druggist in the military dispensary. After the war Heywood moved on to Minnesota, and after living for brief periods in Minneapolis and Faribault, he settled in Northfield in 1867. He went to work as a bookkeeper and was apparently good at it; after four years of taking care of the accounts of the S. P. Stewart Lumber Yard, Heywood hired on as bookkeeper with the bank in 1872. His wife, Lizzie Adams Heywood, was a virtuous and respected Massachusetts lady, and the couple lived with Heywood's five-year-old daughter by a previous marriage.

Heywood was much respected and trusted in Northfield. Besides his duties at the bank, he was treasurer of the city of Northfield, Carleton College, and the Northfield Board of Education. Heywood's picture shows a dark-haired, serious man with a neatly trimmed full beard and mustache. Though he may not have had a strong constitution—the breakdown of his health during the war shows that—this quiet, pleasant man was iron inside.

The assistant bookkeeper for the bank was a young man called Alonzo Bunker, known to Northfield as Lon, a slim, handsome man with a drooping Wyatt Earp mustache. Like Heywood, he was a New Hampshire man, born in the town of Littleton. His parents brought him to Minnesota in 1855, when he was six. After some time in the public schools, he became a printer with the *Mantonville Express*, then a schoolteacher, then a student at the St. Paul Business College, from which he graduated in 1869.

By 1871 Bunker was a student at Carleton College, still working as a printer on the side. Worn down by trying to work and attend school at the same time, he joined the bank in 1873 as a bookkeeper. He also worked as an accountant and taught bookkeeping at Carleton College. Bunker was newly married at the time of the raid; his wife, Nettie, was a Red Wing girl who taught in the Northfield public school. She was teaching on the day of the raid.

The third bank employee was a temporary assistant bookkeeper, Frank J. Wilcox. Wilcox was another New Englander, born in Massachusetts in 1848. Son of a Baptist clergyman who moved to Northfield when Frank was ten, young Wilcox attended both public school and a college preparatory course at Carleton. He graduated from the University of Chicago in 1874 and returned home to Northfield. Wilcox was single, a dark-haired man with a Smith Brothers beard; he would stay on with the bank and in time would become its assistant cashier. On that sleepy afternoon he was working on the books with Bunker. Heywood sat just a few feet away, dealing with some of the bank's correspondence.

So this was Northfield, and its small, busy bank, on the warm, Indian Summer afternoon of September 7, 1876. It sounds like the sort of town everybody would like to live in, busy, law-abiding, cultivated, the hub of a fertile, blooming country.

It was about to become a battlefield.

CHAPTER FOUR

THOSE GENTLEMEN
WILL BEAR WATCHING

Autumn comes early in Minnesota, ushered in by a delightful bite in the early morning air and an awe-inspiring panoply of colors as the trees prepare to lose their leaves. Still, midday can be warm in September, even this far north, and so it was on September 7, 1876.

The raiders rode in from the west through a smiling, pleasant autumn day. The citizens who saw them noticed their fine saddle horses. And some probably noticed that all of them wore long linen dusters, although these were not unusual garments for travelers in those days. A duster kept at least some of the dust off a traveler's clothing—and for a criminal a duster came in handy to cover up pistols and cartridge belts. One story of the raid puts five of the raiders in Northfield early in the morning and asserts that citizens thought two of them had visited Northfield about a week before, stopping at the Dampier Hotel.

Two of the bandits had eaten some lunch about midday in John Tosney's restaurant, on Water Street near the Cannon. Or, according to another account, four or five of the bandits walked into a restaurant run by J. T. Jeft. These men, according to this account "loitered in front of Scrivers Hardware until noon" before they went off to Jeft's to eat lunch. It's said that all five bandits ordered the same thing: ham with four eggs apiece. While they ate, they talked loud enough to be heard all over the restaurant, one or more

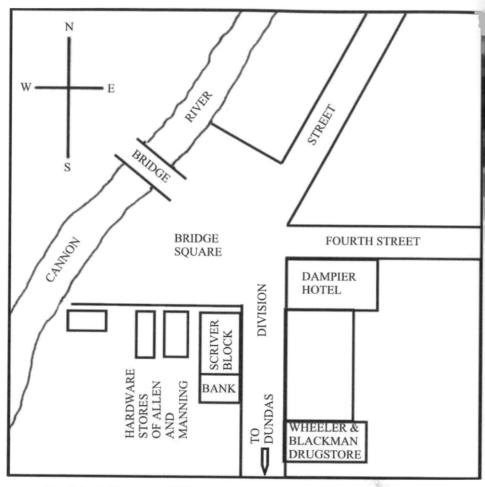

Northfield, Minnesota, 1876

of them offering to bet anybody a thousand dollars that Northfield would vote Democratic in the election coming in November. After finishing lunch, they departed, "walking with bold reckless swaggers and looking as if they could be hard to handle."[1] If this tale is true, it is proof that these gang members showed no spark of common sense. If you're going to rob a bank and don't want to be remembered, you don't offer that kind of bet in a loud voice in a Republican stronghold.

There's another story that at about the same time two or three of the other raiders, probably Frank James, Bob Younger, and Charlie Pitts, dropped in at the Exchange Saloon, about a block from the bank, in the three hundred block of Division Street, the main commercial thoroughfare of Northfield. The three partook of ardent spirits at the Exchange—heavily by one account. More important to our story, they also bought a quart of whiskey to take along with them and then mounted up and crossed the river to join the rest of the gang for the final planning session.

And then the time had come to get on with the raid. It was about two o'clock, according to the best contemporary history of the raid.[2] Another account relates that the five backup men were to ride to the edge of the town and "wait there until the clock in the belfry of the Lutheran church struck one. That was to be the signal for the wild dash into Northfield, both groups timing themselves so they would reach Bridge Square within a few minutes of each other." The same account has the three inside men eating lunch at Jeft's restaurant, just "a few doors up the street."[3] And then the three loafed around in front of Manning's store until the church bell struck the hour.

It is most probable that the gang rode toward the bank in three units, as they had planned. As is usually the case in outlaw history, there is no agreement about what happened next. The best guess is that Pitts, Bob Younger, and one of the James boys—probably Frank—were the first unit, the inside team, although at least one excellent history says the inside unit was composed of Bob Younger and the James brothers.[4] Other sources say Bob Younger went inside, accompanied by Jesse and Charlie Pitts,[5] or have Pitts and the James brothers entering the bank.[6]

As the three men rode abreast across the Cannon River bridge onto the square, they passed Adelbert Ames, his brother, and his father walking down from the First National after a board meeting. They were headed for the Ames Mill, just across the Cannon on Water Street. As the three bandits passed the Ameses, one lifted his hat to them. "Hello, governor," he said, and the greeting made

Adelbert Ames wonder. "No one here calls me governor," he said, adding, according to one tale, "those men are from the South and are here for no good purpose."[7] Ames did not have much longer to think about this strange greeting, for it would be only a few minutes until the devil was loose in Northfield.

The first three riders were also spotted by a citizen named Francis Howard, who was standing at the west end of the bridge. Howard did not like their looks, enough so that he followed them a little way, until he met Elias Stacy, who was standing on the sidewalk also watching the riders. "Stacy," said Howard, "those gentlemen will bear watching," and Stacy agreed.

Howard and Stacy watched the three outlaws cross the square, ride on past Manning's hardware emporium, and turn the corner onto Division. The outlaws left their horses in front of the bank, tossed their reins over the hitching posts, and walked back to the corner of the Scriver Block. There they sat down on some boxes stacked in front of Lee and Hitchcock's dry goods store under its enthusiastic sign, Good Goods Cheap! They tried to look as nonchalant as possible—at least for three strangers in long dusters— and began "whittling the boxes, like the most commonplace loafers."[8] One account of the raid says that the inside men entered the bank briefly and changed a bill *before* they sat down on the corner.[9] This story is unlikely. It would have been a pointless act, since the decision to rob the bank had already been taken. And if the advance party had cashed a bill, they would know where the bank kept its currency drawer; in the event, the robbers never located the drawer. Even more convincing, neither surviving bank employee mentions such a visit.

Harry Drago insists that as the Lutheran church bell chimed one o'clock, Bob Younger, Chadwell, and Miller galloped into town "yelling like savages, their guns barking. As they thundered across the bridge, Cole and Jim Younger swept in from the west, their .45s cracking."[10] This vivid tale is certainly stirring but certainly incorrect, for there is no evidence that anybody fired a shot until some of Northfield's citizens realized that something was wrong inside the bank and began to shout an alarm. Moreover, there would be no reason to whoop, holler, shoot, and rouse the town as long as the robbery inside the bank proceeded quietly.

Another story relates that on the Wednesday or Thursday before the raid, two of the outlaws had called on Trussell's store while the merchant was selling a citizen a plow. The visitors had asked questions about the road system in the area, slightly arousing Trussell's suspicions. The strangers "talked well and behaved well," however, and were on their way in a half hour or so. One of the pair was the rider of a fine bay horse. And now, on this warm afternoon, Trussell saw at least one of the same men ride back into town. Again he became suspicious but relaxed when Elias Hobbs assured him that he was sure the men were cattle buyers.

As the bandits rode into Northfield across Bridge Square, J. S. "Sim" Allen, whose hardware store was just west of the bank, became suspicious. Shouldn't we, he asked merchant Trussell, "tell the boys at the bank to be on the look-out?" Trussell laughed, now that he was convinced that the horsemen in long dusters were cattle buyers. There was no reason, he said, for frightening the employees of the bank. Sim Allen was not convinced. "Who are those men?" he said to Ino Acker. "I don't like the looks of them." And then, as two more mounted men came into town across the Cannon River bridge, Allen instinctively jumped to the right conclusion: "I believe they are here to rob the bank."[11] Allen later said that he "suspected their mission and immediately went to the corner of Lee & Hitchcock's store watching their movements."[12]

Cole Younger and Clel Miller were the two riders Allen had seen riding up toward Division Street along the same route across Bridge Square. Miller was calmly smoking his pipe. Cole was puzzled to see the first three outlaws sitting on the boxes, since the robbers' plan called for the raid to be aborted if there were "too many people on the street." According to his account, Cole turned to Miller in surprise: "Surely the boys will not go into the bank with so many people about. I wonder why they did not ride on through town." But then, as Cole and Miller approached, the first three outlaws got up from their boxes and walked south along Division Street to the bank door. "They are going in," said Miller, and Cole began to get anxious. He turned to Miller: "If they do the alarm will be given as sure as there's a hell, so you had better take that pipe out of your mouth."[13]

Francis Howard was getting anxious, too. As the first three outlaws headed for the bank door, he turned again to Stacy and other citizens near him, including Allen. "There is a St. Alban's raid," Howard said, and Allen immediately started for the bank door. Howard's last remark takes a little explaining: his reference was to a daring 1864 attack on the town of St. Alban's, Vermont, by Confederate lieutenant Bennett Young and a couple of dozen men. The raiders succeeded at first, robbing three banks, but then were forced to flee by a pack of angry citizens; only about half of the invaders made their escape into Canada, just fifteen miles away.

Whatever Cole's misgivings may have been, once the raid had begun there was nothing for the rest of the outlaws to do but see it through. Miller got off his horse in front of the bank, opened the door to peer inside, closed it again, and then began to walk up and down in front of the door. Cole dismounted in the middle of the street and pretended to adjust his saddle girth. One citizen at least saw through his charade, noticing that the girth was already so tight that the horse's belly ridged up on both sides of its webbing.

The last three outlaws, Jim Younger, Bill Chadwell, and the other James brother (probably Jesse) rode across the bridge and stopped near it, ready to charge into town yelling and shooting to clear the streets in case there was trouble in the bank. They would also a provide a convenient covering force if the raid went bad and the gang had to beat a fighting retreat.

By this time, a couple of oddities should have been obvious to anybody out on Division Street. Cole's fiddling with a girth in the middle of the street and Miller's marching up and down in front of the bank entrance were hardly activities calculated to escape notice. And they didn't. What the gang did not know is that at least some citizens had heard a report of nine riders approaching Northfield. Even those who had not heard the story had to wonder at the presence of a number of duster-clad horsemen in town, especially because in settled Northfield most people traveled in wagons or buggies.

A. R. Manning was in his hardware store in the building just next to the bank, facing Bridge Square. He looked up from dealing with a customer as firing broke out on Division Street. Two riders were galloping across the square, firing their revolvers, and Manning at first thought they were advertising a show that was to be given that night. But then somebody yelled something about robbing the bank, and Manning knew there was trouble.

So did Mrs. John Handy. She was shopping in a store right across the street from the bank, chatting with W. H. Riddell. Mrs. Handy happened to hail from St. Alban's and knew all about bank robberies. As Riddell put it, she was "evidently suspicious of the movements of the strange horsemen and hardly paid any attention to me."[14] Mrs. Handy soon noticed the flash of steel from the bandits' revolvers and forthwith betook herself out the back door of the store. Riddell, less wise and more curious, went out his front door onto Division, intending to see what was afoot at the bank.

Still, most citizens were not alarmed. Some took the strangers to be hunters in town for the prairie chicken season, then in full swing. Others believed the riders had something to do with promotion of a circus or a Wild West show. Even after the shooting began, a citizen named Van Amberg, busily building a chimney on a Division Street house, was convinced that the shooting had something to do with the governor being in town. R. C. Phillips, who worked for Manning, heard the first shot and asked his boss what it was. Manning replied, "I think it's that show that's going to be here tonight." Some residents continued to believe the riders were advertising a show even after the shooting began. At least one, Steven Budd, at first thought the strangers were cattle buyers. A few Northfield people concluded that the pistol-waving riders were only celebrating drunks, and others paid no attention at all, intent on their own business.

Northfield's dentist, Dr. D. J. Whiting, was in his office on the second floor of the Scriver building, above the bank and reached by the outside stairway from Division. From his window, which fronted on the square, he noticed horsemen riding by but thought little of it. Then came the gunshots, but still the doctor did not take alarm. Let him tell the rest:

> Soon I heard firing and saw doves flying. I thought the boys across the street were shooting and went to the doorway at the head of the stairs and saw several men on horseback riding up and down the street firing revolvers, swearing and yelling in the wildest manner.

Whiting watched the riders order a man on the street to run. When the man simply walked on down the street, they pursued him, firing and shouting at him to get off the street.

> About this time, some of them saw me and sent a shot at me, ordering me back. I was wondering all the time what all this meant. A lady in my office said there was to be an Indian show that evening and the show men were advertising.[15]

A. O. Whipple, whose law office was at the south end of the second floor of the Scriver Block, dashed into Whiting's office. If the doctor still had doubts that there was trouble, Whipple banished them. There's a gang in town, the lawyer said, and they're robbing the bank.

Whiting's patient, young Adeline Murray, stepped out onto the landing with Dr. Whiting to see what the commotion in the street was all about. One of the outlaws spotted the pair, yelled at them, and drove a slug into the casing of the landing door. "Addie," said the dentist with masterful understatement, "this is no place for us."[16] It wasn't, and some of the other townspeople were also beginning to take alarm. One man sprinted back across the Cannon River bridge shouting, "There's fifty men over there shooting everybody on the street!"[17]

If some of the townspeople were not immediately wary of all the riders in linen dusters, others were very suspicious indeed and willing to take a closer look. Two who *were* uneasy about the activity around the bank were Sim Allen and Henry M. Wheeler, a young Northfield man home from medical school at the University of Michigan.

Wheeler was on the east side of Division, sitting on a chair under an awning in front of a drugstore in which his father, Mason, was a partner. A passing farmer had spoken to Wheeler, wondering why there were so many saddle horses in town, and somebody else had said that "eight men came out of the woods to the west of town on saddle horses, and I think it means something." And so when the first bandits approached the bank, Wheeler became suspicious: he got up and walked down the sidewalk until he was across the street from the bank door. One source says that Wheeler recognized the riders, even knew their names, because "[t]wo of them had stayed at the Dampier Hotel ten days before."[18] Maybe the faces were familiar, because some of the men had been in Northfield earlier in the day or week, but there is no other evidence that any of the gang had stayed overnight in town.

As Wheeler walked down closer to the bank, Allen was standing on the west side of Division about opposite the Dampier Hotel talking to another citizen. When the three bandits went into the bank, he tried to follow them inside. Wheeler, Budd, and Riddell watched as Clel Miller grabbed Allen by the collar, shoved a revolver under his nose, and ordered him with a stream of profanity "not to holler, for if he did he'd blow his damned head off." Francis Howard said later that Miller "drew his revolver and swung it over his head, began shooting in the air and shouting 'Get out of there, you sons of bitches!'"[19] At this first shot the three remaining bandits charged across the square into Division Street, pistols in both hands, firing and yelling the usual expletives, "get in, you sons of bitches!"

Allen, unimpressed by Miller's pistol, pulled away and ran toward his store at the front of the Scriver Block, yelling an alarm as he ran. Just exactly what he shouted is lost, but it was enough to alert the whole town. "Get your guns, boys, they're robbing the bank!" he roared, according to one account, as he ran back toward his store. Budd took to his heels as well, afterward remarking wryly that he had "thought it safe to go that way too."[20]

Wheeler joined in the hue and cry, shouting, "Robbery! They are robbing the bank!"[21] Cole and Miller immediately mounted and began to yell at Wheeler, snapping a couple of shots over his head. "Get back," one outlaw yelled, "or I'll kill you!" When the shooting started, J. A. Hunt came out of the jewelry store five doors south of the bank, only to be confronted by Jim Younger, mounted and firing a revolver with each hand. Shouting and cursing, he ordered Hunt back inside the shop. As Riddell began shouting the alarm and Wheeler ran, the outlaws galloped up and down Division, shouting "Get in! Get in!" and spraying pistol bullets in all directions. As the firing started, Stacy ran into a store on the corner and kept on going until he reached a vantage point on the roof.

At the sound of shooting the three outlaws posted by the bridge galloped across the square yelling and shooting at anything that moved. Everywhere citizens ducked for cover. Phillips, not satisfied with Manning's explanation of the first shot, went outside and around the corner, where he met John Archer and John Tosney. "They're robbing the bank," the men shouted, and then Phillips saw more outlaws (he thought there were five) galloping from the bridge across the square, spraying bullets "right and left and shouting, 'Get in, you sons of bitches!'"

Cole wrote later that the alarm was given just as Miller closed the bank door. Somebody shouted, "Robbers in the bank!"

> A man came up to the bank, and then started to run away, whereupon Miller drew his pistol down on him and cried out, "Stop, or I'll kill you!" The man halted, but soon began to move off slowly, and I called out "Don't shoot him; let him go!"[22]

This is clearly a reference to Sim Allen's attempt to enter the bank, although Cole's self-serving version of what he said to Miller is not reflected in any other account of the raid. Cole says he also kept Chadwell from shooting Allen as the covering party galloped in from the bridge to help out on Division Street. At about the same time, according to Cole, the "man on the buckskin horse"—Cole's euphemism for one of the James boys—"passed on up the street fifty or a hundred yards south of the bank," and Cole and his brother Jim stopped in front of the bank. By now people all over town could hear the steady hammer of gunfire, Northfield's church bells had begun to ring the alarm, and dogs were barking furiously, adding to the racket along Division Street.

Up at Carleton College a matron and the wife of one of the trustees ran into the school crying orders to "keep the girls off the street." The matron then promptly fainted, and a professor's wife helped get the female pupils up onto an upper story, believing for some reason that the bandits would next attack the college. "Every girl was to take an axe and we went all of us to the third floor, determined to make a good resistance."[23] Northfield's women, it appears, were every bit as courageous as their men.

If things were bad out on Division Street, they were much worse inside the bank. J. L. Heywood, the acting cashier, and Wilcox and Alonzo Bunker were taken entirely by surprise. Bunker looked up from his accounts at the sound of footsteps, prepared to greet a customer. Instead he was confronted by the unwinking eyes of three revolvers and three hard faces telling him to throw up his hands. Bunker momentarily wondered if somebody was playing a joke, until the three bandits climbed over the counter and explained why they were there. It went something like this: "We're going to rob this bank. Don't any of you holler. We've got forty men outside."[24]

Bunker found himself "looking those revolvers in the face, the hole in each of them seemed about as large as a hat." "I was commanded," he said, "'to throw up your hands.' Under the circumstances, this seemed the most appropriate thing to do, and I 'threw them up.'" In later years Bunker wrote of telling this story to another man, who emphatically agreed with the rightness of Bunker's response: "I tell you boss, I'd a 'frowed up all de hands I had, and wished I had mo'."[25]

Wilcox, who turned at the sound of "some confusion and a rush from the door," confessed he "was something more than startled by the presence of three men with pistols in their hands." He thought that the three robbers inside the bank were Pitts, Bob Younger, and Frank James. "It was evident," said Wilcox later, "that they had been drinking, as the smell of liquor was very strong." Wilcox remembered that one of the robbers said, "Throw up your hands, for we intend to rob the bank, and if you halloo we will blow your God damned brains out." "We could not," said Wilcox simply, "do otherwise than comply."[26]

Whatever the robbers said, they made it pretty plain that they were serious. One of them—Bunker said it was Frank James—then confronted Heywood with "a flourish of his revolver," asking whether he was the cashier. "No," said Heywood, which was at least technically true, and Bunker and Wilcox answered in the same way. The bandits picked on Heywood, however, because he was the oldest man present and was sitting at the cashier's desk. "You're the cashier," Frank James said. "Open that safe damn quick, or I'll blow your head off!" Or maybe it was, "Now open the safe you son of a bitch." One version of the raid has Heywood trying to "go limp and slip to the floor," but that comment is neither supported by any other account nor in keeping with the stout heart of J. L. Heywood.[27]

The vault door stood open, and one robber now ran to the vault entrance and stepped inside. One version of the raid says this outlaw was Jesse James. At this Heywood sprang forward and tried to slam the vault door. Wilcox said that Heywood managed to push the door closed, shutting the robber inside so that the others had to "release the incarcerated robber." Whoever the robber in the vault was, Wilcox described him as "a slim, dark-complexioned man with a black mustache . . . who appeared to be the leader."[28] The description seems to fit Charlie Pitts better than Jesse James.

Nobody knows whether Heywood was actually trying to shut one of the bandits in the safe or just trying to slam the door and lock it. The uncertainty has not stopped some writers from speculating on Heywood's intentions, even to the point of inventing a train of thought. For instance this, from a very early account titled *The Northfield Tragedy*: "If I can but get that ponderous door closed," thought he, "and spring the bolts upon the scoundrel, the villians [*sic*] will be baffled, and my integrity saved from suspicion."

Frank James and Charlie Pitts dragged Heywood back and shoved their revolvers in his face, snarling, "Open that safe now, or you haven't but a minute to live!" or something like it. I can't open the safe, Heywood told the bandits. It has a time lock on it, he said, but the bandits didn't believe him. "That's a lie!" one said, and the three threw the helpless bank man around the room. Still full of fight, Heywood shouted "Murder! Murder!" and was rewarded with a smashing blow to the head from one of the bandits' revolvers. He crumpled to the floor behind his desk, and Pitts, brandishing a knife, said, "Let's cut his damned throat." Pitts pulled the blade across Heywood's throat, leaving a superficial cut, and two of the bandits dragged the poor battered Heywood back toward the vault door and partway inside.

Still trying to intimidate the semiconscious Heywood, one of the bandits shoved a pistol up close to his head and fired. The slug flew into the vault and tore into a tin box of papers and jewelry in safekeeping for one of the bank's clients. Bunker, hearing the shot and seeing Heywood motionless on the floor, thought the bandits had killed him. Wilcox remembered that the bandit he considered the leader ordered another outlaw—probably Pitts—to "go into the vault and try the safe." "All right," said Pitts, "but don't let him lock me in there."[29]

Had the furious bandits only tried the door of the safe, they would have found it open. Although the door was closed and latched, nobody had turned the combination dial. It would have opened at a touch. In spite of his mistreatment, Heywood never told the outlaws the safe was open, and in spite of brandished pistols and repeated threats, the younger bank men would not tell them either. Bob Younger kept his revolver trained on them while he nervously rummaged through drawers and rifled through papers on the bank's desks. He found nothing, even though two nearby counter drawers contained a great deal of money.

At one point Bunker, still clutching the pen he had been using when the bandits entered, realized it was "not as 'mighty' as the revolver just at that time" and tried to lay it down. Bob Younger "sprang at" Bunker, shoving his pistol in Bunker's face. "Here," the bandit said, "put your hands up, and keep 'em up, or I'll kill you."[30] He then forced Bunker and Wilcox to get down on their knees behind the counter.

Bunker, under the muzzle of Younger's gun, still thought about repelling the invaders. He remembered a .32-caliber Smith and Wesson pistol lying on a shelf beneath a teller's window and began to sidle closer and closer to it while Younger's back was turned. Pitts saw Bunker move, however, and snatched the little pistol off the shelf before the bookkeeper could reach it. Dropping it in his pocket, he chided Bunker: "You needn't try to get hold of that; you couldn't do anything with that little derringer anyway."[31]

Bunker managed to stand up about this time, determined to try to get out of the bank. Younger turned on him, demanding, "Where's the money outside the safe? Where's the cashier's till?" Still intent on protecting his employer's assets, Bunker pointed out the small-change box on top of the counter that contained coins and a little currency. "There's the money outside," he said. Ordering Bunker back down on his knees, Younger began to empty the drawer into a grain sack—standard bank robbers' equipment. He dropped in a handful or two, and then, in Bunker's words, "it seemed to occur to him that the 'claim he was working, panned out but little.'" Angry and swearing, he turned to Bunker, now back on his feet: "There's more money than that out here. Where's that cashier's till? And what in hell are you standing up for? I told you to keep down!"[32]

Younger pushed Bunker back down on his knees, shoved his pistol against Bunker's temple, and pushed Bunker's head down against the floor. "Show me where that money is, you thus-and-such, or I'll kill you!" Bunker stubbornly said nothing, and Younger went on searching vainly, missing some $3,000 in currency neatly arranged in a drawer just beneath the small-change box Bob had just cleaned out. It was only part of more than $15,000 on hand in the bank that day.

Bunker said later that he thought his time had come: "I cannot tell the sensation I experienced, but I know many thoughts flashed through my mind. I thought of my wife, my mother and my Maker, and felt reconciled to die." And so, before Pitts or anybody else could enter the vault and try the safe door, Bunker decided it was now or never, what with poor Heywood apparently either dead or badly wounded. With Bob Younger's head turned away from him, Bunker jumped to his feet and bolted for the room at the rear of the bank, called the "directors' room," and the back door. In a couple of steps he got out of the bandits' line of sight, and Pitts shouted and turned to chase him. As Bunker dashed for the back door, Pitts caught sight of him and fired a shot at the running man. The pistol ball snapped past Bunker's ear, and he lowered his shoulder, smashed into the double blind across the open back door, and burst into the daylight of the alley between the bank and Manning's hardware store.

As Bunker ran for the shelter of Manning's, Pitts appeared in the bank door and fired again, missing Bunker, and then the outlaw fired again from the bank's rear steps. This time the ball tore through Bunker's right shoulder, close to the shoulder joint, barely missing the big subclavian artery. Bunker, feeling like he had been hit with a board, staggered but kept his feet. He turned away from Manning's and sprinted across a vacant lot, headed for a doctor's office a block away. Pitts gave it up and turned back into the bank, for the roar of gunfire was rising higher and higher out on Division and Cole Younger was yelling at the men inside the bank. "The game is up! Better get out, boys. They're killing all our men!" Or, according to Hunt, "Come out of there, we are getting all cut up here!"

Cole kept trying to get the inside men out of the bank by firing at the windows on Division Street. According to Cole's narrative, his brother Bob finally emerged from the bank, but the others still did not. The hammer of firing on Division Street grew louder and louder, and Cole ran back to the bank door again, frantically shouting to the bandits inside, "For God's sake, come out!"

About then the other two bandits backed out of the bank, carrying almost nothing in the way of loot. And as they fell back, the last man to climb back over the counter paused a moment for an act of pure, pointless savagery. Heywood, battered and bleeding and only partly conscious, had struggled back onto his feet and staggered toward his desk. Wilcox watched as the last man turned and "with the expression of a very devil in his face put his pistol almost at Heywood's head and fired the fatal shot."[33] The killer shot gallant Heywood through the head. The banker fell dying on the floor of the bank he had tried so hard to protect.

To this day nobody knows for sure which bandit fired the fatal shot. Cole at first called the shooter only "the last man to leave the bank" and said the killer thought "he [Heywood] was going for a pistol." Jesse James has been repeatedly blamed for the wanton killing. One somewhat suspect book, *This Was Frank James*, tells it this way. Jesse confronts Heywood, demanding that he open the safe. And then:

> "I will do no such thing," said the brave cashier.
> "Open it," said Jesse, "or you die like a dog."
> "I will do my duty," said the cashier.
> "Then die," said Jesse James.
> Jesse James never repeated his word the second time. The
> cashier fell, dead.[34]

This version is patent moonshine: it has Heywood killed *before* Bunker made his dash out the back door of the bank and appears to place the Northfield raid *during* the Civil War, while "Quantral" was still leading his guerrilla band against the Yankees.

Although he was perfectly capable of such wanton murder, it is highly unlikely that Jesse was the man who shot the cashier. Later Cole wrote that Charlie Pitts, "in his liquor," was the killer.[35] Blaming Pitts for Heywood's death was convenient, of course, because dead men tell no tales. However, there is considerable reason to believe that the killer was in fact Frank James. In still another version of his story, drawn from a manuscript Cole gave to the Stillwater prison physician A. E. Hedbach, Cole said,

> The last man to leave the bank told me that as he was leaving the bank and jumped on the counter he saw Miller lying in the street, and at the same moment saw one of the clerks spring up and run towards the desk. . . . [He] ordered him to stop and sit down, . . . but he kept on and as my informant jumped from the counter he leveled his pistol and fired. The man fell. . . . [We] learned after we were captured that it was J. L. Heywood.[36]

Cole's glib explanation is a little hard to swallow. It is difficult to imagine poor, battered Heywood "springing up" and "running" anyplace, and Cole refers to the killer as "the last man to leave the bank" and "my informant." Cole's account sounds like an attempt to excuse the killing of Heywood and to cover the trail of his old friend Frank James. Bunker wrote later that the killer *was* Frank James and that Frank fired while Heywood, now on his feet, was leaning on a table in the center of the room. Frank climbed onto a desk, Bunker wrote, "between the Cashier's desk and Teller's window, and turning, reached back as near Heywood as possible, and deliberately shot down into his head, killing him."[37]

Dallas Cantrell agrees that Frank shot Heywood. But according to Cantrell, Frank's crime is even more plainly premeditated murder. Frank turned and fired at Heywood once, according to this story, but missed as Heywood hid behind a desk. In spite of the thunder of gunfire on the street outside, and in spite of Cole Younger's frantic call to "for God's sake, come out!" Frank followed Heywood, shoved the muzzle of his revolver almost against the bank man's face, and pulled the trigger.[38]

Harry Hoffman, in "The Youngers' Last Stand," tells us that Frank James "noticed a gun lying under the cashier's window, but didn't pick it up." And then "the cashier quickly made a leap for the gun which lay by his window. He was shot and instantly killed."[39]

Now Heywood was nowhere close to a window when the gang charged into the bank, and nobody else mentions another pistol in the bank. Moreover, Hoffman conveniently omits any mention of the terrible beating the gang gave Heywood. For these reasons we can dismiss Hoffman's account as an embroidery on Cole Younger's self-serving story that the shooter thought Heywood might be trying to reach a weapon.

The highly unlikely story of Heywood reaching for a gun has been repeated by several other writers. Drago, for example, says Jesse "glanced back and saw Heywood reaching under the counter, as though for a gun."[40] Frank Triplett tells his readers that Heywood (he calls the bank man "Haywood") was killed: "as the last robber was just about reaching the door he sprang to a drawer where he kept his revolver, but before securing it the rear robber turned, and divining his purpose, fired and killed him."[41]

Wilcox, however, ridiculed the whole notion that Heywood ever sprang anywhere or reached for anything: "[H]e . . . was reeling toward the desk in such a condition that anyone would know he was not reaching for a pistol and could not have used one had he held it in his hand."[42]

Much later Cole is said to have told Todd George, an insurance and real estate man in Lee's Summit, Missouri, that Frank James had killed Heywood. In fact, said George, he asked Cole who had done the murder, and Cole told him, "Ask Frank James, he knows who killed the cashier." George was even concerned that he might be quoted "and thus become an enemy of the remaining members of the James family or of some of Cole's kin."[43]

George also said that Cole told the same story to one George Williams at Monegaw Springs. Hoffman wrote long after that, "If I could say who rode the dun horse—they would then know who killed the cashier."[44] Frank James had bought a dun horse in Red Wing shortly before the raid. On the other hand, longtime Northfield columnist and historian Bill Schilling insisted, "[A]ll witnesses of the tragic shooting of acting cashier Heywood said at the time that it was the rider of the buckskin horse who left the bank last and fired the fatal bullet."[45]

Pitts could have been the killer, although Bunker said Pitts did not return to the room behind the counter but instead went back up the passageway to the front door. Still, Bunker could not know anything personally from the moment he crashed through the blinds on the rear door and ran for his life. He may have learned from Wilcox that Pitts ran and Frank James shot Heywood, or he may have simply surmised it. His is only part of the evidence that it was Frank James, not Jesse James or Charlie Pitts, who shot down the battered, half-conscious Heywood.

While the inside men were brutalizing Heywood, young Wheeler was driven from the street by gunshots and shouted threats. He ran to his father's drugstore, where he customarily kept his rifle. Remembering that he had left the weapon at home, he sprinted straight through the store and ran for a neighbor's house, where he thought he might get a gun. Changing his mind again, Wheeler turned into the Dampier Hotel, and there he found an "old army carbine," probably a single-shot, paper-cartridge Sharps. When the hotel clerk, Dampier, managed to scrounge up four old cartridges, Wheeler climbed to the third story of the hotel and got his old rifle into action.

At the same time Allen was in his hardware store handing out weapons and ammunition to anybody who wanted them. Next door Manning learned of the robbery from Allen and began to look for a weapon of his own. Manning is described as tall and thin, with a slit mouth, "prominent nose and remarkable eyes." Those eyes were striking, so large in Manning's narrow face that they seemed to be "making a complete, painstaking appraisal of everything they looked at."[46] Those remarkable eyes were about to see very clearly over the sights of a rifle.

Manning's clerk, Phillips, "took the guns and revolvers [they] had and threw them out on the show case." Later Phillips said that he remembered handing Manning a "single shot Winchester"

(Steven Budd, who saw Manning fighting, agreed, but Bunker remembered that Manning's weapon was a Remington). But Phillips, according to his account, gave his boss the wrong shells, so that Manning had to return to the store for the proper ammunition. Another account says thnat Manning snatched a handful of cartridges from a pigeonhole in his desk. Manning himself, without mentioning Phillips, later said,

> I remembered I had a rifle in the window that I had practiced with the spring before. . . . I jumped for that, pulled the cover off, and put my hand up and caught a lot of cartridges that lay there loose and put them into my pocket and started for the bank, loading my gun as I ran.[47]

However he got himself properly equipped, Manning courageously ran for the corner of the Scriver Block fronting on Division Street, where unalloyed hell had broken loose.

Most Northfield residents could only run for cover, helpless as the outlaws galloped screeching and firing up and down Division Street. Merchants hastily locked up their valuables, and the postmaster threw his registered mail into his safe and slammed the door. Somebody thought to notify Carleton College and the Northfield school that the town was under attack, but otherwise the wildest confusion reigned in the streets. Nobody knew how many outlaws were attacking the town, only that there seemed to be lots of them, blazing away at any window in which a citizen's face appeared. The five hoodlums galloping up and down Division Street, shouting, cursing, and spraying bullets, must have seemed like an army. Some of them at least were firing a revolver in each hand.

One citizen, Peter Youngquist, ran to his team of mules, who were panicked and trying to break loose from the hitching post. "Get in!" yelled one of the bandits and shoved his pistol against Youngquist. But Youngquist simply ignored the revolver and the threat, repeating that "all he wanted was to care for his mules." Another citizen had even more pressing business on the street. Carl Onstad sprinted down the wooden sidewalk of Division Street to snatch up his tiny son, ignoring the bandits' shouted commands and brandished pistols. E. S. Bill and his wife were in the back of the Shatto store with friends when the firing began. Bill ran to the door but quickly returned to soothe the ladies. "Don't be alarmed," he said, and then added, alarmingly, "they're robbing the bank."

Shatto quickly produced a weapon from his quarters, a dubious firearm described by the Northfield *Independent* as a "long-barreled, ancient-looking pistol." Bill grabbed the weapon and went out toward the street, "turning over the gun in his hands to discover its mechanism."[48] Before Bill could do any damage to the bandits—or himself—one of them saw him and snapped a shot over his head, breaking a window. There is no record of Mr. Bill taking any further part in the battle of Northfield.

But resistance was beginning. Elias Stacy borrowed a shotgun from Allen's store, and about the time Cole called out the inside party, Stacy got a charge of "chicken shot" into Clel Miller as the bandit mounted his horse. Another account says the shooter was Joseph Hyde, one of the clerks in Allen's hardware store.

Whoever shot Miller, the charge was too small to kill him, but it hit him in the face hard enough that he swayed in the saddle or, in some versions, knocked him clear off his horse. At least three other citizens got into the battle with borrowed shotguns, and if their birdshot was also too light to inflict a mortal wound, it had to hurt and confuse the outlaws, who must have been wondering what kind of hornet's nest they had stumbled into. Phillips was by this time blazing away from the corner with a pair of revolvers from Manning's stock. For the bandits galloping up and down the street, things had gone sour in a hurry.

Cole Younger would blame the bandits' failure on an abundance of ardent spirits. The inside men, he said, had shared a quart of whiskey before the raid. Pitts had admitted as much to him, said Cole, during their flight out of town. "I never knew Bob to drink before," wrote Cole much later, "and I did not know he was drinking that day until it was all over.[49] [W]ith all my faults, and I am sorry to say they were many, whiskey drinking was not one of them, and I never had confidence in a man who drank that he would do the right thing or what was expected of him when he was under the influence of whiskey."[50] He wrote to a friend later,

> [A]ll of the trouble was caused by a quart of whiskey which I learned afterward one of the three men had concealed, and between where they left us in the woods and town they had drank most of it and were drunk. That accounts for them not shutting the door of the bank and not coming out according to our agreement when I called to them that the alarm had been given. Had it not been for the whiskey there would not, in all probability, have been a man killed.[51]

Years afterward Harry Hoffman said Cole told him that the plan had called for Bob Younger to stay at the bank door while Cole went inside the bank. But, Cole said, when he realized Bob had been hitting the bottle hard, he sent Bob inside, because Bob was too quick on the trigger when he'd been drinking.[52] The statement contradicts the tale Cole told in *The Story of Cole Younger*, that he had no idea anybody had been drinking and would have aborted the raid had he known anybody was working on a bottle. But then, Hoffman also has the inside men entering the back of the bank through a door instead of jumping the counter, and he says they "scooped into sacks all money on the counter and in drawers," when we know the bandits missed one drawer filled with a substantial amount of cash.

Moreover, it makes no sense to send a drunk into a situation in which he would surely confront unwilling bank employees face to face, rather than keeping him outside, where Cole could watch him, and where he would not be tempted to shoot unless the raid went bad. We'll never be sure which version is the truth—or whether either of them is true. Marley Brant, in her excellent book, *The Outlaw Youngers*, guesses that the story about Bob and others drinking on the raid was an invention, a yarn concocted by Cole to explain the embarrassing rout of a large band of experienced and famous bandits by a handful of ordinary citizens, Yankees at that.[53]

Maybe so, for Cole was never slow to embroider on reality. But Wilcox commented on the strong stench of whiskey emanating from the three bandits inside the bank. And a Northfield man remembered many years later that before the raid he had seen the outlaws "carousing around in a saloon."[54] It therefore seems probable that all three *had* been drinking. If so, Cole had to have known they were and later seized on the whiskey as a convenient excuse for failure.

In later years Cole often repeated his story about the whiskey. "It had always been his policy," he said, "when they were planning a robbery never would he permit liquor in their camp the day before." The night before Northfield, however, "the other boys were very much intoxicated." He continued, even in old age, to blame the whiskey for the fact that anybody was killed.

Other writers picked up on Cole's lament. One called Bob Younger "a bit fuzzy in his reactions," adding the probably invented statement that although he "could handle his liquor better than Bob . . . Frank was inclined to be a bit trigger happy and belligerent."[55] One embroidered story of the raid has Pitts and Chadwell drink "the better part of a quart bottle of whiskey," rendering themselves "too befuddled to remember their instructions" and arousing the "suspicions of those in [the] bank before the squad who was to ride down the street got under way."[56]

So maybe whiskey did contribute to the fiasco on Division Street. However, if in fact there had been considerable drinking the night before, if indeed the inside men had been at the bottle earlier the same day, neither Cole Younger nor Jesse James thought it important enough to demand that the attack on the bank be delayed. When the gang assembled for final briefing just before the raid, the fact that three members of the gang had been hitting the bottle must have been obvious to everybody. If they passed their bottle back and forth on the way into Northfield, surely Cole or Jesse or both would have noticed. It seems most probable that there had indeed been a good deal of drinking the night before and that at least some of the outlaws indulged in a bit of the hair of the dog on the day of the raid. It follows that nobody thought

it an important matter at the time, but later booze became a wonderful excuse for failure.

Whether Old John Barleycorn did or did not have something to
do with what happened at the bank, the major reason for the gang's
discomfiture was not whiskey but a bunch of angry citizens, and
chief among these were Henry Wheeler and Anselm Manning.
Manning and Phillips got back to Division Street and looked for
targets. Seeing the heads of two men above the backs of the teth-
ered horses, Manning raised his rifle, but both men ducked. Rea-
soning that the horses belonged to the outlaws, Manning shot one
of them and slipped back around the corner of the Scriver Building to reload. He worked the breech lever of his rifle, but nothing
happened. The spent cartridge was still jammed in the chamber,
and Manning sprinted back to his store for a ramrod to knock the
cartridge hull loose.

Returning to the corner with a fresh round in the chamber and
thoughtfully carrying the ramrod, Manning fired at a figure between
the horses and the bank door. His round glanced off a wooden post
and may have gone on to slam into Cole Younger's thigh, for Cole
was hit about this time. Whoever fired the bullet, it left an ugly
wound. Manning jacked another round into the rifle, stepped
around the corner again, and pulled down on Chadwell, sitting his
horse in the street. Adelbert Ames had run back from the bridge
after the alarm went up and stood close to Manning. "Manning
had a trembling hand," said Ames later, "but took deliberate aim
and shot the moving horseman nearly a block away, through the
heart and dropped him dead to the street."[57] It was fine shooting,
though perhaps Chadwell was something less than a full block
away. Manning later remembered that Chadwell was sitting his
horse, watching the south side of Division Street "more than half-
way up the block."

Or maybe, according to witnesses James Law and H. B. Gress,
Chadwell was galloping down the street near the corner shooting
at Manning when Manning shot him down. Law remembered that
Chadwell rode down the street past the corner and, seeing Manning

with his rifle aimed, turned and shot at him while making the turn. Chadwell's horse then carried him back down Division Street toward the bank. At least one other citizen, a Mrs. Kingman, agreed. She too saw Manning's bullet strike Chadwell, but she thought the bandit fell almost in front of the bank.

> I saw him reel in his saddle and nearly fall off. He threw his left arm around the horse's neck, and that turned the horse up the street again and he came as far as my door, where he fell off and died, after a short period of intense suffering.[58]

Gress remembered that Chadwell "dropped to the side of his horse and turned and started back from whence he came, but soon fell off in the street and died there."[59] With Chadwell crumpled in the street, his horse sensibly retired from the fray, trotting off to a nearby livery stable. Wherever Chadwell was when Manning fired, the merchant knew his bullet had struck home: "I saw him wince and dodged around the corner and re-loaded." Manning's bullet tore through Chadwell's heart and the bandit toppled from his saddle into the dirt of Division Street, in front of Lockwood's store.

One source credits a merchant called Bates with running a courageous bluff about this time, a bluff that may have saved Manning's life. Bates was the manager of Hanauer's clothing store, which was situated roughly opposite the bank. Bates was inside his store chatting with a commercial traveler named Waldo, up from Council Bluffs. Their interesting talk about trusses was interrupted by the hammer of gunfire just outside the store.

Bates ran to his front door with a shotgun, only to discover that the weapon would not fire. He grabbed an empty revolver and "at just the right time, in just the right spot, he bluffed a shot at one of the mounted raiders. But it was enough to cover, momentarily, Manning's exposed flank." One version of the fight then says Bates heard "from somewhere above his head . . . the blast of a heavy explosion . . . the shot that was perfectly timed to back Bates' bluff with the empty pistol."[60] Waldo's contribution to the defense seems to have been limited to calling out helpful advice to Manning: "Take good aim before you fire!"[61]

Meanwhile Wheeler was sniping from his window in room 8 on the third floor of the Dampier Hotel. He first fired at Jim Younger, but the round went high: men shooting downhill tend to shoot above their target. Younger did not see where the shot came from, and Wheeler reloaded and used his second cartridge on Clel Miller, already bleeding from Stacy's load of birdshot. Miller was mounted, apparently bending down to adjust his left stirrup, and this time Wheeler had a steady rest on the windowsill and his aim was true. Miller pitched out of the saddle with a hole in his shoulder, almost exactly the wound Pitts had inflicted on Bunker. But Wheeler's bullet had severed the subclavian artery, and Miller was dying when he hit the dust of Division Street.

For a little while Miller stayed on his knees, calling out something to the other bandits. We'll never know what it was, although Dr. Whiting, who watched him, thought he was giving orders. After Miller collapsed, Cole dismounted, ran over to him, and turned him over. It was about that time, according to Cole, that a bullet smashed into Cole's left hip. Cole wrote later that he had been hit by a pistol ball, which he thought came from an upstairs window somewhere north of the bank. Hurt but still mobile, Cole picked up Miller's revolvers and pulled himself back onto his horse.

Dr. Whiting watched one bandit ride across the street "hiding his body Indian fashion behind his horse." As he reached the other side of the street, the outlaw dismounted, and Manning shot the horse (presumably the same horse other accounts say was shot in front of the bank). Another raider—we don't know which one— was hiding behind a lumber wagon close to the corner. About this time, however, Dr. Whiting was finally driven back off the stair landing by a bullet that slammed into the wall just over his head, showering him with plaster.

"I thought I was pretty nearly hit for the fellow aimed at me," the dentist said afterward. "Things were getting too hot for them and they were shooting apparently to kill." And then he added, with marvelous understatement, "I thought it was not prudent to go to the window again, so soon opened a window further south in the building."[62] By this time Bunker had made his break for freedom out the back door of the bank, and Cole Younger was again shouting at the bandits inside to clear out of the bank. Outside, two of the bandits were hunkered down behind the dead horse, firing north down Division Street, until one of them, probably Cole, ran to the bank door, yelling at the bandits inside, "For God's sake, boys, hurry up; it is getting too hot for us!"

Up and down Division Street the bandits were taking a terrible beating. Chadwell and Miller were down, dead or dying, one horse was dead at the hitching rack, and two other horses had galloped away. Bob Younger, without a horse, ran down the sidewalk toward the corner of the Scriver Building and came face to face with Manning and his rifle. Bob ducked behind the outside stairway that led up from Division Street to the second floor of the Scriver Block, and Manning took cover around the corner of the building.

Dr. Whiting, still watching, thought that Cole, on the east side of Division, was ordering the rest of the raiders to close in on Manning. "Kill the white-livered son of a bitch on the corner," somebody yelled. "[T]hey took deliberate aim at Manning every time he showed himself beyond the stairs. Then Cole ordered Bob to shoot through the stairs, which he did."[63] By one estimate, the riders fired at least thirty rounds at Manning, for many marks of bullet strikes were found on the stairs behind which he had fought.

About this time Colonel Streater, ex-cop Elias Hobbs, postmaster French, and a black citizen named Ben Richardson joined in the battle with astonishing courage and the only weapons available, hurling rocks at the yelling bandits. "Stone 'em! Stone 'em!" roared Hobbs, bombarding the outlaws with "big and formidable missiles, more fit for the hand of Goliath than for the sling of David."[64] Bunker wrote that one of Hobbs's stones struck one robber on the knee, "injuring one of them quite seriously," although another writer said the only wound inflicted by the rock throwers was to skin the shoulder of a horse. Meanwhile, Hyde, James Gregg, and

Reverend Ross Phillips banged away with shotguns loaded with birdshot, and if their loads were too light to do much damage, they added considerably to the general confusion and the robbers' consternation.

Manning and Bob Younger tried to protect themselves and at the same time look for a chance to shoot. While Bob was concentrating on killing Manning, Wheeler, across the street, got a clear shot at Bob. One contemporary account of the raid has a young woman also at his hotel window, "coolly watching the fight throughout." Pointing to Bob Younger, the story goes, the comely witness told Wheeler: "Only aim as true as you did before," said the brave girl, "and there will be one the less to fight."[65] Thus inspired, young Wheeler fired again, and his shot smashed Bob's right elbow. Hurt but still full of fight, the outlaw shifted his pistol to his left hand and kept on trying to get a shot at Manning. Dr. Whiting watched Bob from his office window, "when suddenly he took his revolver in his left hand, jumped in the air, turned clear around, threw out his right foot as if kicking at the stones thrown by Hobbs and Streater."[66]

Bob kept on shooting at Manning, turning once to snap a shot through a store window at storekeeper Bates, whom Bob may have thought had fired the shot that smashed his elbow. This may be the round that raked across Bates's cheek and ear.

By this time another citizen, J. B. Hyde, had gotten a shotgun into action, and his weapon was loaded with lethal buckshot. Hyde may also have hit Bob Younger. The Rice County *Journal* opined that it was Hyde's shot that smashed into Bob's arm and that Wheeler's rifle bullet struck Bob in the leg.[67]

Phillips was banging away with his revolvers to no apparent effect, standing on the third step of the outside staircase, close to Manning, when Bob Younger drove a bullet through the step he was standing on. Manning told him to get down, and Phillips sensibly did so. Somewhere along the way, somebody, maybe Wheeler, hit Jim Younger in the shoulder. One account of the fight on Division Street tells that Bob's return fire put a bullet through Wheeler's cheek. However, there is no evidence that Wheeler was injured in any way, and the same dubious story erroneously makes Wheeler a full-fledged doctor and has him firing at the bandits from his "office in the Scriver block."[68]

Now Wheeler, hurrying to load his last cartridge, dropped it, and the paper burst, spilling powder across the floor. Wheeler ran for more cartridges and met Dampier who was already on his way back with more ammunition. Wheeler quickly returned to his window, ready to get back into the war.

Harry Hoffman vividly described the chaos on Division Street:

> [O]ne of Cole's bridle reins was clipped by a bullet; he quickly reached for his knife and cut the other rein close to the bit. Guiding his horse with knee and hand . . . Cole's horse now reflected the training he had received . . . responding to every pressure of the knee. Bullets screamed and spat with a thud on the pavement; guns flamed and roared; Cole felt a sting in his side, another high on his shoulder; his hat was shot away, the horn of his saddle was ripped loose and hung there swaying in the wind.[69]

Down on the street, Manning was reloading on the move. Unable to get a clean shot at Bob Younger, he now started out to run around the building, intending to cut through the alley and circle in behind Bob's shelter under the stairs. But the outlaws had a belly full of Northfield. They were whipped and they knew it, and all that mattered now was to get away from these infuriated townspeople. Cole told Pitts to help him get Miller up on Cole's horse but gave up the attempt when he realized Miller was dead. By the time Manning got around the Scriver Block and back onto Division and Wheeler had returned to his window with more ammunition, the gang was galloping for safety, south down Division.

In all probability the outlaws had intended to leave town the way they had come, across Bridge Square and over the Cannon River bridge. But that way lay the deadly rifles of Manning and Wheeler, and the bandits had had quite enough of them. The outlaws were a battered lot, thoroughly beaten. In addition to Cole's thigh wound and Bob's shattered elbow, Jim Younger had been hit in the shoulder, possibly by Wheeler's rifle. It is also quite possible that either Jesse James or Frank James had been wounded, probably in the leg or thigh, but that is not certain. Hoffman wrote that Jesse was "shot on the chest," but there is no other evidence to back up his statement.

Without a horse, Bob Younger left his shelter beneath the stairs, calling to his comrades, "For God's sake, boys, don't leave me!" Some accounts of the raid say Bob swung up behind his brother. Hoffman, for example, wrote that "Cole's horse . . . whirled at the precise second, putting Cole in position to reach down and grab Bob by the belt and pull him onto the horse behind him." And he added, perhaps unnecessarily, that "the feat performed that day by Cole Younger and his educated steed was not only miraculous, but seemed impossible."[70] Perhaps impossible is the right word.

By contrast, Cole wrote that he shouted to Jim Younger to catch Miller's horse for Bob to ride. Jim did so and helped Bob to mount. Cole says he then got the horseless Pitts up behind him, and the surviving bandits galloped madly for safety, Jim leading the horse to which Bob clung desperately. Phillips and Stacy fired a couple of shots after them, but by then the outlaws were a block away and there were too many citizens in the way for the defenders to keep on shooting.

Norman Van Buskirk, who owned a shop on the west side of the Cannon bridge, had watched the robbers ride across the bridge and into town. He was intrigued that they were all mounted in a town where saddle horses were uncommon and that they wore "kind of uniform" dusters. Even so, Van Buskirk paid little more attention until the roar of firing broke out across the river along Division Street. Startled, he had started across the bridge to see what was happening when one of the raiders came galloping wildly out of town, shouting, "Get back, you sons of bitches!" and firing "so close that I could hear the bullets whistling." Van Buskirk took the sensible course: "I got back making far better time than I did going over. When I got out of range I turned and saw that they were preparing to go away and very shortly after they rode out of town."[71]

The fight was over. For all their hard-case reputation, for all their yelling and shooting, for all the blood spilled, the gang had made off with $26 and some change.

The streets of Northfield were quiet now, save for the barking of dozens of dogs and the frenzied clanging of every bell in town, and the citizens began to leave cover to wander down Division Street and stare at the detritus of war. A horse lay dead near the bank, and two strange men in bloody linen dusters lay sprawled in the street. One citizen thought Miller was still alive and said later, "I had all I could do to keep the boys from shooting him with their little pistols."[72] The citizens gaped at friends and neighbors carrying weapons and warily inspecting the bandits' remains. The facades of the downtown buildings were pocked with ragged scars of bullet strikes; broken window glass littered the street. George Bates stood holding the flattened pistol ball that had grazed his cheek and came close to ending his life. The whole thing was astonishing, the sort of horrible, outlandish event that nobody imagined could happen on the quiet streets of Northfield.

And then it got worse, it got uglier, as Heywood's body was found inside the bank. The cashier was

> lying prone upon his face with his brain and blood oozing slowly from a hole in his right temple. A huge spot of deep red clotted blood and blood stain upon the matting behind the counter told where the murdered bank official had fallen. Upon his desk there lay a blotter besmeared with blood and small particles of brains. His desk was also similarly smeared with the brave man's brains.[73]

As Northfield's citizens watched in horror, Heywood was carried from the bank. Dwight Davis brought his buggy around, and the dying cashier was loaded in and driven away toward his home, tenderly held in the arms of Dr. J. W. Strong, the president of Carleton

College. In twenty minutes Heywood was dead, without having regained consciousness. Mrs. Heywood was at home and had heard the dreadful news of her husband's death before Dr. Strong could reach her. The banker's lady was as strong as her husband had been, for when she heard how Heywood had died, she said simply, "I would not have had him do otherwise."

Now there was news that still another innocent citizen had been mortally wounded in the gunfire on Division Street. He was a Swede named Nicolaus Gustafson, a thirty-year-old immigrant from a town called Fiddekulla. Gustafson had come to Minnesota only recently, in spring 1876, bringing with him his eleven-year-old nephew, Ernst. A local historian said he was a blacksmith by trade, perhaps employed by the Hagen Wagon Company, two blocks south of the bank on Division Street.

Gustafson lived with relatives in Millersburg, some twelve miles west of Northfield, where a number of other Swedes had settled. On the day of the raid he and several other Swedes had come to Northfield with a neighbor who had a team of mules. Each of the Swedes represented a family, and all had come to Northfield to shop for supplies. Gustafson spoke very little English, and his lack of understanding may well have been his undoing. It was only his first or second trip to town.[74]

When the raid began Gustafson was on Fifth Street, one block south of the bank and around the corner from Division, not far from the Bierman Furniture Company. Down in Bierman's basement was John Olson, a carpenter who had just finished hanging a door at the foot of the basement stairs. Curious at the sound of firing outside, the carpenter went up to the street in spite of cries from outside on the street, "Robbers in the bank!" One of the outlaws jammed a pistol barrel against Olson's head. Get back inside, the bandit ordered, "offering to help him if he did not obey orders." When the outlaw was distracted by a citizen trying to get his little boy off the street, Olson ran back to the basement. As he did so, he saw a man fall in the street outside—perhaps Chadwell—and met Gustafson about ten feet from the basement entrance.

As they met, a slug struck Gustafson in the head. Gustafson fell backward against Olson. Olson staggered but kept his feet and made for the shelter of the basement stairway. He scrambled to the bottom of the stairs, only to find the door locked behind him. Olson began to worry about the Swede then, and started back up toward the street. But, he said, "as soon as my head was above the sidewalk the robber caught sight of me and told me to 'sit right still where you are, or I'll kill you, too.'"[75] Olson obeyed, but he was startled to see the wounded Gustafson run toward the Cannon River. By the time Olson could leave the basement, he met Gustafson coming back. The wounded man had gone to the river to wash himself.

It is a reasonable hypothesis that when Gustafson went outside to see what was happening, he could not understand the bandits' shouted orders to get inside and was shot down in the street when he would not obey. "I'll kill you, *too*," said the bandit who threatened Olson. Olson got the wounded man up to what he called "the Norwegian Hotel"—a hostel frequented by Norwegian immigrants—and called a doctor. Gustafson was conscious and able to speak, and at first it was thought that his wound was not fatal. The doctor determined, however, that the ball had fractured his skull and driven a piece of bone into the brain. Gustafson would linger a few days more, but the injury would prove mortal.

The Swedish community worried that Gustafson had been killed because he saw something or someone in particular and feared the outlaws would return to attack them. The people with whom the injured man had come to town traveled quickly back home, and there the men of the Swedish community stood guard in shifts for three whole weeks, sharing their single firearm between the sentries.

To this day nobody knows for certain who shot Gustafson. There is no evidence that anybody saw the slug strike him. Although Drago's account of the raid says Wheeler "saw young Gustavson [*sic*] felled," the statement is uncorroborated. Cole Younger and Clel Miller are likely candidates, as they were assigned to cover the street outside the bank. A citizen remembered that one bandit he thought was Cole "was, during the time the firing was going on, on the southeast corner of the block."[76] Jim Younger may have fired the round that killed Gustafson, for he seems to have stayed close to Cole outside the bank.

Bunker wrote later that Cole murdered Gustafson, probably reflecting the general opinion of the town. But the best candidate is the "man on the buckskin horse"—almost surely Jesse James—who may have been farther south on Division Street than were any of the other outlaws. If he was indeed a hundred yards south of Cole, that would have put him at or very near the corner of Division and Fifth Streets, close to Bierman's furniture store and close to Gustafson and Olson.

Gustafson's murder is often attributed to Cole, despite the absence of definitive proof. In 1897, during an attempt to win a pardon for the Youngers, many affidavits were sent to the Minnesota statehouse asserting that Cole killed Gustafson. Whoever fired the fatal round, it seems likely that one of the robbers shot Gustafson down when he did not respond to orders. Cole Younger argued, "Neither Jim nor myself fired a shot in that part of the City. We were in front of the bank and our stray bullets went north over Bridge square; I believe the bullet that wounded him was fired by a citizen at us, the ball passing up the street southward."[77]

Cole always maintained that the Swede was hit by a glancing shot from Manning's or Wheeler's rifle. Since we can account for most of the rounds fired by both men and theirs were the only rifles in action, it is unlikely that either they or any other Northfield citizen fired the fatal shot. Olson agreed, for, as he said, to strike Gustafson "the ball would have had to turn the corner about ten or twelve feet." Olson thought the killer had to be the bandit "guarding the corner. He was there during the entire time I was out of the cellar and was shooting all the time in every direction."[78]

Olson's account helps to eliminate Cole as Gustafson's killer, for another citizen said later that Cole rode back to the bank door from the corner to the front of the bank, shouting to the inside men, "[C]ome out. . . . [W]e are getting all cut up here!"[79] Olson was very clear about the possibility that Gustafson was hit by a bullet from farther north on Division Street: "From the position in which Gustafson was when he was shot, it was physically impossible for him to have been killed by a ball from the guns of any of those defending the bank."[80] And Olson should know.

The mystery deepens, for Cole later wrote, without preamble, "If any of our party shot him it must have been Woods," one of the aliases he contrived for two of the robbers. Cole does not explain why he said this. Perhaps it was another attempt to exonerate himself; or maybe he was really saying—at least obliquely—that one of the James boys shot Gustafson. Cole's somewhat cryptic statement is consistent with the hypothesis that Gustafson was murdered by the "man on the buckskin horse," whom we can guess was Jesse James.

A block or so away from the blood-splashed bank, Bunker was having his shoulder treated. His wife of just a year, a teacher in the Northfield school, had found out about the raid from two or three women, who told her to "keep the children in, as the town was full of desperados, who were 'sacking the town.'" One of them said there had been firing at the bank, and then somebody else added that Heywood had been killed and Bunker had been wounded. Mrs. Bunker got permission to leave her class—people paid strict attention to their duty in those far-off days—and somebody else told her that her husband was dead. A friend borrowed Captain Ames's team, collected the anxious Mrs. Bunker, and drove her off to find her husband very much alive.

Down along Division Street, the men and women of the town stared curiously at the bullet-pocked storefronts—one citizen said Skinner's store, across the street from the bank, was "riddled with bullets."[81] And the townspeople stared at the two dead strangers lying in puddles of their own blood, or, as one sensational account had it, in "a pool of seething gore." Neither man carried any document that might identify him, and both men would remain unidentified for some days. The Rice County *Journal* reported that the bandits had left behind a grain sack labeled "H.C.A.", with a few dollars in it, and one of the linen dusters. "Probably," quipped the paper later, "the Bank would send these by Express, if they can get their address."[82]

The dead men's hands, said the Rice County *Journal*, showed no sign that they were workingmen. Nobody seems to have felt much sympathy for them, certainly not the newspaper: they were to be consigned to "potters field, such a field, to the purchase of which Judas' money was devoted more than 1,800 years ago, because the money was the price of blood." The *Journal* reserved its sympathy for the "splendid and innocent horse. . . . Let us put the horse in his own peaceful heaven. He looked like a thoroughbred."[83]

In time the corpses were carried indoors, either into an empty granary or a vacant building next to Morton's store. One citizen remembered going out into the empty streets of Northfield that night and discovering that the only light burning in the town was a lantern standing on the counter in the vacant building next to Morton's. Inside, the bodies of the two outlaws lay on the floor. The next day the remains were carted out into the square for the convenience of the curious, who thronged about to get a glimpse of all that was left of Chadwell and Miller.

And then, on the day after the raid, Norman Van Buskirk met two Cannon Falls men on the street in Northfield. The visitors asked where the dead bandits were, and Van Buskirk led them to the place. One of the Cannon Falls men, Cal Peterman, recoiled in horror. "For God's sake, Norman, don't you know that man? Why, that's Bill—Bill Stiles, my brother-in-law!" Maybe so. The tale is consistent with the story that Stiles had a sister living close to Northfield.

It also fits in neatly with the account that a "heavily veiled woman"—possibly his sister or another of Stiles's relatives—was seen to lay a flower on the chest of each of the dead men. A related story says that a man asked permission to examine the bodies, since he thought one might be "a missing brother-in-law." "How can you tell? asked the officer. "By a bullet scar under his left arm," the man replied. Sure enough, one of the corpses carried such a scar.[84] The man who inquired is not identified, but as the corpse was apparently that of Chadwell/Stiles, it may well have been Peterman who sought and found the identifying mark. (The wildest of the Jesse James books asserts that Stiles wasn't killed at all but "escaped from his wounds and some Swede was buried in his place." He died, says this account, of old age in California in the late 1930s. Clel Miller also miraculously escaped and died "a natural death in Murray, Arkansas.")[85]

On the morning of September 8, according to the Rice County *Journal*, both of the dead outlaws were stripped and cleaned up for the inquest that was scheduled for that afternoon. The coroner, Dr. Waugh, came up from Faribault for the occasion. His verdict clearly did not require in-depth investigation, and he duly announced that "the two unknown men came to their death by the discharge of firearms in the hands of our citizens in self-defense and in protecting the property of the First National Bank of Northfield."

Anybody who had a story about the raid must have told it to his neighbors. One described the "leader of the gang." He was clean-shaven, about five feet six, slim but muscular, and with a fair complexion, which sounds a lot like Jesse James. This man wore both a cape and a duster and, oddly enough, white cotton gloves. One description said three of the outlaws had a "sharp, shrewd aspect, and would be taken rather as gamblers of the flashy sort than desperate highwaymen."[86]

Not all of the citizenry were heroic during the battle of Division Street. John Archer, horse trainer and resident joker, ran to hide in an icehouse southwest of the Manning and Allen stores. In those days the winter ice harvest was buried in sawdust to preserve it, and into this itchy mess Archer dove headlong. He had no sooner gotten himself well covered in sawdust than another fugitive jumped into the icehouse and landed on top of him. Feeling suddenly insecure, Archer fled the icehouse and ran for the banks of the Cannon River. Later he described his sprint in appropriately horsey terms: "I struck a forty gate, but John Tosney took the pole and went by me so quick I thought I wasn't goin' at all, and felt they'd ketch me sure."[87]

Archer was no more pusillanimous than a German furniture dealer named Miller, whose repair shop and store were located just south of the bank. Miller was hard of hearing and was forever trying to find his sons, one of whom was named Robert. And so when one of the bandits yelled at him, "Get off the street, you thus-and-such," Miller cupped a hand to his ear and asked, "What d'ye say? Robert on the street?" The response he got was a pistol shot and a shout from the robber. Miller took to his heels forthwith, dashing through his shop, out the back door, and up the rear steps to the bank.

Peering through the double blind that covered the bank's rear door, Miller was horrified to see a figure hurtling toward him. In fact, this apparition was Alonzo Bunker running for his life, with Pitts close behind him. As Bunker came crashing through the blind into the alley, Miller tumbled down the bank steps "heels over head," as Bunker later put it. Miller then dove through his basement door, and Bunker ran on. Ever after, Miller insisted that "another robber took after him."

Meanwhile, a Norwegian tailor, Hamre by name, left his shop south of the bank and came up Division Street toward all the excitement. Spying a robber, he inexplicably yelled, "Came on! Came on!" Horrified when the bandit did exactly that, Hamre fled down Division Street, not stopping until he and his family were safely hidden in his basement. He "vas not scared" he avowed afterward, but because his wife was nervous he thought it best to keep his family company in the cellar. Hamre was less distressed than Mrs. John Ames, who was driving her horse-drawn phaeton when the shooting began. There were bandits in town, somebody said, and Mrs. Ames stopped her team and dithered. "John! John! she screamed, running round and round her carriage. "Where's John! Oh, I want John!"

Other stories of the raid abound, and after all the years nobody knows whether they're true. One tale was about the unarmed cit-

izen who simply stood on the street and shook his fist at the robbers in futile fury. Then there was the man who tottered out onto
the square with "an old rusty gun" and shook it at the bandits. He
was too drunk to fire a shot in anger, and the robbers paid no attention to him.

Long after the smoke blew away, excitement ruled in the streets
of Northfield. As Adelbert Ames wrote, "Every old musket, shotgun and pistol was drawn from its hiding place and put on duty."
In response to Mayor Ames's cable, lawmen hurried to Northfield,
then on to the west in pursuit of the fleeing bandits. W. H. Revier
and Ames, both armed with revolvers, walked downtown together
in time to see four St. Paul officers riding out of Northfield, "armed
to the teeth . . . we saw them leave the Davis livery barn about 8:00
o'clock, headed for the big timber."

Both of the dead outlaws were left where they fell, "to be
looked at by the world," as Adelbert Ames wrote his wife. "Men,
women and children had their fill. Country folks came in or were
in town and sat in their wagons by the dead bodies and chatted
by the hour . . . women and children. All the women and children
in town nearby went to see . . . ."

One of the abiding curiosities of the Northfield raid was the
bandits' failure to use anything but pistols during the fight on Division Street. Contrary to what you see on the silver screen and read
in lots of western novels, the gun that won the West was made by
Mr. Winchester, not Colonel Colt. Any man who expected to be in
a serious fight chose a shotgun for short-range and a rifle for
longer-range work, yet the bandits used neither. Good repeating
rifles were widely available, too, from the 1866 and 1873 Winches-
ters to the reliable seven-shot Spencer of Civil War fame.

Now it is true that all of these men had roots in the bushwhacker
days in Missouri and Kansas, and the bushwhacker's favorite
weapon was a revolver—preferably several of them—used as a rule
from horseback. And no doubt the hurrahing of a quiet town was
more efficiently done with a pistol in each hand. Still, these were
experienced outlaws, not tyros, and their failure to at least tell off

two or three of their number to set up a base of fire with rifles argues for vast overconfidence—the shared assumption that the Yankee sodbusters would be a pushover, a walk in the sun. It must have been a shock to learn that just two townsmen armed with rifles had killed two bandits, wounded most of the rest, and driven off the survivors in confusion.

Along the way, one of the dead bandits' pockets—apparently Chadwell's—yielded an interesting find. It was a clipping from the Rice County *Journal*, about a month old, an enthusiastic account of the Northfield bank's wonderful new safe. It's worth quoting:

> The First National Bank of this place is having a new set of doors put into their vault. Two doors will have to be opened before the vault is reached, each fastened with the most approved combination locks. On the inside of the vault will be placed a steel burglar-proof safe having a chronometer lock, thus avoiding the annoyance of having burglars pull the cashier's hair to make him open the safe, as it cannot be opened until a certain hour, by anyone.[88]

No doubt this information would have discouraged the bandits from robbing the bank by stealth, although secrecy and finesse was never the James-Younger style. And so they turned to the old ways, straightforward bullying, hurrahing the town with lots of shooting, pistol waving, and shouting damn-you-get-inside-you-son-of-a-bitch. The gang ran true to form at Northfield, doing exactly what they did best, doing what had worked for them before. But this time they picked on the wrong town.

The Cannon River bridge and Bridge Square, 1876. (Northfield Historical Society Archives.)

The Scriver Block and the First National Bank of Northfield (at left), downtown Northfield, Minnesota. (Western History Collections, University of Oklahoma Libraries.)

The interior of the bank, an authentic and exact modern recreation. (Northfield Historical Society Archives.)

A. B. Bunker, bank cashier. (Western History Collections, University of Oklahoma Libraries.)

Frank Wilcox, assistant book-keeper. (Western Histories Collections, University of Oklahoma Libraries.)

Joseph L. Heywood, head bookkeeper and assistant cashier. (Western History Collections, University of Oklahoma Libraries.)

Adelbert Ames, about 1870, in photograph never before published. (Northfield Historical Society Archives.)

Jesse James in his bushwhacker days, wearing the "guerrilla shirt." Taken in Platte City, Missouri. (Western History Collections, University of Oklahoma Libraries.)

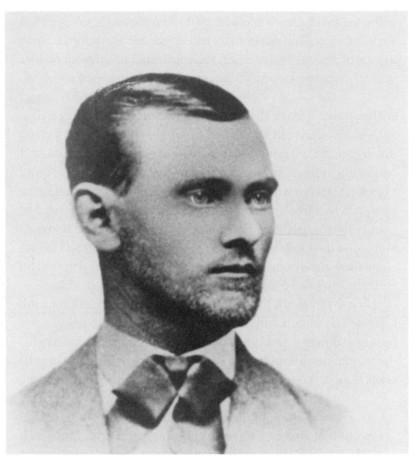

Jesse James, 1875. (Western History Collections, University of Oklahoma Libraries.)

Bob Younger in the Faribault jail just after capture, 1876. (Western History Collections, University of Oklahoma Libraries.)

Cole Younger, captured near Madelia, Minnesota, on September 21, 1876, soon after the raid on the Northfield bank. (Western History Collections, University of Oklahoma Libraries.)

Frank James, in his
respectable years, 1898.
(Western History Collec-
tions, University of Oklahoma Libraries.)

A. R. Manning, the sharp-
shooting hardware merchant.
(Western History Collec-
tions, University of Oklahoma Libraries.)

Dr. Henry M. Wheeler, student turned warrior. (Western History Collections, University of Oklahoma Libraries.

REWARD!

- DEAD OR ALIVE -

$5,000.$\frac{00}{xx}$ will be paid for the capture of the men who robbed the bank at

NORTHFIELD, MINN.

They are believed to be Jesse James and his Band, or the Youngers.

All officers are warned to use precaution in making arrest. These are the most desperate men in America.

Take no chances! Shoot to kill!!

J. H. McDonald,
SHERIFF

Reward poster for the raiders. (Northfield Historical Society Archives.)

 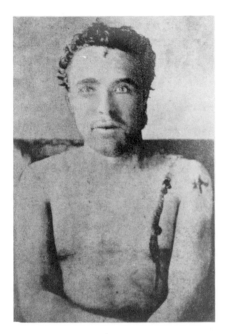

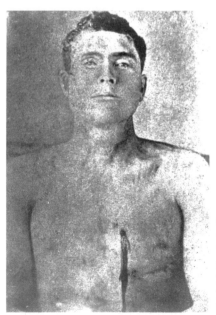

Charles Pitts, top left, killed at Madelia, where the Younger brothers were captured, 1876. Clel Miller, top right, expired 1876. Bill Chadwell, bottom left, killed during the Northfield bank robbery, 1876. (Western History Collections, University of Oklahoma Libraries.)

The Madelia posse that captured the Younger brothers in a fight at Madelia, 1876. Left to right: Sheriff James Glispin, Capt. W. W. Murphy, G. A. Bradford, Ben M. Rice, Col. T. L. Vought, C. A. Pomeroy, and S. J. Severson. (Western History Collections, University of Oklahoma Libraries.)

CHAPTER FIVE

PURSUIT

And so the remains of the gang galloped south out of town, one horse carrying double. They ran their horses abreast, crowding other traffic off the road. "Take the ditch, God damn you!" they shouted, running one old farmer with a wagonload of vegetables into a muddy ditch. Two well-mounted, well-armed Northfielders pursued but lost some of their ardor as they got close to the fleeing bandits. "Nor did," said one account, "they again find their courage return, but they sat there and saw the marauders . . . again boldly dash away."

The outlaws had fled so quickly that they had not stopped to cut the telegraph lines as they had planned, and so, as the citizens gathered in the streets, the telegraph hammered out news of the raid in all directions. Word quickly spread across the countryside, and posses began to form. Farm families looked to their shotguns and watched the roads apprehensively. Back at the Philadelphia Centennial Exposition, bank cashier Phillips received a brief and horrifying telegram: "Bank robbed. Heywood killed two robbers also."[1] Phillips immediately started for home.

The outlaws could be anywhere, and the alarm spread quickly from town to town. In fact, the gang had stayed together. They galloped into little Dundas, the nearest point at which they could recross the Cannon River. Their luck was in; the telegraph operator was not at his key, so word of the raid had not yet reached the town. In Dundas the battered outlaws stopped long enough to wash their wounds. Whether either or both of the James boys had been hit is uncertain; if they had been, their injuries were probably leg wounds. In any case, neither brother seems to have been badly injured.

Others were much worse. Bob Younger's right elbow was shattered and must have caused him tremendous pain; infection would set in, and he would soon begin to spike a fever. Hoffman wrote that Bob "begged them to go on without him and make their escape." As one might expect, Cole's response was predictably heroic and noble: "We rode here together; we will ride away together, or we will die together."[2]

Jim Younger was shot through the shoulder, and this wound would also become infected. One writer has part of Jim's "jaw shot away and both shoulders pierced,"[3] but it is virtually certain that he did not receive such wounds during the Northfield fight. Cole's thigh wound was bleeding badly until he could get it tightly wrapped. It must have hurt terribly to ride; when on foot, he needed a stick to walk. The raiders were a badly battered group, unable to travel with the speed of healthy men.

Mayor Ames of Northfield telegraphed for police help from both Minneapolis and St. Paul. Lawmen also came from both these cities and smaller towns in Rice County and throngs of amateurs joined them. The hunt quickly centered on the area around Faribault, which became a sort of headquarters for the pursuers. Many of the hunters were peace officers, ex-soldiers and other responsible citizens who could be depended upon to act professionally and follow orders.

The police chiefs of both Minneapolis and St. Paul joined the pursuit, along with their chiefs of detectives and dozens of other officers. They were helped—or hindered—by hundreds of ordinary citizens, more than enough to get in the way of each other and the real policemen. Everybody seems to have assumed that the fugitives would head due south. Because of this expectation, strengthened by a false alarm, most of the pursuers concentrated along an east-west cordon running roughly through Janesville. Most of the pursuers seem to have neglected the obvious escape routes to the west, in spite of the efforts of capable leaders such as Rice County Sheriff Ara Barton, who led his posse out of Faribault and sent parties to cover likely bridges, roads, and fords.

Many searchers, however enthusiastic, proved inept. It soon became clear to the professional lawmen that the very number of those hunting the gang was an obstacle to finding their quarry, for most of the men in the ad hoc posses had neither experience nor organization for this sort of thing. Many were no doubt driven by lust for the rewards. The state of Minnesota put up $1,000 a head for the outlaws, and $500 apiece more was offered by the North-field bank. While that whetted the appetite of many of the summer soldiers, there were some observers who questioned their enthusiasm for closing with their quarry. As the Minnesota historian William Folwell dryly commented, "The fugitives had no difficulty in breaking through them. It may be said without impeaching the bravery of any that there was no impetuous alacrity to make battle with six such desperadoes accustomed to pistol-shooting to kill."[4]

That comment may be a little hard on the pursuers, or at least most of them. They had an enormous area to guard and search, much of it a wilderness of forest and brush, river and lake and swamp. And when the moment would finally come to close with the bandits, the amateur hunters would prove to be formidable indeed.

Before the hunt ended, as many as a thousand men were beating the bushes, but the whole effort was uncoordinated and, so far, futile. As Huntington put it in *Robber and Hero,*

> There were also, of course, in so large and hastily-mustered a force, very many who had no fitness for the service . . . and no conception of the requirements of such a campaign. They came armed with small pistols and old fowling-pieces of various degrees of uselessness, and utterly without either judgment or courage. Their presence was a source of weakness to the force. Their fooling indiscretions embarrassed and defeated the best-

laid plans; and their failure at critical moments . . . made them
worse than useless—worse than enemies.[5]

While the gang pushed on from Dundas, southwest toward the
Big Woods, the hunt went forward, with increasing numbers of
hunters in full cry behind them. Meanwhile, Northfield tried vainly
to identify the two dead robbers. There were plenty of photographs
of the corpses, for a Northfield photographer, Ira Sumner, had
propped up the bodies and taken pictures of them, according to the
custom of the day. While Sumner ultimately sold some 50,000 photographs—at $2 a dozen—nobody who bought one in the first days
knew who either of the dead men were. St. Paul mayor James Max-
field chipped in with the somewhat grisly proposal of

> severing the heads . . . from their bodies, and either embalming
> them or putting them in spirits so as to preserve the features of
> their countenance as perfectly as possible, so that, in case the
> authorities of Missouri and Iowa desire to examine them they
> can do so and be enabled to determine whether or not they
> belong to the famous Younger Brothers as some think.[6]

Mayor Ames wisely rejected this novel suggestion. Without any
head-severing, by September 11, it was generally thought that the
raiders might well have been the James-Younger gang, and the
corpses had been tentatively identified as Pitts and Chadwell. On
Saturday a Cincinnati detective had arrived in town and poured
out a positive mine of misinformation. To start with, he positively
identified Clel Miller as Charlie Pitts. He thought Miller had been
inside the bank, because, he said, Miller was in the habit of club-
bing with his pistol and so was probably the one who knocked Mr.
Heywood down with his revolver. The great detective was positive that the wounded bandit—Bob Younger—was surely Frank
James. Jesse, said the Cincinnati man, was always ready for murder and was therefore the man who killed Heywood.

The well-founded suspicion that the James-Younger gang was
their quarry did nothing to help find the surviving bandits. At first,
all anybody knew was that the raiders had galloped away to the

west. The hunters knew the gang had stopped in Dundas, for there they had come upon Philip Empey's hired hand, who was using a horse to haul rails. The outlaws had opened up the hand's scalp with a pistol barrel, stolen Empey's horse for Bob Younger, and ridden on. Two men from Northfield had seen them do it.

The Northfield men, outnumbered, had not intervened but instead followed for a little way. Before stealing Empey's horse, the fleeing bandits had passed up a team driven by W. H. Revier, who worked for the Ames family. Revier was plowing near Ames's farm when he saw six men riding toward him, two of them riding one horse. The outlaws were reloading their revolvers as they passed Revier, who heard one of them say, "Let's take a horse here." One of the others answered, "No, no. Go on further." Ironically, the bandits, who professed enmity toward the Ames family, had passed by the team belonging to Ames. They were fine animals, too, for a pair of them sold the following summer for $450.

No doubt Revier was suspicious of these pistol-carrying strangers. Their bloody wounds must have been obvious to him. Even so, he did not find out what had happened in Northfield until two more mounted, rifle-carrying men appeared on the Dundas road. Revier knew them both—Dwight Davis and Jack Hays—and they told him of the carnage in Northfield, then pressed on in pursuit of the outlaws. "Believe me," said Revier, "I lost no more time in getting home." Very quickly the Ameses also appeared, carrying weapons, and Revier was told to arm himself and stand guard in front of the farmhouse.

The fleeing outlaws stopped at a farm owned by Robert Donaldson. There they asked for a pail of water, apparently to wash Bob's injury. When Donaldson asked what had happened to Bob, somebody told him that he had killed a "blackleg" called Stiles in Northfield and had been wounded in the fight. The gang's next recorded stop was that evening, at a saloon in the hamlet of Shieldsville. There are at least two versions of what happened next.

In the first, as the robbers slaked their thirst they also soaked rags in water, probably to cleanse their wounds. Before they could get on the road again, Bob passed out and fell from his horse. One of the bandits, probably Jesse, got Bob back in the saddle and told a local citizen, "We're going to hang that damn cuss," explaining that Bob was a horse thief. The local went back into the saloon and immediately four other citizens came to the door, only to find themselves looking down the barrels of the bandits' pistols. The gang rode out of Shieldsville in a hurry but were chased by the four men from the saloon and fourteen more local citizens. The gang abandoned Empey's horse and got clear of their pursuers only after some shooting.

The other version, Cole's, is quite different. Cole says the men at Shieldsville were a posse from Faribault who "had left their guns outside a house." In this account, the gang forced the posse back inside, away from their weapons, while they watered their own horses. Homer Croy says there were "rifles and muskets lined up on the porch and a posse wolfing down vittles inside." William Folwell, an early historian of the raid, generally agreed with Cole's version. The posse left their weapons in their wagon, outside the place where they were "comfortably refreshing themselves," when the bandits appeared. They "watered their horses, exchanged some pleasantries, peppered the pump with bullets as an object lesson in pistol shooting, and rode on."[7]

The posse followed, and a firefight ensued some four miles west of Shieldsville without damage to either side. One may wonder at the story of a bunch of possemen going off to hunt outlaws but leaving their weapons outside while they bent the elbow. If the story is true, it verifies the accuracy of Huntington's acid comments on the somewhat dubious competence of some of the amateurs out beating the bushes for the gang.

The correspondents were out in force as well, for this was the biggest manhunt anybody had ever seen. One newspaperman somewhat grandiloquently headed his stories "Headquarters in the Saddle," which must have reminded some Civil War veterans of a Union general who used the same pompous heading for his reports—a habit that had prompted some wit to comment that the general had his headquarters where his hindquarters should have been. This correspondent, like most of the others, never saw hide nor hair of the fleeing outlaws.

On Friday, September 8, the gang approached a ford in the Little Cannon River but found it guarded by a three-man picket. The guards fired on them, but the outlaws simply turned back into the woods and waited. In a short time the guards departed. The gang pushed through the ford and vanished into the forest on the other side. One account of the raid has the guard detail taking to its heels in panic, "one leaving his time-honored Prussian musket in the brush, and another losing his valuable set of false teeth."[8]

So far the bandits' luck seemed to be holding, for they had made good their escape as far as the Big Woods. This wild area seemed designed to be a sanctuary for hunted men. There were farms and small settlements in the Big Woods, but it also contained thick timber, draws, bogs, creeks, lakes, and heavy brush where the gang could expect to find good cover.

And then it began to rain. The downpour, which fell in torrents on and off for the next couple of weeks, was both good news and bad for the fleeing bandits. It made the going very bad, both for tired horses and for men in pain. At the same time, it virtually obliterated their tracks, and for a while the hunters lost all idea of where their quarry might have gone. Everywhere householders and isolated farmers looked to their weapons and feared the coming of night.

One man, nine years old at the time of the raid, later remembered how he and his four-year-old sister trembled at the thought of the raiders. The children were alone on their parents' farm near Madelia and spent the nights huddled together in a big chair, "fearing at every noise" and convinced "that the wicked men were at the door seeking shelter and meaning harm to us children." The same man remembered a tale that the gang had a falling-out nearby: "Some wanted to return to Missouri, now their guide was dead, but the Youngers decided to go on. Years later when I worked as a brakeman on the Missouri and St. Louis Railway, that crossing was still called Younger Brothers Crossing."[9]

The sheer number of the pursuers gave the gang an advantage nobody could have predicted. On more than one occasion the outlaws pretended to be possemen searching for those devilish robbers, and the subterfuge got them food and horses from farm families eager to help, or too much alone to ask questions of these "lawmen." The pursuit was also hampered by bad information, the inevitable well-intentioned false reports that the gang had been sighted here, there, and over yonder too.

The possemen masquerade worked again as the outlaws approached the Cannon River, then swollen from hours of steady rain. The gang found an unsuspecting road crew that directed the "peace officers" to a nearby bridge, over which they might continue their pursuit of the Northfield robbers. Crossing safely, the fugitives ran head-on into a posse led by one Captain Rodgers, turned back across Lake Tetonka, and evaporated into the forest on the other side.

That same afternoon the gang approached Janesville. They had managed to supply themselves with four fresh horses and kidnapped a farm boy to guide them. Moving into LeSueur County, they stopped at another farm and forced two boys to take over the guide duties as far as the road to Elysian, in an area of swamps and lakes. Over the owner's objections, they swapped two tired horses for two fresh ones at a farmhouse, and later stole two more mounts out of another farmer's field. Finally, late on Friday, September 8, they made camp between Elysian and German Lake.

Here they turned loose their stolen horses, which promptly went home, and huddled miserably beneath the dubious shelter of blankets suspended from brush. The rain continued to fall. The combination of aching, infected wounds and the miserable weather was wearing the bandits down. One of the possemen commented afterward that he never suffered more from cold than he did that night on picket duty when he was trying to block the gang's escape route toward the southwest.

The next day, Saturday, the ninth—or Sunday, the tenth, depending on which account you read—the gang abandoned their remaining three horses, callously leaving them tied to trees, and continued on foot. Sore-footed, using strips of their underwear as socks, they hobbled on and that night camped near the hamlet of Marysburgh. Early in the morning they could hear the bell of the Catholic church there calling the faithful to early-morning services.

As crippled as the outlaws were, it is difficult to understand why they decided to trudge on on foot. Maybe they thought their horses were too well known, particularly since one of them was a "yaller hoss," said to be quite conspicuous. But if that is so, why would they release the horses they had just stolen? Surely they must have reasoned that the reappearance of the stolen mounts would tell the pursuers that their quarry might now be traveling on foot. Perhaps they intended to steal more horses. But if that is the case, why would they abandon *all* their horses, including mounts for Bob and Cole, before they had obtained new ones? Hoffman thought he knew the answer: "The day after the raid [the day is wrong] the six bandits found that horses made them too conspicuous, so they abandoned them and went into the woods on foot, dodging, creeping, hiding."[10]

Just maybe the gang thought they might steal a march on the hunters, who were all looking for men on horseback, although surely it must have occurred to them that six battered men on foot, one or more of them limping badly, would draw at least as much attention as the same number mounted. Whatever their motives, the six tired outlaws struck out on foot, and the spot where they had abandoned their horses was not discovered until Tuesday. Until then the search was still concentrated in the area around Elysian. Assuming they were now three days behind the gang, some of the hunters gave up, not only the discouraged fairweather possemen and bounty hunters, but also some of the hardheaded professionals, who reasoned that the gang had gotten clean away.

But they had not; they were moving far too slowly. The gang rested for a day on an island in the midst of a swamp, then made a few miles more the following night. On Sunday morning they trudged slowly on, making another four miles before camping again. They made one more short march, reaching a point only some two or three miles from Mankato. There they found a deserted farmhouse and moved in, grateful for the shelter, and stayed there Monday night, all day Tuesday, and Tuesday night as well.

Added to their pain and weariness was hunger, for the outlaws were living mostly on green corn, watermelons, and the occasional chicken, all stolen from farmers along their line of retreat. After one particularly successful scrounging session, the gang hid in a thicket long enough to light a small fire, hiding it with a blanket hung from a tree branch. How the smell of their stolen chickens and turkey must have made their mouths water, these soaked, hurting, half-starved fugitives. And how it must have broken their hearts to have to run before they could eat, spooked from their feast by a small posse that included Northfield mayor Ames.

On Wednesday, September 13, the fugitives captured a farm manager in the woods not far from Mankato. This man, Thomas Dunning, could have a posse on their trail if they released him. What to do? As Cole put it later,

> [I]t was proposed by one of our party that we shoot him, to which I said: No, we will not kill him. It will be easier to run away from all the men he can put on our track than it would be to get rid of the memory of having killed an innocent man who has never wronged us, and who said he had a wife and children depending on him for their support.

Then, again according to Cole, "the one who made the proposition" suggested that Bob Younger, the worst hurt of the outlaws, should decide what should be done with Dunning: "If we turn this man loose he will have the whole country after us in twelve hours, and with your broken arm we cannot possibly get away." Bob, of course, nobly refused, saying he'd rather be shot dead than have that man killed.[11]

And so the decision was taken neither to kill the man nor to leave him tied to a tree, for he might well die there in the woods, undiscovered. The robbers extracted a promise from Dunning not to reveal their whereabouts, and Dunning was turned loose.

There are conflicting stories about what Dunning did next. In one, he concluded that "a bad promise was better broken than kept" and immediately told his story to the farmer for whom he worked.[12] In a second version, however, Dunning tried to keep his promise, but "he acted so strangely that [his employers] noticed it. . . . [T]hey commenced to question him and after a period of approximately three hours he finally admitted the real cause."[13] So now the hunt was back on, full force. Many of the fainthearted and reward seekers returned and new men joined up, until the hunters were again about a thousand strong.

Some sort of organization was achieved under Gen. Edmund M. Pope of Mankato, a Civil War veteran, who got some sort of picket line established along the Blue Earth River. But even with the bridges and fords covered, the robbers got through. It seems the railway company told Pope they would guard their own railroad bridge, and Pope stood down his own sentries. As luck would have it, of course, the gang picked the railroad bridge to cross, and the guard detail—two men and a boy—did not have the courage to try to stop them.

Once across the Blue Earth River, the outlaws kept moving. They managed an impromptu feast on some stolen chickens, and by Thursday, the fourteenth, had found their way around Mankato. Here they stopped to take counsel together, for they suspected that by now, despite his promise, Dunning would have told his story and the hounds would be baying behind them once more. Bob and Jim Younger were in very bad shape, especially Bob, and Cole had great trouble walking. Bob volunteered to let the others go on without him, but his brothers would have none of it.

And so the gang split up, and again there are two entirely different stories about how that came about. For here the James brothers elected to go on alone. One version of the parting makes it acrimonious and has Jesse suggesting that the outlaws ought to shoot Bob, so that everybody else could move faster. This version is widespread but almost surely a fiction. Cole Younger, although he had managed to get both of his brothers into trouble with the law, was still deeply loyal to them. I believe that, despite his friendship for Frank James, Cole might well have killed Jesse James for even suggesting that Bob be abandoned. Cole himself consistently denied that Jesse ever mentioned killing Bob and said that in fact Jesse wanted Cole and Bob to ride two horses the gang had recently stolen. This is the way Cole is said to have put it in his 1916 "deathbed statement" to Jesse James's son and Cole's friend Harry Hoffman:

> During the night, Bob's arm had taken a turn for the worse and he was suffering great pain and I told Jesse and Frank to take the horses and go. And this they did. Their acts and treatment of us were honorable and loyal.

Hoffman later wrote that Cole "wanted all his friends to know" that the widely circulated story that "Jesse and Frank had deserted the Youngers when they needed them most" was false.

> Cole told us that day—that story was untrue. The two men who escaped was in every way honorable—Cole was very anxious for J.J. Jr. to have that information.[14]

Croy tells us the outlaws "crept through" the town of Mankato by night (why creep through a hostile town when you can go around it?). Anyhow, according to Croy, the battered robbers tiptoe past Bierbauers's Brewery in the gloom but are terrified by the sudden scream of a whistle in the night. It comes from Boegan's Lumber Mill and it only marks the midnight shift-change, but the outlaws flee in terror, thinking they have been discovered. It is about this time, Croy says, that Jesse takes Cole aside; this is Croy's version of their conversation. Jesse began it:

> "We'll have to do something about Jim."
> "What do you mean?"
> "You know what I mean. He's holding us up and we may all be captured."
> "He's doing the best he can."

"It's either him or us. I'm going to shoot him."
"If you shoot him, I'll kill you."

At which Cole drew his revolver and called Frank James over. Frank sided with Cole, the story goes, and Jesse went off alone to sulk. It is at this point, Croy tells us, that the gang decided to split up, and the James boys broke off on their own.[15] Or, if you prefer another version, Cole answered Jesse's proposal like this:

> Jesse, we will separate now and here. If Frank shares your sentiment, and if Charley Pitts thinks the same way, you can take them with you, you curs![16]

Carl Breihan, master of all manner of undocumented dialogue, created an equally unlikely conversation between Jesse and Cole. Jesse begins it by telling Cole, "What I propose is a horrible thought, but . . . ," and finishing with a long oration about the need to kill Jim, who "cannot live." The other bandits "looked at each other. They seemed hardly able to believe their own ears" (the reader has the same trouble). Cole, of course, is not having any and responds in such purple prose as this: "'Damn you, Jesse James' hissed Cole, 'you are a cold-hearted devil!'"[17]

This fable has been repeated again and again in the folklore of the James-Younger gang. It is unsupported by any proof, and Cole adamantly denied anything of the sort ever happened. In fact, he denied it again on his deathbed, where for the first time he admitted the James boys were both part of the Northfield raid. As he lay dying, he told Hoffman how the story got started.

> I know when that story was invented and why—myself and brothers were awaiting trial in prison—the detectives were trying hard to trick us into acknowledging that the James were at Northfield. So one day a detective came to my prison and said "Cole, we heard about Jesse James trying to induce you to kill Bob so you could all escape—and we also heard what you told him. The public is going to give you a lot of credit for your loyalty to your brother and it should go a long ways in the jury's consideration when your trial comes up."[18]

Cole then said he told the detective to "try another dodge," for he could not know anything about what had passed between the fleeing bandits. The story appears to be unmitigated fantasy, not only because Croy and Breihan had no reasonable way of discovering the conversation among the bandits, but also because their versions of the conversation differ markedly.

It is indeed very hard to believe that Jesse would make such a suggestion, considering the close friendship between his brother and Cole Younger. There is no logical reason to think Jesse would prefer killing Cole's brother to striking off on his own with Frank, as the two ultimately did. Moreover, both Bob and Cole were seriously injured as well and would have slowed the James boys down almost as much as Jim would.

Honorable or not, the James boys struck off on their own and on the night of the fourteenth were spotted as they tried to pass a bridge near Lake Crystal. All the bridge guards were asleep save one, but he didn't hesitate to open fire. The brothers were riding double, the story goes, and when guard Richard Roberts fired on them, the horse jettisoned both riders and made off on his own. Both brothers escaped into the night, leaving only a hat as a trophy for the bridge guard. Roberts may have hit one or both brothers, but if he did, he did not slow them down.

The James brothers now found a pair of good grey horses to steal. Riding bareback, they made much better progress. The story goes that they continued to pass themselves off as lawmen. According to Huntington's *Robber and Hero*, in spite of being without either saddles or bridles, they "had no difficulty in getting food and information from unsuspecting people, who found only too late how they had been imposed upon."

Traveling night and day, the brothers made for the Minnesota border with Dakota Territory, and in time they abandoned their tired greys for a pair of black horses, also stolen. One of these horses turned out to be blind in one eye, the other totally so, and so, early on Monday morning, September 18, they stole two more grey horses and pressed on toward the west and safety. Somewhere along the way, according to Alonzo Bunker, Frank and Jesse were ambushed by a single boy, a courageous lad who

> stepped behind a tree till they passed him, and he was sure they were not innocent men, when he blazed away with both barrels, the charge taking effect in Frank James' thigh, inflicting a painful wound. Not knowing how many were in pursuit, the bandits lashed their horses to a run and escaped.[19]

An early account of the raid confirms that a Mankato youngster named Richard Roberts fired on two fugitives as they crossed a small creek near Lake Crystal. This version also says that they were riding double, and their horse threw them both. On no obvious evidence, the chronicler assumed that "[t]he two men must have been hit in the legs" but then went on to say that both "dashed into a cornfield nearby," hardly a description of anybody recently punctured by a rifle bullet.[20] The horse departed in haste, leaving the fugitives on foot.

There is no confirmation that either of the James brothers were wounded, but several sources say that Frank or Jesse, or both, had been shot at Northfield. It is possible that Frank was hit again by the kid with the shotgun—or maybe that was the first time he was wounded. The one thing that is certain is that if either James sustained a wound, at Northfield or after, it did not slow them up. Hoffman spun a piteous yarn about the brothers' flight "westward, ever westward." As Hoffman told it, Jesse was hurt so badly that his "wound had become unbearable; he could go not further." At that point, Hoffman wrote, Frank walked "down to the river," where he found "a sturdy little rowboat." Frank returned for his brother, and the two stole the boat. "The oars splashed lightly and skiff scudded swiftly into the gloom and was gone," presumably downstream toward safety among friends in distant Missouri.[21]

According to *The Northfield Tragedy*, written in the year of the raid, two men, probably the James brothers, came to a house north of Luverne, Minnesota, and asked for breakfast. They were riding grey horses and using straw for saddles and "loops of rope" for stirrups. And, he said, they "seemed very lame, and shuffled along, unable to lift their legs." One of the strangers "gave evidence of a bad wound in the right side, and could scarcely sit up to eat breakfast." Both weary men had trouble remounting and had to climb onto their host's fence to get back on their horses.

Another tale tells of Jesse and Frank stopping at a farm near Valley Springs in what is now South Dakota. They asked the farmer, Nels Nelson, for a drink, and Nelson obligingly indicated a bucket sitting on the well platform. Before Jesse could get off his mount, however, his thirsty horse thrust its nose into the bucket and began to drink. When Nelson offered to fill a fresh bucket, Jesse bitterly commented, "I'd rather drink out of a pail used by a horse than by some men I know."[22] We'll never know the reasons for Jesse's black anger, but his mood was surely not improved by many days of hiding, running, and hard living and by a badly bruised ego. He must have been deeply embarrassed by the realization that he and his professional Missouri hard cases had been routed by a handful of Yankee sodbusters and storekeepers.

The brothers' last brush with northern law seems to have occurred somewhere around Luverne, down in the southwest corner of the state close to the borders of Iowa and the Dakota Territory. They had stopped twice in the area to cadge meals, and one suspicious householder had ridden into Luverne and raised a posse. These citizens, eager but amateur, "with rusty firearms and forgotten revolvers dragged forth," gave futile chase. At one point they closed within about half a mile of the fugitives, but the stolen greys were not tired enough to be caught. One account of the James brothers' flight relates that they had a brush with a pursuing posse near Yankton, during which Frank killed a man, but this seems to be just one more fable in the deathless mythology of the outlaw brothers.

Beginning to feel confident that they had escaped the swarm of possemen back in Minnesota, the James boys started to feel their oats again. According to one source, they "exchanged salutations with the driver of the Yankton stage" and were apparently the ragged pair who held up one Dr. Mosher, a Sioux City, Iowa, physician. Dr. Mosher (or Moshier) had hired a first-class livery stable horse and was on his way to take out Mrs. Robert Mann's troublesome goiter. Mrs. Mann lived near Kingsley, Iowa, a day's ride away, but the doctor was not sure exactly where.

The tale of Dr. Mosher's kidnapping is part of the folklore of the Northfield raid. On Sunday, September 17, the story goes, the good doctor was nearing his destination, anxious for specific directions to his patient. Trying to find somebody who could help him, he made the grievous error of repeatedly hailing two riders he saw ahead of him. They turned out to be big trouble. When the doctor finally caught up with these unhelpful horsemen, he asked them why they had not waited for him. At that, the strangers, distinctly hostile, asked the doctor what *he* wanted. "You are the man we want," they said and drew their revolvers. You're a St. Paul detective. We hate detectives, and we're going to kill you. They were sure, they said, that the doctor matched the description of this St. Paul lawdog, which they had in a letter one of the outlaws carried, ostensibly from his wife.

We're the James brothers, they told the doctor bluntly; do you know about the Northfield bank raid? Yes, said the doctor; he had read about it. The only proof the doctor could offer that he was a healer and not a policeman was his scalpel, but that impressed the bandits enough that Jesse took time to stop at a farmhouse in the area. There he asked whether there was in the neighborhood a Mrs. Mann who had a problem with a goiter. There was and she did, said the farmer helpfully, and Dr. Mosher's life was spared.

After that Jesse swapped his tired horse for the doctor's excellent livery mount, and the three men rode on together. At another farm the brothers convinced the owner that the doctor needed a fresh horse and a saddle, which were kindly provided. For several hours more the three rode on, until Frank saw the lights of another farmhouse ahead. After taking the doctor's clothing in exchange for the rags one of them had worn, Frank drew his pistol. "Doctor,"

Frank said, "suppose you leave your horse here and go to that farmhouse and stay overnight. Run, doctor, run!"[23]

Most versions of this tale have the brothers forcing the doctor to tend to Frank's leg wound. However, the most probable version says the doctor did not repair a wound, for the injury was minor, and ten days old to boot (if that is so, what about the fable of the boy who ambushed the fleeing brothers, and what of Hoffman's anguish over Jesse's overwhelming pain?). A later newspaper account says only that the doctor reported that one of the fugitives had a bullet wound "near the right knee."[24] Drago went a step further, asserting that Dr. Mosher removed a "slug from Jesse's thigh," allegedly suffered during one of "three or four brushes with the posses that were scouring the country for them."[25] After releasing Dr. Mosher, the brothers probably made tracks across southeastern Dakota, crossed the Missouri somewhere near Springfield, and headed for Columbus, Nebraska. There they sold their horses and bought train tickets for Omaha and found their way back to Clay County.

Most of this is guesswork, at least from the point at which the pair held up Dr. Mosher, but it seems their most likely route away from danger. Like the tale of the kidnapping of Dr. Mosher, the saga of the brothers' flight is replete with other yarns. One author speculates on the conversations Jesse and Frank may have had along the way. The same writer tells us that the brothers, "still possessing plenty of cash from the Rocky Cut haul," bought their meals en route. Maybe the brothers *were* still well stocked with money, though the other gang members had little money when they were killed or captured. And, says the author, they had "Frank's wound" dressed in Sioux City, where they bought "new outfits of clothing." Could be, of course, but such things belong in the realm of pure speculation.

Whether either James brother was actually wounded in or after the Northfield fight remains uncertain. There are many stories that one or both had been shot, probably in the legs, and one version has both men shot through the leg with a single bullet. One source says Jesse called on a Fulton, Missouri, doctor named Yates "a few months later" to be treated "for the gunshot wound in his thigh."[26] The Northfield *News* also reported that Mosher saw that one man had a bullet wound "near the right knee which the robber told he received at Northfield; and the pants the doctor had to take had the bullet hole near the knee."[27]

There remains at least one more interesting story of the James boys' flight from Minnesota. Writer Carl Breihan told the story of the editor of the Sioux City *Democrat*, who heard Dr. Mosher's story of his kidnapping and whose "sympathies were with the hunted men." He therefore learned of the law officers' plan to catch the Jameses, and especially of a scheme to "patrol the Missouri River in small boats." Having somehow misled the posses and "thwarted" the plan to patrol the river, the editor and a friend managed to fall in with Jesse and Frank, and the editor

> explained his scheme to the outlaws. In return for his help, the James boys were to reveal unknown facts to him concerning their lives and escapades. Frank and Jesse at first thought it was just a joke and got a big laugh out of it. But since they did not know the topography of the land . . . they accepted the editor's offer of assistance. The editor and the man with him were well known throughout that part of the state and, of course, the two bandits who were riding with them excited no suspicion.

And then, says Breihan, the editor helped the brothers steal a skiff, in which they paddled off safely, south toward Missouri. The editor experienced, he said, "the greatest thrill of his entire life . . . to sleep one night lying between Frank and Jesse James."[28] Breihan said he got this story from a descendant of "two pioneer sheriffs," but the whole thing sounds like the editor—or somebody—made up the whole fantastic tale to sell lots of newspapers . . . or maybe books. Hoffman also said that the brothers drifted south along the river in a boat, the "skiff" Frank found on the riverbank. They moved at night and laid up by day, hidden in willows along the banks, until they reached a relative's house in what is now north Kansas City. Hoffman does not mention the adventuresome editor.

Where Jesse and Frank went after winning clear of the northland remains unclear to this day. They may have gone into hiding in Texas or Kentucky. By the following summer they had settled with their families in Tennessee, and by autumn 1879 Jesse had raised a new gang and was back in business. Frank stayed out of trouble somewhat longer, but by July 1881 he was back on the owlhoot trail with Jesse. In that month and year they stopped a Rock Island train near Winston, Missouri, robbed the express car, and brutally murdered the conductor and a passenger. Folklore says the killing of the conductor was by way of vengeance, and so it may have been. He was William Westphal, supposed to have been the conductor on the train that carried Pinkerton's agents on their way to attack the James farm back in 1875. A captured gang member swore the killing was done by the James boys.

Tales of the James boys' flight from Minnesota were legion, then and afterward. One has Jesse going off on his own while the others are resting in a deserted farmhouse. Jesse hitches a ride with a boy named Ben Williams who is driving his team home. Mentioning the Northfield raid, he asks Williams whether he would take Jesse for "one of them." Jesse then asks Williams whether he can get a bed and supper at Williams's house, and Williams says he can. No, says Jesse, we really can't do that, because I'm Jesse James, and he places the boy's hand on his leg, where he has a bullet wound.[29] The story strains credulity. Even Jesse, always something of a daredevil, would hardly announce his presence in hostile territory, sending young Williams on his way no doubt to raise the hue and cry in the countryside all around.

Probably the best of the James fables is a reprise of the old "desolate widow" tale, related by a Northfield man named John Hengen. According to Hengen's story, the fugitive bandits stopped at a house to ask for food, and the owner, a widow, said she would cook two chickens if they would help her catch them. One of the Jameses promptly pulled his revolver and blew the heads off both birds, an unlikely notion: the first chicken may be easy enough, but hitting a running hen spooked by the explosion of a black-powder pistol?

After their chicken dinner, the bandits gave the widow $20, and she broke into tears. She owed $1,500, she said, which she could not pay, and the banker was on his way to "put me off the farm because I can't make my payment."

Miraculously, one of the outlaws just happened to be carrying $1,500, which he handed to the widow. Get a receipt, the bandits told her, and departed. When the banker arrived with the sheriff in tow, he was duly paid and handed over a receipt. And then, the story goes, the gang lay in wait for the banker and relieved him of his $1,500. It's a nice story, but there's probably not an ounce of truth in it. Aside from the fact that the same tale is told of the Jameses and set in entirely different places and times, it is highly unlikely that the outlaws, wounded, pursued, and far from home, would part with any money at all, and then take the time to hide in a thicket and ambush the banker.

The wondrous tale of "the desperate widow and the heartless banker" also appears elsewhere in the folklore of the James brothers. In one version it happens somewhere in northern Missouri and the amount that Jesse ponied up was $1,400. In another, Jesse saved a widow's old homestead at Monegaw Springs. The story shows up again in the Ozarks, where the amount the widow requires is only $800. Still another account—this one supposedly told by Frank James—reduces the mortgage payoff to only $500 and places the incident at a farmhouse somewhere in Missouri.

As if this tale were not overworked enough, it is also told about the Younger brothers. In this version of the fable, the desperate widow is Hannah, an elderly part-black, part-Indian woman living in her small cabin near Roscoe, Missouri. The reference may be to Aunt Hannah McFerrin, who lived about three miles from Monegaw (although her cabin was large and as late as 1874 her husband was living). About to lose her little place, she told the Younger boys, who advised her to write the banker: send a messenger with the mortgage papers and note and she would pay in cash. The boys then furnished her the money. Once the note was marked *paid*, well sure enough, the Youngers waylaid the messenger and got their money back.[30]

Or maybe it never happened at all, as I am inclined to think. It's a nice story (it's told about Butch Cassidy, too), but it has the ring of pure fantasy. It partakes of the same unreality as the story of Jesse related by one Uncle Dick Henterton, whose story is said to have appeared in the *Denver Post* in 1890. It seems that during an 1879 train robbery near Glendale, Missouri, "an old lady in black gave Jesse James $70 in greenbacks and then cried, 'That is all I have in the world. My husband's corpse is in the baggage car.'" Jesse wept, the story goes, gave the lady back her money, and kicked in $200 of his own. That was Jesse, said Uncle Dick, friend to the poor and oppressed. Why, "once in Liberty, Missouri, he gave his coat to a shivering old man."[31]

This tender myth about the widow and her mortgage sharply contradicts another fable widely circulated by apologists for the brothers. Judge Thomas Jefferson Younger may have started it during a trip to St. Louis. Judge Younger, who had just finished ridiculing the notion that the Younger brothers had been part of the Otterville robbery, now had some trouble denying the boys had been at Northfield, seeing that they were now resident in the Faribault jail. Well, said the judge, "the boys have carried out the threat made a year ago, that if not let alone they would have the benefit of it," because they were hounded and persecuted and could not live in peace, and so on.

And the judge did his bit to perpetuate the invincible outlaw myth. Why, said the judge, Cole said the only reason the boys didn't kill their pursuers was that they knew they would have to leave Bob behind, and he would have "suffered punishment from his exasperated captors. Cole said he could have killed twenty of his pursuers had he desired to do so."[32]

The same story quoted Cole Younger as having "protested against" the Northfield strike. But, said the paper, "it was the James boys that persisted in it," a plain admission, if true, that Frank and Jesse were indeed in the raiding party, Cole's denials to the contrary notwithstanding. The James boys, said the judge, were actually headed for "the British Dominion" where they would settle down and live in peace. But, sadly, the Jameses gambled away their money and then borrowed everybody else's and inconsiderately lost that, too. And that, the story goes, is why they robbed the bank; the poor boys just couldn't travel without money.[33] And if that, as westerners used to say, ain't a load of horsefeathers, I'll put in with you.

All of this is a part of the great Jesse James fable, right along with the story that Jesse remained a God-fearing Christian all his days. This tale is also worth telling, if only to illustrate the astonishing mythology that grew up around notorious outlaws and was swallowed hook, line, and sinker by the credulous. It goes like this. It seems in later years a minister reproached Jesse and urged him to stop the things he was doing.

> Jesse: "If you tell me just how I can stop, I'll be glad enough to stop; but I don't intend to stop right under a rope!"
> Minister: "Well, anyhow, you ought not to forget your religion."

At which, the story goes, Jesse showed the parson his New Testament. Said the minister afterward, "Never in my life have I seen a Bible so marked up, showing such constant usage."[34]

Well, maybe so, but you have to wonder how dedicated Jesse was to the Ten Commandments. Although Jesse apparently embraced the Baptist Church in Clay County in 1868, it's a little hard to equate devoted Bible reading with shooting men you don't know because they don't take kindly to being robbed. Still, from later years, there is the instructive story of Deacon Jim Miller, who spent a good deal of time in churches—Jim said he was a Methodist—in between expeditions here and there to kill people for hire. Deacon Jim was a well-known churchgoer for years, at least until 1909 when the citizenry of Ada, Oklahoma, snatched him up for one of his murders-for-hire committed in their town. And then, in a nearby stable, they switched off Deacon Jim without either benefit of clergy or any perceptible due process of law.

Mythology to the contrary, real people in southern Minnesota reacted to the pursuit of the bandits with fear, like Carolyn Murray, sister of Dr. Whiting's comely patient. "I hardly slept for a week," she said later. One gloomy night was especially terrifying, for she and her family heard something—or somebody—stop outside the house. When the family opened the door, they saw two white horses. Carolyn screamed and ran out of the room, for the latest rumor was that the raiders might return and that they had stolen two white horses. In fact, the two white horses turned out to be the property of a peddler.

For many weeks nobody in southern Minnesota knew for sure whether the surviving bandits would reappear to steal and kill. Perhaps they or their friends might come back with more hoodlums at their backs and vengeance in their hearts. That fear and unease was yet another legacy of the James-Younger gang. And, according to the *Northfield News*, it was not until 1917 that Minnesota banks once again remained open during the noon hour. After Northfield, banks all over the state had closed for lunch rather than leave a single employee on duty. "The present custom of closing the banks during the noon hour," said the paper, "is declared to be merely a survival of an old precautionary measure which was the aftermath of the James-Younger raid on the bank in Northfield."[35]

If Minnesota was now rid of the James brothers, the citizens could not relax, for it still remained to settle with the Younger boys and Charlie Pitts. The hunt went on.

CHAPTER SIX

SHOWDOWN AT
HANSKA SLOUGH

Though Frank and Jesse James had won clear, the Younger boys and faithful Charlie Pitts were still within the pursuers' net. As they moved more and more slowly, hungry and hurt, the fates were closing in. The outlaws were heading for a crucial bridge near Madelia, which for a time had been guarded by a picket that included Col. Thomas Vought. He was the owner of Madelia's Flanders House hotel, where Cole Younger had stayed before the raid, and the two men had spoken at that time. After it appeared that the gang had gotten away, the picket stood down and the bridge remained unguarded.

Vought remembered his friendly chat with Cole at the hotel, however, and he especially recalled Cole's interest in the geography of the region. He cautioned Oscar Sorbel, a boy from a farm near the bridge, to be alert for the outlaws. Oscar was excited by the manhunt. He had visited the colonel and the rest of the picket at the bridge and told the colonel more than once that he wished he could have a go at the outlaws with his father's gun. As it turned out, Oscar was destined to do a good deal better than that.

On the morning of September 21, while Oscar and his father were milking, the boy saw two men walking by the Sorbel log cabin farm near Linden Lake. They greeted Oscar courteously, but something about them made the boy turn to his father. "There go the robbers," he said, but at first his father paid little attention. "No," he answered, "they was nice men." Oscar showed his father the imprint of the outlaws' great toes in the mud. "I will show you," said the boy, "how nice men they are." But the elder Sorbel was not persuaded.[1]

Oscar was sufficiently sure to set down his milk pail and follow the pair, asking neighbors about them, sure that he had seen some of the Northfield outlaws. At one point, trying to spot the fugitives, Oscar even climbed onto the roof of a house, but he could not locate them. Returning home, Oscar discovered that the two suspicious men had returned to his family's farm along with two more men like them. They were on a fishing trip, the strangers said; they had asked for food and gotten it. Finally yielding to his son's entreaties, Mr. Sorbel let the boy take a horse and head for Madelia, some seven or eight miles away over roads sloppy with two weeks' steady rain. As he went, rather like Paul Revere, Oscar called out that the robbers were near, but nobody listened. Not until he got to Madelia, where he headed for the Flanders House and Colonel Vought.

There was something convincing about this excited, muddy boy on a tired, muddy horse, for the colonel *did* pay attention when nobody else would. In *Jesse James Was My Neighbor*, Homer Croy produces some dialogue between the excited youngster and the landlord of Flanders House:

> "I've found the bandits!"
> "What did you do with them son?"
> "Well, they're still there. They're four of them."
> "That's a big haul. Have you had breakfast?"[2]

Whether this somewhat suspect dialogue ever took place, Vought grabbed his rifle and got his horse, and a posse began to form. Watonwan County sheriff James Glispin rode along with Vought, and other men from Madelia and neighboring St. James joined in until a substantial force was on the heels of the tired outlaws. The local men sent a rider ahead, warning threshing machine crews to unhitch their horses and make for open country. The search did not last long, for about six miles from Madelia the fugitives were discovered by the posse as they began to enter Hanska Slough, a marshy area on the edge of Lake Hanska. Glispin yelled at them to surrender; when they ignored his command, the posse opened fire at long range, hitting nobody.

The gang disappeared, moving as quickly as they could, and the posse gave chase. The outlaws fled across the shallows of Lake Hanska, and the possemen had trouble getting their horses to follow. They managed to find crossings, however, and quickly gained on the outlaws. Glispin and two men pursued from one side; Vought and posseman Dr. Overholt closed in from the other. At one point Overholt squinted down his rifle barrel and tried a shot at long range. The doctor didn't hit anybody, but he shot well enough to hit the stick with which Cole Younger was laboriously walking.

Sheriff Glispin and a posseman named Will Estes also fired on the fugitives, nicking the shoulder of one of the outlaws and putting a bullet through another man's shirt. Just after noon Estes and Glispin traded more shots with the gang, and return fire grazed Glispin's horse. Estes returned to town for more ammunition, sending on toward Hanska any reinforcements he chanced to meet along the road.

One of the posse's aims was to keep their quarry on foot, for they could see the gang making feverish attempts to find horses. The outlaws pushed down the bank of the north fork of the Watonwan River, shouting across the stream to a farmer named Andrew Anderson. We're lawmen, they yelled, and we're chasing bank robbers, and we need you to bring your horses over the river to us. But Anderson wasn't having any, no doubt put off by the ragged, battered appearance of the "officers." Instead, he drove his horses away from the river and the desperate outlaws.

The outlaws crossed over themselves, and hesitated near Anderson's granary, as if they were considering making a fight of it there. But then they pressed on, moving toward two hunters named Thompson, a father and son from St. Paul. The Thompsons had horses, too, a pair of livery teams they had hired from Colonel

Vought. The Thompsons were apparently made of stern stuff, and they did not run or try to drive off their horses. Instead, they stood their ground, clearing the birdshot from their shotguns and replacing it with goose loads, plenty heavy enough to drop a man.

Reading the omens correctly, the outlaws turned away along the Watonwan, finally going to ground in heavy brush along the riverbank. Pitts and the Youngers found themselves trapped in a rough triangle of about five acres, a small jungle of grapevine, willows, elders, and wild plums. On the north side lay an S curve of the Watonwan River. South, at their backs, rose a steep bank, which ran down to meet the curving river at each end.

There was no place left to run.

Harry Hoffman later quoted some lines of dialogue he said passed between the trapped outlaws. "Cole," said Charlie Pitts, "we are entirely surrounded; there is no hope of escape—we had better surrender!" Cole, however, was not prepared to quit. "Charlie, this is where Cole Younger dies." Pitts's response, according to Hoffman, "much impressed" Cole, "for he talked of it years after: 'All right, Captain, I can die just as game as you can. Let's get it done.'"[3] Whatever his other sins might have been, Charlie Pitts was loyal to the death.

The posse now hurried to make sure every exit was covered, although they could not see the bandits through the thick vegetation. By this point the posse had grown substantially, and men were spreading out on both sides of the river. There were plenty of guns to keep anybody from escaping that five-acre trap, at least as long as daylight lasted. With nightfall, however, there was every chance one or more of the outlaws might slip through the cordon and escape. The leaders of the posse were not about to take that chance.

By now, effective control of the posse had passed to Civil War veteran Capt. W. W. Murphy. Murphy was a Pennsylvanian by birth, an adventurous sort who had spent some time in the California gold country before returning to Pittsburgh when the Civil War erupted. He was an able soldier who rose from a second lieutenancy in Company G of the Fourteenth Pennsylvania Volunteers, to command that company. Murphy was a seasoned veteran, who carried on his body the marks of a gunshot wound and two saber cuts received in fighting at Piedmont, Virginia. A respected citizen, he had served in the state legislature. Now he was a farmer and stock raiser near Madelia, but for this afternoon he took command as he had in the old days, and he did it well.

Murphy got a line of a couple of dozen men in place on the north side of the Watonwan so that no outlaw could escape in that direction. Other citizens held the bank south of the thicket where the gang had gone to ground. Then Murphy crossed to the south bank, gathered the men there, and suggested a quick solution to the situation. Let's go in after them, he proposed, a suggestion likely to make even strong men blanch. For walking into an almost impenetrable five acres of brush after invisible gunmen is a most uninviting prospect for the bravest citizen. It is especially intimidating when the quarry are desperate, armed with a couple of revolvers apiece and prone to shoot people, and have absolutely nothing to lose. Even so, Murphy got six stout volunteers.

Sheriff Glispin said he'd go, and Colonel Vought said he would too. Though Vought was landlord of Madelia's Flanders Hotel these days, he was a veteran soldier like Murphy. He had served the whole Civil War in the 14th Wisconsin Volunteer Infantry and afterward became one of the pillars of Madelian society. Vought was a New Yorker by birth, forty-three years old in the year of the raid. He had lived in Wisconsin since he was sixteen, worked as a lumberman and hotel employee, and married before the Civil War. In the days afterward, he first ran stage lines, then bought the Flanders House when the railroads began to put the stage lines out of business.

Glispin, Irish to his bootheels, was a Massachusetts man. He had sold agricultural implements for a while, but at the time of the raid he was in his second term as Watonwan County sheriff. He was not a big man, no more than five feet six inches tall, but he was famous for his courage and strength. He had a reputation as a fistfighter, a terror to opponents much larger than he. He was not a man to back away from danger.

The other hardy volunteers were Charles Pomeroy, James Severson, George Bradford, and Ben Rice, none of them peace officers, none of them Northfield men. Severson was of Norwegian blood, a store clerk by trade, who worked hard and spoke several languages. He was short and somewhat stout but powerful and confident, "the jolliest and most popular young man." "Jim" Severson was something of a ladies' man, known as a hardworking and effective salesman. Like Vought, Pomeroy was born in New York, but his father was an early settler in Minnesota, coming to Madelia in 1855. Pomeroy was a survivor of the Sioux wars of 1862, a solid citizen who served as, among other things, justice of the peace. He, too, was physically strong and level-headed, a good hand in a tight place.

Ben Rice was a St. James man, twenty-four years old, with a local reputation as a dead shot. He had been born in Alabama back in 1851 but had his roots deep in Minnesota by the time of the Northfield fight. He had been a clerk for the Minnesota legislature at twenty-two (his father was a state representative). He was "noted for both the ardent impetuous temperament and the chivalrous manners of the Southern Gentleman."[4] Other posse members said admiringly that he seemed to be in his element on this day.

Bradford was a farmer and businessman, born in 1847 in an Indiana town called Patriot. For some years he had divided his time between teaching school in the winter and farming in the summer. More recently he had been both store clerk and store owner. He is described as a modest soul, much respected in Madelia. For all of his quiet reputation, he would prove to be a doughty fighting man.

Murphy shook these men out into a skirmish line, its right flank within sight of the little river. The volunteers kept four paces or so between men, and they stepped off into the thicket, walking straight into the teeth of a death they could not see. The second you can see the bandits, Murphy told them, open fire and hold low. Or maybe, as another source says, Murphy made a somewhat more flamboyant speech, something like this:

Here is the way we will do it, men. Form a line 15 feet apart and we'll walk right at 'em. When we see 'em demand their surrender if they shoot, shoot them. Shoot to kill, keep on shooting till they surrender or are all dead, or we are.[5]

George Bradford remembered simply that Murphy had cautioned his men to aim low and hold their fire until he had ordered the outlaws to surrender.

Then the little skirmish line pushed off grimly into the dense thicket from its eastern edge. Glispin seems to have been on the far right, with Murphy next to him, the others spread out to their left. For fifty or sixty yards nothing happened, and then somebody in the skirmish line saw the gang, crouched together in a tangle of wild plums, vines, and willows. At the same instant, one of the bandits fired, probably Pitts aiming at Glispin. Glispin and one of his men returned the fire, Pitts went down, and suddenly hell was in session beside the little river.

The posse and their quarry were no more than thirty feet apart, point-blank range, and both sides blasted away furiously. Severson and Bradford were both grazed by outlaw bullets; another slug hit Murphy in the side, over his pocket, shattered his briar pipe, and stuck fast in his pistol belt. The posse stood its ground and returned fire, pouring lead into the heart of the thicket. Murphy emptied both his shoulder gun—probably a shotgun—and his revolver, and Glispin tossed him another pistol. Across the river, other posse members cut loose in the general direction of the outlaws; Bradford remembered their bullets "cutting the twigs over our heads."[6]

According to Hoffman, crippled Bob Younger reloaded for Jim, Cole, and Pitts, but they could not match the posse's firepower. Pitts went down with a round through the heart, and a slug knocked Cole's revolver out of his hand. He snatched up Pitts's .45 Colt, and a second bullet tore the extractor from the pistol. And then Cole was on the soggy ground himself, bleeding from a head wound. Another of the posse's slugs ripped into Jim Younger's mouth, smashing his upper jaw and tearing away his upper teeth, and he went down as well.

The temptation to embroider on this grim little fight has been irresistible for some writers. Cole Younger claimed the outlaws intended to "break through the line and make for the horses." He rose up, he said, "as a signal for the charge, and a volley was fired by himself and comrades."[7] One or more of the outlaws may actually have tried to charge Murphy's skirmish line, but if they did, the attempt collapsed immediately under the concentrated fire from the posse's weapons.

Other writers have also tried to romanticize the Youngers' last, futile fight. One of these tales is worth quoting.

> There was a grim smile upon their drawn faces. The red bandages told of many wounds. Each brother chose his man, and three bullets found their mark in the first exchange. There was another exchange. Cole and Jim Younger sank to the ground. Their shattered bones refused to bear them. . . . Bob Younger stood up between his prostrate brothers. His right arm was helpless by his side. With the other he blazed away. Cole and Jim gritted their teeth and loaded the revolvers as fast as Bob emptied them.[8]

Grim smiles and gritted teeth or not, under the storm of lead from Captain Murphy and his men, the bandits' return fire gradually slackened and died away to nothing. Cease fire, ordered Murphy, and suddenly there was no sound except for the chattering of the river. Surrender, the captain called, and Bob Younger answered. "They're all down but me," he said. "I surrender." And then he stood up, and as he did so a posseman up on the bluff—Willis Bundy—fired on him and hit him again, this time in the chin. Murphy yelled at the shooter, and there was no more firing. Some of the posse members had what Vought called "words of condemnation" for the prisoners, until Sheriff Glispin snapped at them to be quiet. Cole Younger recognized Vought, called him "landlord," and held out his bloody hand. Vought shook it. Captain

Murphy regarded his prisoners sadly. "Boys," he said quietly, "this is horrible, but you see what lawlessness has brought you to."

In a stand-up fight, the experienced gunslingers had come in a distant second, for the posse's guns had done terrible damage. Charlie Pitts was dead, with five slugs in his body. The little revolver Bunker had tried to reach at the bank was still in his pocket. Bob Younger, the only outlaw standing, had been shot in the chest. Jim Younger had five wounds, and Cole had been hit no fewer than eleven times. Cole postured a little by challenging the possemen to fight him hand to hand, but that was only his ego talking. In fact, he and the rest had been badly whipped. Bob asked for a chaw of tobacco, and young Oscar Sorbel borrowed a plug from a posse member and handed it to the outlaw.

One account of the Hanska fight has Cole telling the posse that "with these revolvers he had never before missed a man inside of one hundred yards, and yet that he emptied them into that body of men at less than half that distance, and never killed a man. 'I knew then that it was fate, and so I surrendered.'"[9]

And if Cole had never missed with a revolver under a hundred yards, that wasn't fate; it was a miracle. This line is surely pure invention, for even Cole Younger, with his penchant for blarney, would never make a statement so patently preposterous to men who knew something about handling weapons.

Nobody now knows exactly what arms the two sides fought with, but it's safe to say that it was a mixture of cartridge weapons and cap-and-ball firearms. It is reasonably certain that Charlie Pitts was carrying a .44-caliber Smith and Wesson "Russian," a popular top-break revolver, quick to reload and comfortable in the hand. Charlie also had a cap-and-ball 1851 Navy Colt, a handy .36-caliber revolver, although whether he lasted long enough to fire both weapons is lost to history. Jim Younger also carried a .44 Smith and Wesson Russian, although what other weaponry he may have used is not known.

Cole carried a curious little .32-caliber rim-fire revolver made by Moore. The pistol is a relative popgun, probably a backup weapon, his "hidey-gun." Cole may also have been carrying a long-barreled .45 Colt Army, the famous "peacemaker," which first appeared on the market in 1873. It was not uncommon for outlaws to carry more than one revolver in those days: when Bob Dalton was killed at Coffeyville, Kansas, sixteen years later, he carried no fewer than *three* pistols in addition to his Winchester. Another legend of the raid says that Cole's big Colt was sent, at Cole's request, to none other than Belle Starr, who "used it for several years" and then gave it to one Texas Jack, a member of the Buffalo Bill Wild West Show. One contemporary account simply says the outlaws were "armed with Colt's and Smith and Wesson's six shooters, army size."[10]

What weapons the possemen carried is not certain. Murphy borrowed a shotgun from a neighbor, John Bisbee, and we know that both he and Sheriff Glispin also carried revolvers in addition to their shoulder weapons. Glispin is said to have used a breech-loading "carbine," which could mean anything from a state-of-the-art 1873 Winchester to a military-style Spencer carbine, or anything in between. The other possemen no doubt carried an assortment of shotguns and rifles of all ages and styles, both cartridge and cap-and-ball, certainly of several different makes. Considering the number of holes they drilled in Pitts and the Youngers, Glispin's sturdy men had lots of firepower, which means at least some repeating weapons. One account says Vought and Pomeroy used double-barreled shotguns, Bradford and Severson rifles, the others some combination of carbine or pistol or both.[11]

Once the smoke had blown away, Captain Murphy and his men collected the bandits' weapons and got their prisoners, the living and the dead, into a lumber wagon. At this point, according to Croy, Cole turned to his captors and asked, "Did Frank and Jesse get away?" "Yes," said somebody, at which "a look of relief came over Cole's face, for his loyalty to Frank was touching."[12] This anecdote is a little hard to swallow, too. In the first place, nobody in the posse would have been likely to know at that point whether the James boys "got away." Second, Cole Younger, a veteran campaigner, would hardly have blurted out the names of gang members who had gotten clear, especially not the name of his close friend, Frank James. In other accounts, Frank's question is related otherwise: "Did the other two men get away?" which sounds a good bit more like what really happened.

Accompanied by the rest of the posse, and by a continually growing number of men who had come to help, Murphy, Glispin, and their prisoners set out for Madelia. By the time they arrived, about 6:00 P.M., the citizens of the town had heard about the fight and the streets were full of people cheering the posse. The outlaws, ever eager to posture a little more, raised their hats to the crowd, although the applause wasn't for them. Still, the townspeople were compassionate. Jim Younger's chin was still bleeding badly, and a woman ran out to hand him a white handkerchief, which he shoved against the wound. More and more people crowded into the little town, and a special train brought even more of the curious from Mankato.

Charlie Pitts was lodged in the tiny jail, stretched out on a table covered with a sheet, another sheet covering his body to the waist, his chest bared to show his fatal wound to anybody who cared to view this edifying sight. Many people came by to take a look at Charlie, and many brought their children too, for in those days the sight of a very dead outlaw was considered not only interesting but instructive, especially to the impressionable young.

Still, in spite of the routine exhibition of Charlie Pitts and in spite of the gang's murders in Northfield, the surviving bandits were well treated by the citizens of Madelia. Under guard, they were fed and put in rooms at the Flanders House; they were cleaned up and dressed in fresh clothing; they had their wounds dressed and their filthy clothing washed. All of them were badly shot up, riddled with a combination of rifle bullets and buckshot. Cole carried the most wounds—eleven—although his brothers were probably worse hurt.

The bandits were photographed one at a time, sitting in a chair on the hotel stoop, as mobs of citizens pushed in to stare at these bedraggled desperadoes. While all this was going on, souvenir hunters stole all the buttons from the Youngers' newly washed clothing and for good measure debuttoned the photographer's coat, draped temporarily over the same clothesline.

The robbers were the biggest attraction ever to hit little Madelia, and people came by the hundreds from miles around, wandering through the bandits' rooms to gawk at what little remained of the fearsome James-Younger gang. One contemporary writer estimated that more than three thousand of the curious flocked to the Flanders House to see the dreaded outlaws.[13] Rising to the occasion, Cole Younger seems to have talked almost incessantly. Working the crowd as he loved to do, Cole

> quoted Byron and Shakespeare, and said while he had lived in the South all his life and thought he was familiar with warm weather, Minnesota was the hottest climate he ever struck. He complimented the citizens of Northfield and the sheriff and party in their bravery, but said he had no use for detectives and policemen.[14]

Cole also said he and the others never intended to kill anybody. That was not, he said, "their policy." And he told Captain Murphy that "if he hadn't been in this business he would have been a preacher. He talked about dying and pretended great seriousness and a desire to repent." So at least reported the Mankato newspaper of September 26, 1876. Years afterward Cole's loyal friend Harry Hoffman commented that he'd never heard Cole talk about becoming a preacher, but at the time Cole must have thought the story would be good for his image.

Handcuffed, Cole had his picture taken under a big cottonwood tree and took the occasion to praise the courage of Sheriff Glispin and his posse. He also did a little boastful threatening of Willis Bundy, "who, after we had surrendered and thrown down our guns and I was the only one standing ... shot my brother Jim who was lying on the ground in the chin, a cowardly thing to do, and if I live to be a free man, I will hunt that man down and kill him."[15]

Cole tempered his threat of vengeance with a dollop of piety: "I conceive prayer to exist in every action, every thought, and considering the eventful life I have led, I cannot say I have been a praying person." He went on to praise "that divine mandate, 'Remember thy Creator in the days of thy youth.'" Some observers doubted Cole's sincerity, suspecting he was trying to "play off the pious dodge," especially when Cole implied that he really hadn't tried to shoot anybody at Hanska Slough. What good would it have done, he said, to kill all seven possemen? There were plenty of others left to finish him and his brothers.

One local newspaper account claimed that the Minnesota governor "and others in St. Paul" had sent telegrams to Sheriff Glispin asking that the captured outlaws be brought to St. Paul. The local doctors advised against moving the captives, however, and Glispin agreed. "The plucky little sheriff," said the paper, "says he will not take them to St Paul or elsewhere for needless display, but . . . will deliver them to the sheriff of Rice County." The Youngers still refused to identify their comrades, but photographs of the dead outlaws made their cooperation unnecessary. Most people correctly assumed that the two missing bandits were the James boys.

The captured bandits were outspoken in their gratitude to the people of Madelia, who treated them far better than they expected. Sheriff Glispin and the townspeople were prepared to defend them against a rumored lynching, but the necktie party remained a rumor. On Saturday, September 23, the bandits were handed over to Sheriff Barton of Rice County.

No doubt with a sigh of relief, Sheriff Glispin washed his hands of his notorious charges. In time he would submit a modest statement of his expenses for everything from clothing for the prisoners to grub and beds for the guards. He added $25.00 for carpet and bedding destroyed at Flanders House—no doubt from splashes of blood—and $71.50 for medical care, including "drugs, medicines and appliances." The whole bill came to only $272.30, surely bargain-basement rates for capturing and holding the most notorious outlaws in the land. The sheriff's account asked nothing for the risk and hard work of himself or the volunteers who followed him.[16]

The battered Youngers were now moved to the county jail in Faribault, where the visits by the curious continued unabated. Streams of people paraded through town to catch a glimpse of the terrible Missourians. Some were charmed by Bob's good looks and Cole's inexhaustible line of blarney. Others, however, were not impressed. One man who saw the prisoners commented sourly: "There is nothing good about them. They look as if they hated the sight of every man and would not hesitate to put a bullet through the brains of anyone."[17]

Inevitably, there was, said Alonzo Bunker, "the usual sentimentality and slobbering on the part of weak minded women over these criminals. Bouquets of flowers were presented to the prisoners, and their signatures solicited for autograph albums." During the outlaws' time in Faribault, four thousand or five thousand curious people trooped past the jail to peer at the new celebrities. Even Cole may have tired a little of all this lionizing. Asked to speak to a particular group for a second time, he somewhat arrogantly commented, "No, don't call them back. They are so illiterate that they cannot appreciate the sublime life I have led."[18]

Croy, the source of other unconfirmed tales, says Cole met the president of the Mankato bank on the train to Faribault. According to this story, the banker berated Cole for his evil ways, saying, "You and all the others are a despicable gang and a disgrace to our country."

"Wait a minute," said Cole. "Would you like to know the difference between what you do and what I do?"

"Yes."

"It's very simple. You rob the poor and I rob the rich."[19]

At which, of course, the banker went away much wroth. Although this story is entertaining and fits neatly into the myth of the noble outlaw, it is otherwise unconfirmed and improbable.

A more probable conversation is one between Bob Younger and a reporter from the St. Paul *Pioneer Press*, in which Bob repeated the standard Younger line that the bandits "could have picked off many citizens, as all were dead shots, but did not desire to do murder." Bob also delivered the somewhat small-souled comment that he thought "Haywood [sic] was more frightened than brave."[20]

During the Youngers' stay in Faribault, still another lynching threat was bruited about. This one, too, came to nothing, possibly because of the heavy guard Sheriff Barton maintained at the jail. Still, the threat of a lynch mob did have one tragic effect: a Faribault policeman, on his way to the jail, was killed by a nervous guard when the policeman failed to heed the guard's challenge. At about that time Barton offered Cole the prospect of leniency if he revealed who had actually murdered Heywood. Cole thought about the offer overnight, or pretended to, and in the morning handed the sheriff a note which somewhat dramatically said only "Be true to your friends if the Heavens fall."

Otherwise, Cole kept right on talking. Among other things, he said the gang had chosen the Northfield bank "to get even with Governor Ames as he had driven the James-Younger gang out of Mississippi," a variation on the "looting the South" theme he offered in other times and places. He was also quoted as saying that the gang would never have come to Northfield at all, "if they had not encountered gamblers in St. Paul, who won their money, and they made the raid to get even with the state." Cole also added that the gang certainly didn't intend to kill anybody. Killing people was not their "policy," he said, which sanctimonious statement must have cheered up the families of the dead men scattered along the gang's backtrail.

Cole also earnestly denied that the robbers had intended to kill anybody in Northfield. A visitor from Northfield scoffed at him, describing the bandits' repeated attempts to kill Manning. No, said Cole, they just fired all around him. Then how, said a Faribault citizen, came bullet holes to be in the railing of the staircase behind which Manning fought? Cole could only deny that there were any bullet holes and was at last reduced to saying that he was tired, was not afraid to die, and hoped to prepare for a better world. I wish, said another bystander, that you would soon take your long rest. It was "no use," Cole sniffed, "to talk to illiterate people, they could not appreciate a sublime life."[21]

Cole and the other prisoners also waxed a little sanctimonious, too, for there was lots of talk about the terrible circumstances that drove the outlaws to a life of crime. "If it had not been for the war," said Cole, I might have been something." And the brothers added adjurations to young men about sticking to the straight and narrow, mixed in maudlin references to their own family, and topped the whole pastry off with requests for "the prayers of pious women."[22] It was a bravura performance. On one occasion Cole, presumably intending to be overheard, was discovered soliloquizing in this vein: "I don't believe it—I don't believe it. . . . Byron says 'Death is the end of all suffering—the beginning of the great day of nothingness,' but I don't believe it."[23]

In retrospect, this whole performance smells strongly of the most cynical grandstanding, perhaps in preparation for their pending trial. The Youngers were facing murder charges, after all, and some smidgeon of public sympathy might come in handy when sentencing time came. If any among their listeners were of a doubting nature, he or she might have pointed out that none of the outlaws had ever before given a tinker's dam for anybody else's life or for their family's feelings.

The *St. Paul and Minneapolis Pioneer Press and Tribune* expressed its disgust editorially, with particular reference to Bob Younger, whose good looks made him the special favorite of fluttering, sympathetic ladies.

> Bob Younger had his bouquets in Madelia, and he has his cigars, oranges and nuts in Faribault. We haven't a doubt that Bob could marry the handsomest woman who confers these palatable luxuries upon him, if he did not himself despise the whole simple and gushing set. Bob's sentiment, it should be remembered, doesn't get above a bawdy house.[24]

The fight at Hanska had broken the tension that had hung over all of Rice and Watonwan Counties since the raid two weeks before.

Nobody had been sure whether there might be more bandits on the way to revenge their comrades. As Adelbert Ames put it,

> Yesterday we had dispatches notifying us of the capture of four of the six escaping bank robbers. One was killed, three wounded. This town has been very nervous about robbers, and the news of yesterday seemed to relieve every man, woman and child in town from personal danger. . . . Everybody talks and laughs with everybody else and all is happiness.[25]

News of the capture of the Youngers was celebrated with a monstrous bonfire in Bridge Square, a conflagration that "illuminated the town. Every box, barrel, crate and whatever else in reach that would burn was piled up . . . and things were intensely lively for several hours."[26]

Some of the town's conversation must have concerned the $2,000 reward offered for the bandits' capture. On October 19 Judge Dickinson of the Sixth Judicial District would convene a hearing in Madelia to solve that knotty question, but his decision, joined in by a second judge, predictably failed to satisfy everybody. It particularly galled the Rice County *Journal*, which called the judgment a "strange decision," for it awarded Murphy, Glispin, and the rest of the posse only $50 apiece. "The money," scoffed the *Journal*,

> is ordered to be divided between forty-one different contestants; the men who held the horses, and the men who saw the smoke of battle afar through a spy glass, all sharing equally with the brave seven who went into the brush and did the work.

The *Journal* thought that "the least the seven men who did the work can do is to refuse to take one cent of the paltry fifty dollars," which was of course easy for the paper to say, it not being the *Journal*'s paltry fifty dollars.

At one point a rumor floated around to the effect that a lynch mob was on its way to Madelia to save the state the trouble of a trial, but nothing materialized. One other curious rumor, however, may have had something to it. According to one old-time resident of Rice County, shortly after the raid a number of mills in the county burned down, in fires "supposed to have been started" by "the James gang." The old-timer, only four years old at the time of the raid, could "distinctly remember" two fires that destroyed the Grange Mill and Bean's Mill in Faribault.[27] This story may have a common origin with still another tale of the raid, that an anonymous letter threatened the town with a big fire. Another letter threatened that three citizens would "deliver up the ghost for each man you have killed and wounded."[28] But as usual with poison pen letters, nobody delivered up the ghost, and the town remained intact.

With treatment, the Youngers' wounds gradually improved. The doctor who extracted the rifle bullet from Cole's hip thoughtfully passed it on to Manning, who had put it there, and he carried the slug as a souvenir for years afterward. Eventually, in mid-November, the Rice County district court convened and assembled a grand jury. The prisoners had been guarded around the clock, even though their feet were shackled, and a force of some fifty deputized men was "ready to assemble at the ringing of the firebell." These precautions were designed in part as a safeguard against the possibility of a lynching party, occasional rumors of which still persisted. The Youngers spent their time writing letters and reading. Cole—perhaps overly conspicuously—devoted his attention to the Bible.

On the second day of the judicial term, as the grand jury considered the evidence before it, the Youngers had two callers. The callers who appeared with remarkable timing were their sister Henrietta—called Retta—who struck the citizenry as "a very pretty and prepossessing young lady," and an older woman described as an aunt, "a lady of the highest moral character." Despite their presence, on the next day the grand jury returned true bills against all three for bank robbery, for assault on Bunker, and as accessories to Heywood's murder. Cole was charged separately in Gustafson's death.

The brothers were immediately arraigned before the city justice of Faribault, all three accused of having "without the authority of law and with malice aforethought killed and murdered Joseph L. Heywood by shooting him with a pistol there and then loaded with leaden bullets." The complaint added that the offense "is not bailable," which probably came as no surprise.

On November 20 all three brothers pleaded guilty to first-degree murder. As the court construed the penal law of Minnesota, that plea entitled them to a life sentence, instead of death. According to Hoffman, admittedly a dubious authority, Cole Younger made an impassioned speech to the court before sentencing. In fact, the speech Hoffman relates does sound something like Cole, for it was the same old litany of Civil War oppression and the ills of the Younger family. All that aside, said Cole, "I feel responsible for leading my brothers into the deplorable situation we now find ourselves. I would willingly suffer death in any form—if, by doing so—my brothers could go free." This plea, says Hoffman, produced a remarkable effect in court: "Every eye was moist. The tears streaming down the faces of many, both men and women. The Judge buried his face in his hands and for several minutes would not proceed."[29]

Judge Samuel Lord, tears or no tears, had some words of his own for the brothers: "While the law leaves you life, all its pleasures, all its hopes, all its joys are gone out from you, and all that is left is the empty shell." Over the long, dreary prison years to come, two of the Younger boys would discover just how prophetic Judge Lord's somber words were.

Two days later the brothers were on their way to the state prison at Stillwater. And there, "rough men used to rough ways," they became model prisoners. On admission to the prison, Cole gave his occupation as "farmer," an honorable profession he had practiced precious little over the long years since the war. As time dragged by in the Stillwater prison, the brothers graduated to better jobs: Bob became a prison clerk; Cole was appointed a nurse in the prison hospital; Jim was in charge of mail distribution and the library. And all through the later years of their imprisonment, faithful friends never gave up their efforts to obtain a parole or a pardon for the Younger brothers.

The leader of the parole campaign was W. C. Bronaugh, Confederate veteran and farmer from Clinton, Missouri. Bronaugh first called on the brothers in 1884, while he was on his honeymoon trip, of all things. Thereafter, apparently out of pure sympathy, he fought for seventeen long years, writing countless letters and traveling to Minnesota whenever he could. In time he would win the ear of former Minnesota governor William R. Marshall. As the years passed, Bronaugh also enlisted the aid of onetime Rice County sheriff Ara Barton and ex-warden A. J. Reed and obtained piles of letters from prominent Minnesotans and a round-robin petition signed by nearly every member of the Missouri legislature. Even Captain Murphy, the victor of Hanska Slough, was moved to recommend clemency.

On the other hand, many other Minnesotans were quite content to let the surviving Youngers rot in prison for all eternity. It is fair to say this feeling was especially strong in Northfield, where Heywood's memory remained green. Alonzo Bunker, for example, was not in a forgiving mood, then or long after, for he wrote in 1894,

> Since they have been incarcerated in Stillwater prison, requests for pardon . . . have been presented to different Governors, but without any apparent effect. Such action on the part of Governor of Minn., would result in his political death, as the present generation will not forget the wanton murder of faithful Heywood. . . . Cole and Jim are still "making buckets," the first and only useful employments of their lives.

"Cole and Jim Younger are in Stillwater state prison for life," Bunker added, "and Frank James in (perhaps a worse place) Texas. None of the murder gang having a single good deed to his credit, to ease the way into eternity."[30]

Even during the Younger brothers' time in prison, the mythology continued and grew. One story had it that even the widow of cashier Heywood signed a petition seeking their release, a claim she flatly denied. Cole did his considerable bit to add to the fable as well, writing in his somewhat fanciful autobiography that two former guerrillas "committed small crimes that they might be sent to prison and there plot with us for our escape." One of these, said Cole, "served a year in Stillwater prison without ever seeing us."[31] Well, maybe, but the story sounds like more stuff cut from the whole cloth, entertaining but without foundation in fact. As late as 1965 the Stillwater prison was still patiently answering inquiries about Cole's astonishing claim.

And so Bronaugh and the Youngers had to wait a long time. Among other obstacles was the reasonable demand from the Faribault mayor that the Youngers demonstrate their good citizenship by revealing who had actually murdered Heywood. In 1881 Governor Pillsbury turned away a request for clemency from the brothers' uncle, Littleton Younger. "When I think of poor Heywood," the governor said, ". . . and when I remember how your nephews murdered him in the coldest of blood, intense indignation fills my breast. . . . [D]eath would have been a juster and more righteous penalty."[32] The widow of the Pinkerton agent murdered in 1874 weighed in with a telegram insisting that the governor reject the brothers' applications for parole.

Finally, in 1901, far too late to be of any use to Bob Younger, dead of tuberculosis in 1889, the Minnesota legislature extended the privilege of parole to prisoners serving life sentences. Immediately afterward the parole board freed Jim and Cole. On July 11, 1901, they at last walked free. Cole was still telling his stories, this time to a Minnesota parole officer:

> In one of the fights that Butler's troops had with these raiders, the property of the James Brothers was destroyed by fire and old Mrs. James, mother of the brothers and an old Aunt of the Younger brothers, was shot resulting in the loss of her arm the same being amputated at or near the shoulder.[33]

The brothers swore vengeance against Butler, Cole said, discovered he had interests in Northfield, and rode north hoping to find either Butler or his money. If the agent remembered Cole's story right, the old bandit was still at it, making a good story even better, cobbling together pieces of separate tales and perpetuating the fable about the oppressed southern boys and the brutal carpetbaggers.

One last small story remains to be told about the raid itself. Homer Croy tells it and says he got the details from Frank James's son, Robert, who lived in Excelsior Springs, Missouri, not far from Kansas City. According to Croy, after the Northfield fiasco Jesse showed up in Dallas, where Belle Starr was "dealing faro." Here's the tale, and the reader may judge how much credence is to be placed in it.

"I thought," said Jesse, "maybe you'd like to know what happened."

Belle did, of course, and Jesse proceeded to state the obvious:

"It was bad. . . . I never did want to go to Minnesota. Cole didn't either, for that matter. He's in for life. . . . But he may get out. I hope so."

Belle said she hoped so too, and Jesse went on.

"I have to keep moving all the time. It's not like the old days. . . . [P]eople don't want to take me in any more. The papers tell where I've robbed a bank or a train—I haven't been there at all. That helps throw them off. I'll never be taken alive. I've made up my mind to that. Never."[34]

It's a pretty story, but probably just that much more mythology. There is no evidence that Belle dealt faro in Dallas or anyplace else. In fact, for at least a part of the summer of 1876 she seems to have been in Missouri, not Texas, although her movements after that remain unclear. In any case, there could be no logical way to discover such dialogue. Jesse was killed in 1882, and Belle was murdered seven years later. Since Croy was six years old when Belle was ambushed and does not mention any source for the Dallas conversation, it seems likely that the whole incident is invented.

As for Northfield, the story of the raid would live on. The town's pride in the courage of its citizens would not diminish with the years. Long after, the story of the citizens' bravery was told each year in the town schools on the anniversary of the raid. And at the end of the story, the storyteller would finish by asking, "Who is the hero of the Northfield Raid?" And the children would shout in return, "Northfield!" As late as 1907 an article in the Northfield *News* said proudly,

> It was here that lawlessness met its Waterloo, and from here the news went out over America that Missouri methods did not go in Minnesota. This was thirty years ago, but the memory of that day is still green in Northfield. . . . It is the event which differentiates Northfield from all sleepy towns everywhere. It marks it as a place where heroism is ready to assert itself.[35]

In the midst of its pride, however, Northfield never forgot its own humanity. This proud story of the repulse of the outlaw gang shared the front page with the warm tale of Tom Sardine, the Northfield cat who loved to attend church, trotting up the aisle with a "cat-like tread" and sitting reverently by the pulpit all the way through the final hymn.

The *St. Paul Pioneer Press* summed up the gang's dreary performance in terms of profit and loss:

> The Northfield robbers may have finally escaped from the boundaries of Minnesota, but it will be long before they or the like of them will ever choose this state as the theatre of their crimes. Their account with Minnesota up to date is as follows: eight blooded horses worth a total of $1200; eight McClellan saddles and bridles, totaling $200; eight partial suits of clothes, totaling $200; expenses while in state, $200; less ten nickels captured at Northfield, totaling 50 cents; for a net loss of $1,799.50.[36]

Which pretty well illustrated the colossal failure of this celebrated raid. But it did not count the blood.

CHAPTER SEVEN

THE TWO WHO GOT AWAY

One of the most hotly debated questions in the history of the outlaw West is whether Frank and Jesse James were present at Northfield. If they told anyone they were there, their confidence was never violated, and they never came close to an outright admission themselves. Nor did any of the Younger boys, being "true to your friends if the Heavens fall," as Cole put it. Cole stuck to his story in *The Story of Cole Younger, by Himself*. Cole, doubtless well aware of the difficulty a dead man has defending himself, laid the blame for Heywood's death on Pitts and again denied that either of the James boys was part of the Northfield raid.

There were reasons, Cole wrote, why the James and Younger brothers could not work together in the Northfield raid. There was trouble between him and Jesse. It dated back to 1872, when the outlaw George Shepherd got out of jail after serving his term for the Russellville robbery. Jesse told him Shepherd was gunning for him. Shepherd and Cole met at the house of a man called Hudspeth, and the two men spent a long nervous night sleeping in the same bed. In the morning Cole confronted Shepherd and learned that Shepherd meant him no harm. Cole's bitterness toward Jesse grew deeper when Jesse wrote one of his usual "not me" letters after the robbery of the county fair cashier. Cole was angry that Jesse included in the letter a statement that Cole Younger wasn't one of the county fair robbers, for that was the first time Cole's name had been mentioned in connection with that outrage. For these and other reasons, Cole wrote, "Jesse and I were not on friendly terms at any time after [the] Shepherd affair, and never were associated in any enterprise."[1]

Over the years many others also denied that the James brothers were at Northfield—not only the usual apologists, but also thoughtful people who ignored a unanimous press and a torrent of popular fiction and concluded that there was no absolute certainty that the brothers were part of the raid. Until his last moments on earth, Cole consistently denied that the James boys were along on the Northfield attack. As he explained in *The Story of Cole Younger,*

> Every blood-and-thunder history . . . declares that Frank and Jesse James were the two members of the band that entered Northfield who escaped arrest or death. They were not, however. One of these two men was killed afterwards in Arizona and the other died from fever some years afterward.

Cole does not explain how he learned the fate of his two anonymous cohorts. Much of Cole's self-magnifying book rings false, very like Emmett Dalton's two books, produced after his arrest and imprisonment for murder done during the Dalton gang's fiasco in Coffeyville, Kansas.

Support for Cole's denial came from a statement by George W. Batchelder, the Faribault attorney who drew the unenviable task of defending the Youngers after their capture. Batchelder and John Nutting, president of the bank, returned home from the Philadelphia Centennial Exposition with their families when they received news of the robbery. They arrived about the time the gang was brought down near Madelia.

Batchelder's clients convinced him that the James brothers were not at Northfield. According to a statement given later by Batchelder's son:

> There had been bad blood between the two gangs and Cole had actually gone out with a gun looking for him. This was because there had been so many crimes unduly credited to the Youngers

when they knew that the James boys were responsible . . . . I remember that they told my father in my hearing that it was not the James brothers but a man by the name of Dalton and that the other man was someone who had lived in Rice County and had led the way both going and coming. I have forgotten his name. . . . I also heard them say that Pitts was the man who shot Mr. Heywood. . . . Pitts went into the bank with Cole, but he had been drinking.[2]

"Dalton," of course, is not one of the names Cole later invented for the two mystery bandits and which he used in his book. Neither, according to Cole, did Cole go inside the bank. Moreover, we know that there was never bad blood between Cole and Frank James, then or afterward. So the story the Youngers told their hardworking defense lawyer seems to have been more of Cole's moonshine, probably invented to protect Frank James.

And there is still more evidence. Many years later, C. E. Hinton of Minneapolis wrote the Northfield News to say that at the time of the raid he was studying medicine in the office of two Faribault doctors. While dressing Cole Younger's wounds one day, Hinton posed the question everybody in the territory had been asking, whether the James brothers were the two bandits who got away. According to Hinton, Cole replied, "If it were the last words I was to speak, I would swear, if needs be, the James boys were not with us on this raid. Further we have not seen one another for about eighteen months."[3]

As one of the Otterville outlaws, Hobbs Kerry, named both the James and the Younger brothers as being involved in that robbery, Cole's dramatic denial lacked persuasive power. The Otterville bank had been raided only the previous July, a good deal more recent than "eighteen months." There is the outside chance that Kerry made it all up, but Otterville has all the earmarks of a James-Younger enterprise, and its timing was perfect for acquiring a grubstake for Northfield.

Still, lacking an admission by either James brother that they were present at Northfield, some writers have been reluctant to conclude the brothers were among the Northfield raiders. I am not. There is a great deal of evidence that, taken together, convinces me that both Frank and Jesse James were on the raid, that both of them were probably guilty of murder during the fighting along Division Street, and that they were the two bandits who escaped the posses beating the bushes for the fleeing survivors of the gang. To be sure, there is no indisputable evidence that the James boys were present, but there is enough to convince me that they probably were the two who got away.

The most persuasive reason to believe that the James brothers were both part of the Northfield raid came from Cole Younger himself, by way of Harry Hoffman, unquestionably a close and loyal friend of both Frank James and Cole Younger. Hoffman had done a lot of things in his time, but in his later years he was a peace officer in Jackson County, finally becoming marshal for the county. And on a Sunday in March 1916, it was Hoffman who got an urgent call that Cole Younger was near death and wanted to talk to him and Jesse James's son. Hoffman collected James, and the two sat at Cole's bedside while Cole told them about Northfield.

I'm dying, said Cole, and it can't hurt anybody now to tell you what actually happened. The James brothers *were* there, Cole said, but there he stopped, for he would not tell who murdered cashier Heywood. Later Hoffman added that he could say that neither Jesse James nor Cole Younger had killed Heywood but that he could not say "who rode the dun horse at Northfield, because it was he who killed the cashier."[4] Hoffman hedged on his obligation by failing to deny that Frank James bought a dun horse to use in the robbery. While some have speculated that Frank shot the bloodied, half-conscious Heywood in "self-defense," no hoodlum attacking and robbing an innocent citizen can raise that ancient defense, whether or not the criminal thinks the citizen is about to resist.

There has been some speculation that Frank was probably present but that Jesse was not. The point is that the raid was sloppily planned, that Jesse would never have tolerated the other men drinking on the job, and that had Minnesota authorities thought

Jesse was part of the raid, they would have indicted him or issued a warrant for his arrest, which they did not.

It's unlikely that Frank would be so far afield without Jesse. Moreover, it's by no means clear that the outlaws were Jesse's men to command, for both Cole Younger and Frank James were older and experienced. As for the drinking, we don't know how the drinkers behaved, nor do we know precisely how Jesse felt about having a horn or two before a raid. As for the planning, the plan was not elaborate. It did not vary from that behind any other typical James-Younger raid: yell, shoot, bully; cow the locals with your noise and your firepower.

At the time of the raid and afterward, it was commonly believed in Northfield that the James boys were the two escaped bandits. Contemporary belief is worth paying attention to; it is generally pretty close to the truth, and it often tends to be more dependable than later revisionist history. There is also the simple circumstance that the Youngers and the Jameses, whatever their differences, had run together for a long time, at least seventeen years in fact. Again and again they had successfully raided and robbed as a team. It is illogical that they would break up a winning combination. Moreover, whatever hard feelings may have existed between Cole and Jesse, Jesse remained Jim Younger's friend, and Cole and Frank had long been close friends and would remain so as long as they lived.

Then there are the names Cole Younger later gave to the two mystery riders: Howard and Woods. Everybody knows the saccharine ballad about Jesse James, who was living under the alias Howard when he was murdered by "that dirty little coward" Bob Ford. Woodson was Jesse's middle name, and Frank had lived in Nashville in the 1870s as Ben Woodson. Cole's use of two names so close to the aliases the James brothers themselves used seems more than coincidental.

Carl Breihan, prolific writer on the West, claimed to have access to an "almost verbatim statement made by Cole Younger in reply to questions asked by a close relative; with the strict promise that it should not be revealed while either Cole Younger or Frank James was alive."[5] Without naming the relative, Breihan printed the following version of that (perhaps apocryphal) interview:

> Q: Cole, were the James boys in with you at the Northfield raid?
>
> A: Yes, they were, and using the names of Howard and Woods.
>
> Q: Why then did you state they were not and that Howard and Woods were the real names of these other two men?
>
> A: Simply to protect Frank James. If it was thought for a minute that Jesse did not do the killing of the cashier, Heywood, then Yankee Bligh and several detectives from St. Louis would have swooped down on Frank and tried him for the killing. . . .
>
> Q: Who, then, did kill Cashier Heywood?
>
> A: It was Frank James, and to finally answer the question of who rode the dun horse at Northfield, it was Frank James. It was stolen . . . in Kansas City, I believe it was. He was noted to be a sprinter. . . .
>
> Q: It is true that Jesse wished to kill your wounded brothers in order to make escape a sure thing?
>
> A: Yes, Jesse did suggest this and I believe he would have carried it out had he been permitted to do so. Frank would never think of such a thing.[6]

Breihan's report of the interview should have answered forever the question of whether Jesse and Frank were present at Northfield, as well as who murdered the helpless cashier, but it did not. For one thing, none of the Youngers ever agreed that the incident happened. Cole said that the Youngers and the James boys parted friends. For another thing, Breihan's books, including the one reporting the interview, have been roundly criticized for gross inaccuracy and worse.[7] In *The Complete and Authentic Life of Jesse James*, for example, Breihan quotes Cole Younger as saying the "dun horse" was stolen "from a man named Stewart or something like that, in Kansas City, I believe it was." Which makes you wonder how the horse got to Minnesota, seeing that the gang almost surely traveled north by train and bought horses when they arrived.

Moreover, Cole had already covered Frank's trail as best he could with his tale that Pitts had killed Heywood. Frank would have been in jeopardy only if Cole had changed his "Pitts did it" story; nobody would suspect for a moment that Frank did the killing instead of Jesse, or Charlie Pitts.

Another persuasive item of proof is that of bank man Alonzo Bunker, one of the two living men who saw the three inside bandits at very close range. Bunker remained convinced that one of the inside men was indeed Frank James. On a trip to Dallas in 1892, he says, he saw Frank James. "But [I] made no effort to renew our acquaintance, as I was greatly impressed at a former meeting."[8] As Bunker saw the gang's inside men at what was literally point-blank range, it seems to me that his opinion deserves considerable weight. And there is no reason to doubt Bunker's story, or his conviction that Frank James and Charlie Pitts were two of the three inside men. If Bunker was right about these two and Bob Younger was the third man inside with them, not only were the James brothers present at Northfield, but Jesse James is eliminated as Heywood's killer.

Bunker's conclusion was shared by the Rice County prosecutor, George Baxter, who tried vainly to get Frank James returned to Minnesota for trial, although no indictment was issued. In addition, there is the evidence of Dr. Sidney Mosher, who saw the two men who kidnapped him at close range for a substantial period. Over the hours he rode with his two kidnappers, the doctor had every opportunity to observe and remember every feature.

Then there is the evidence of Cole's parole officer in Minnesota, F. A. Whittier. In a letter written in 1924 he described Cole as a "dreamy sort of fellow" who told an extraordinary tale to explain why the gang chose to attack little Northfield. It was Butler, Cole said, arch-carpetbagger Gen. Ben Butler. Butler's troops, according to Cole, had a fight with Missouri raiders, in the course of which "the property of the James Brothers was destroyed by fire and old

Mrs. James, mother of the brothers and an old Aunt of the Younger brothers, was shot resulting in the loss of her arm being amputated at or near the shoulder. . . . [T]he James Brothers swore vengeance against Butler." Cole told Whittier that the shooting of Mr. Heywood was "no doubt" the result "of the James Brothers being determined to get even . . . and they assumed that Mr. Heywood was a relative of the Butler family or the Ames family."[9] Assuming Whittier's memory and honesty are to be trusted—there are no grounds to doubt either—there is even more reason to believe that the James boys were at Northfield. Whittier warned that he told the story "only as one of Cole Younger's yarns," but taken with the other evidence, the tale probably contains some truth.

And it is reasonably certain that Cole told the same peculiar story more than once, if repetition is some indication of truth. The Stillwater warden, replying to an inquiry in 1930, said that Cole "claimed that troops of General Butler . . . maimed their aunt, the mother of the James boys, and that they swore to avenge the deed. . . . [T]hey sought to ruin him financially through this robbery."[10] Now, the "mother of the James boys" was not related to any of the Youngers, unless the boys called her "aunt" out of courtesy. The only relationship between the two families was this: Zerelda's second—and short-lived—husband, Ben Simms, had a niece, Augusta Inskip, who married an uncle of the Younger boys. Save for this tenuous connection, no relationship existed between the two families, certainly none of blood.

Still other versions of the raid place Jesse James inside the bank. Both of Marley Brant's excellent histories of the Youngers say Jesse was one of the inside men and took the lead in kicking Heywood around. In fact, both books flatly say that it was Jesse who put a knife to Heywood's throat, ordering him to open the safe or he'd "cut [his] damn throat from ear to ear."[11] And as late as 1907 the Northfield *News* wrote of Heywood's murder that "Jesse James, drunk and mad turned and shot him through the brain in dastardly revenge."

Both of Ms. Brant's books conclude that it was Frank James who finally paused as he left and coldly shot the cashier in the head, and I agree. Although the brutal attack on Heywood is consistent with Jesse's style, it is difficult to imagine Bunker forgetting the faces of the men inside the bank, especially the face of the one who shot him. The probabilities are, therefore, that it was Charlie Pitts who took the lead in brutalizing Heywood, as well as shooting Bunker as he fled. Jesse probably did not enter the bank at all but was part of the third group of three bandits whose mission was to terrorize the citizens on the streets of Northfield.

And one more minor fragment of evidence remains. At the time of the raid the two escaped robbers were both thought to have been wounded during the attempt on the bank. Many years later, in 1978, a bullet was found in Jesse's original grave and was "traced by Missouri historians to the Northfield foray."[12] According to a Clay County historic site superintendent, the 1978 dig unearthed a ".38 caliber bullet fired from a Smith & Wesson pistol of the kind that came onto the market in 1875."[13]

A Northfield historian theorized that the .38 slug came from the gun of a "Minnesota farmer," from whom Jesse and Frank had tried to steal a horse. The slug "passed through Frank's leg and struck Jesse's leg."[14] Perhaps, but assuming the slug came from Jesse's remains, there is no way to prove that it dated from the Northfield fight, although pistols were probably fired at the gang in the fighting along Division Street. Nor could the bullet have come from the nameless Minnesota boy hiding behind his tree, for he used a shotgun.

All these things considered, there is ample reason to conclude that the James brothers were with the gang that struck Northfield and that Frank James killed Heywood. We'll never know whether Frank killed Heywood out of pure meanness or out of anger because Heywood's attempt to close the vault door injured Frank's arm or shoulder. There is no question, however, about the friendship that existed between him and Cole Younger, plenty of reason for Cole to blame Charlie Pitts for the cashier's death. Faithful Charlie was dead, of course, and dead men can't contradict you. The friendship between Cole and Frank is also reason enough for Cole to deny that either of the James brothers was present at Northfield: if he protected his friend Frank, he had to protect Jesse too. The brothers worked together, and it is unlikely anybody would have believed Cole had he said Jesse was present and Frank was not.

CHAPTER EIGHT

THE YEARS AFTER

The dirty little coward, who shot Mr. Howard,
He laid Jesse James in his grave.

As every red-blooded schoolboy knows—or used to know—the dirty little coward was Bob Ford, killer and would-be member of the James gang. In 1882, at the home of Ford's sister, he and Dick Liddell shot down the bucktoothed outlaw Wood Hite, also a sometime gang member. Not long after the Hite killing, Ford graduated to much bigger game, although he was careful not to risk his own neck. This time Bob and his brother Charlie were out to kill Jesse James himself. And they had an advantage no lawman could have: their quarry trusted them and invited them into his home. Jesse was living in St. Joseph with his family then, on Lafayette Street, under an assumed name.

The Fords were in Jesse's St. Joseph home to plan still another robbery, ironically a strike on the bank in little Platte City, Missouri. Platte City was a bustling little town not far from the Missouri-Kansas line, the very same hamlet in which Jesse had his famous guerrilla ambrotype portrait made during the bushwhacker days so long ago. And there in St. Joe, having won their host's confidence and eaten his salt, the Ford brothers cold-bloodedly did Jesse in.

Bob Ford very sensibly plugged Jesse from behind, after he had stood up on a chair adjusting a picture on his wall. Ford waited until Jesse had laid aside his guns, too, something the veteran outlaw seldom did. Nobody knows for sure whether Ford killed Jesse out of hate or jealousy, or because Governor Crittenden offered him a reward and a pardon to kill Jesse, or just because he saw a chance to move from nobody to somebody in one quick jump. Ford seems to have been a wannabe desperado, and perhaps he felt that the single act of exterminating America's most notorious felon might make him a famous badman.

A good deal of public outrage followed Jesse's death, an odd combination of hero worship and general resentment at the shabby way in which he was killed. The inscription on Jesse's tombstone reflects that anger:

> Jesse W. JAMES
> Died April 3, 1882
> 34 years, 6 months, 28 days old
> Murdered by a coward whose name
> is not worthy to be printed here

Over the years the floorboard in the room where Jesse died was rubbed nearly concave, scraped by throngs of the morbid to retrieve a smidgeon of what might be Jesse's blood. The adulation of Jesse James continued unabated. But it is not fair to characterize all Missourians as uncritical fans of a professional outlaw. No doubt a good many of them, including some citizens of Clay County, were relieved, even pleased, to hear that the notorious Jesse James had at last departed this earth for good. The *History of Clay County* put it this way:

> At any time within the past fifteen years five hundred men could have been raised in an hour to capture the James boys. Dozens of the best citizens of all classes have frequently volunteered to accompany the officers in their search for the bandits, and have lain night after night in the woods and watched roads and bridges, and done everything in their power to vindicate

and uphold the law. Even when Jesse James was shot in St. Joseph a public meeting at Liberty applauded the fact and indorsed [sic] the manner of his taking off.[1]

Jesse spent a time buried at the old homestead where his mother could keep an eye on him. She charged twenty-five cents to have her picture taken with visitors, another two bits for admission, and the same fee for a pebble from Jesse's grave. While it is said that she was not squeamish about replenishing her pebble supply from a nearby creek, that is only rumor, and the tourists didn't know the difference anyway. In 1902, however, Jesse was moved to the Kearney cemetery under a nine-foot stone obelisk, which immediately became fair game for the curious. Souvenir hunters descended on the new burial site as they had on the St. Joe house, and chipped away enough pieces that the monument had to be replaced.

Perhaps the public's righteous anger at Jesse's death might have been less had they known just how badly off the famous outlaw left his family. For long-suffering Zee James had to sell off many of the family possessions for ready cash, in spite of the efforts of editor Edwards and others to raise money for her and her children. One of the pitiful family assets sold off was Jesse Jr.'s little dog, Boo, which brought five dollars.

It is a little hard to care much about any man who is capable of winning an honest living for those who depend on him, but remains an outlaw, living from crime to crime. There is some evidence that Jesse may have explored a more peaceful line of work between robberies. For instance, there is the story that he rode the Santa Fe Railroad to Las Vegas, New Mexico, in 1879. There he put up at the Old Adobe House, a hotel run by a "former Santa Fe freight conductor" who knew him. He stayed in Las Vegas a month or so, exploring "the sheep business and other opportunities" but found nothing to suit him.

And so much for all the persistent tales of unrecovered loot rumored to be stashed here and there around Missouri. Maybe there were piles of gold coins, greenbacks, and bearer bonds secreted someplace by the outlaw brothers and never found. If there were such treasures, however, poor Zee James did not benefit. And even if Jesse never told his wife where the loot was hidden, Frank presumably would have tapped the hoard to help her. Kin stuck together in those days, and Frank was not only Zee's brother-in-law but her first cousin as well. Had Frank known of buried loot—and he would have—surely Zee's latter days would have been somewhat easier and Jesse Jr. would not have had to give up his pet.

You can still visit the house in which the Fords killed Jesse James. The house is much traveled. It's at 12th and Penn Streets these days, although when Jesse was killed it was located farther north. In 1939 it was jacked up and moved over to the highway, the idea apparently being to more easily attract tourists. Fortunately, the house was bought in 1977 and donated to the Pony Express Historical Association, which wisely moved it back to its old neighborhood. It's a museum these days, about a block from the site where Jesse was gunned down.

Not far away is Patee House, also well worth visiting. Patee House was the hotel, then called World's Hotel, at which Zee James stayed after Jesse's death. Before that it had served as Pony Express headquarters. In 1865, seven years after it was built, its owner, Patee, was in financial trouble. He sold lottery tickets on his own hotel in an attempt to turn a dollar and get rid of the building. Interest in the lottery was not what Patee thought it might be, and he had to take the last hundred tickets himself. That turned out to be a fortuitous circumstance, because one of Patee's tickets was the winner. Today the income from the house where Jesse died helps support both the James home in Kearney and Patee House.

You can also visit the James farm today. It's nicely restored and furnished. Part of it is a log cabin, perhaps the oldest building in the county; the front part of the building is an "Eastlake" addition, a kit of precut parts quite popular in its day. There are reenactments held there too, as there are in Gallatin and elsewhere. And in Liberty you can visit the museum, on the site of the first daylight bank robbery in American history. It has been splendidly re-created, including a beautiful calendar clock, said to be one of only four in existence. When I visited, a pleasant worker there told me the tale that Frank James said Jesse did the only killing that day, the shooting of seventeen-year-old Jolly Wymore. And there is a story that Wymore's family later received a letter of apology from Jesse James. The tale may be apocryphal, but even if it's true, anybody can sign someone else's name to a letter. On balance, it is reasonably clear that Jesse was not part of the Liberty robbery and probable that Frank was not there either. But then, a legend is a durable spirit and hard to exorcise.

Whatever the reason Bob Ford pulled the trigger on Jesse James, he passed into history as "the dirty little coward." Ford was duly convicted of murder, but Governor Crittenden pardoned him as he had promised. Now famous, or at least notorious, Ford toured with a stage troupe, telling the story of how he had killed the fabulous outlaw Jesse James and giving an exhibition of pistol shooting. His brother Charlie traveled with him for a while, and the brothers were paid $500 a week, very tidy wages for the time. As it turned out, however, many of the audiences were often hostile, and so in time Bob signed on with a freak show. He had enough of this after two years on the road and moved on to run a saloon in Las Vegas, New Mexico, a wild enough place in its own right.

And so Ford had his brief season in the sun and then reverted to what he'd always been, a small-time punk. His brother, surely a co-conspirator in Jesse's murder, literally died of shame. He shot himself to death in a patch of weeds, preferring suicide to the loathing with which he was received by many Missourians. Bob was apparently unmoved by nobler motives and in time drifted from Las Vegas to Creede, Colorado, then a boomtown overflowing with the silver of the Ethel and the Holy Moses and swarming with miners and prospectors, whores, gamblers, and thieves. There Ford opened a saloon, and when his place burned down he reopened in a board-sided tent, a jerry-built shack in a wild, jerry-built town.

There he prospered for a while, at least by the standards of Creede, peddling booze to perpetually thirsty miners. And then, on an 1892 trip down to Pueblo, he got crossways with another ex-Missouri hard case, one Ed Kelly. Kelly was a tough cob, a relative by marriage to the Younger boys, then still languishing behind bars in faraway Stillwater. Ford accused Kelly of stealing a diamond ring from him when they shared a room in Pueblo and kept grumbling about the incident when he returned to Creede. Kelly heard about Ford's loose mouth, took umbrage, and went to Creede to shut Ford up.

Another version of the tale calls Kelly a deputy sheriff who had led a raid on Ford's establishment early in 1892. Ford was wounded, the story goes, and even went out of business for a while. And then, just after he reopened, Kelly took a shine to Ford's mistress and appeared at Ford's place with the intent to terminate his rival.

Whatever moved Kelly to vent his spleen on Ford, he showed up in Ford's place carrying a Bowie knife and a revolver, but before he could try conclusions with Ford, Ford's bartender and his bouncer threw Kelly out of the saloon. Getting tossed out of Ford's grubby establishment didn't improve Kelly's foul temper. He left the saloon all right, but only temporarily. He was sufficiently irritated to return with a borrowed shotgun to avenge his humiliation. And he did, after Ford was a little slow getting to his own weapon. He blew the killer of Jesse James into eternity by the shortest route, driving one of Ford's collar buttons clean through his throat.

While the death of Ford did not noticeably diminish mankind, it was nevertheless homicide without legal justification. Kelly went to prison for the killing and got out in 1900. Four years later, having learned nothing, he tangled with an Oklahoma City policeman, who ran him into jail for a day or two. Kelly was too humiliated to forget the arrest. One day he encountered the officer on the street and struck at him with a revolver. They raise tough cops in Oklahoma, and this one turned out to be quicker than Kelly was; he wrestled Kelly's gun around until Kelly ate his own bullet.

We left Clel Miller and Bill Chadwell, alias Stiles, quite dead in the street near the bank, their bandit careers ended for good, or so it must have seemed. Although both bandits were soon to be buried, neither one was destined to stay put very long. Indeed, both were about to embark on a second career. They were helped by young Wheeler, the heroic medical student, who cannily suggested that as cadavers were much in demand for medical school dissection, the fresh corpses shouldn't be wasted. In the words of a descendant of Northfield men, this argument appealed to "men of weight" in the town, who "allowed that since Wheeler had killed him, he was entitled to him."

That applied to Miller at least, and Chadwell was also deemed suitable material for dissection. Both men traveled to Ann Arbor, although precisely how they got there depends on which version of the story you read. Anyway, one story has it that Wheeler, lacking a handy spot to keep cadavers, prevailed on a friend to help him (the friend's name varies depending on who tells the tale). The friend—or maybe friends—stored Stiles and Miller in a barrel—or perhaps it was a lead-lined "pickling box"—until Wheeler could remove the remains to the University of Michigan, his alma mater. The strong probability is that Wheeler's helpers were Dampier, son of the owner of the Northfield hotel, and Clarence Persons, as both young men were also studying medicine at the University of Michigan.

The story gets even better at this point. Confronted later by a hired man asking to be paid early, one of Wheeler's friends opened up the box to show the terrified hired hand "the last man who asked . . . for his pay before he was entitled to it." The alternative ending to this tale is that the hired hand found the body and asked about it: the friend replied that it was the remains of a hired hand who wouldn't do what I told him to. At which the hired hand fled, never to reappear.

However they traveled, there is a tradition that both outlaws made it to Ann Arbor in time to assist their new owner and his friends in medical school. On his way into the laboratory, Wheeler asked a freshman to help carry one of the new cadavers inside. Obliging and maybe envious, the freshman asked Wheeler where he had come by his very own cadaver. "I shot him," answered

Wheeler. And, again according to legend, the freshman fainted dead away.

Another version of the tale has Wheeler, helped by Dampier, another medical student, stashing both cadavers in barrels in Chub Creek until school began in the fall, then shipping them north to Ann Arbor. In a different account the bodies were sent off to Ann Arbor in barrels marked "Fresh Paint." In those days paint was usually shipped dry, as pigment, and mixed at its destination when the time came to use it. "Fresh paint" was no more than paint that had already been mixed. That label would account for the sloshing of the brine solution inside the barrel. [2] Still another version has Stiles shipped off to Ann Arbor labeled "salt pork."

The *Michigan Quarterly Review* declared that Wheeler "was chosen to lead the hastily organized posse." Engaged in preparing to chase the fleeing survivors of the gang, Wheeler turned to Clarence E. Persons, his Michigan roommate and fellow medical student. On the way out of town with the posse, says the *Quarterly Review*, Wheeler hailed his friend Persons and gave him quick instructions:

> Clarence, you had better see if you can get the bodies of the two fellows who have been shot and perhaps we can land them in Ann Arbor for dissecting material. You see what you can do while I am gone.[3]

Sure enough, as the story goes, Persons went off to the cemetery in the gloom of night. The *Quarterly Review* agrees that Persons had help from young Charley Dampier. The two collegians dug up the earthly remains. In this tale the shipment to Michigan is also made in kegs disguised as fresh paint. That Clarence Persons was one of the body snatchers is conclusively proven by the diary—still extant—of his uncle, which contains the cryptic entry that Clarence "shipped two barrels mixed paint."[4] That Clarence's uncle made the entry without explanation suggests strongly that the diarist knew precisely what was in the barrels of "paint."

The *Michigan Quarterly Review* relates that late in 1876 "friends of one of the slain bandits"—probably Miller's family—appeared

September 7, 1876:
"O & I take C. ???? pile a load of hay 16.80 lbs. and plows in a.m.
& draws straw till 3 p.m. then goes to town. I cut corn & C.
draws straw. Eight robbers ride into Northfield & attempt to rob
the bank but but Heywood would not unlock it for them they
kill him and I hear Bunker through the shoulder. Manning & H.
Wheeler each kill a robber & wound another & kill one horse
they then leave.

September 8, 1876.
I go to town to see the dead men this morning and I ran manure.
O. helps Weeks thrash with his team and Nelly to draw straw
in p.m. I finish cutting corn in p.m. C. does some work tonight.

Sat. September 9, 1876
A rainy day core and string apples is about all we do today.
Clean up a load of wheat just. Night Clarence, Orville & Wife
come home today & Albert comes at night. C. ships two barrels
of mixed paint this morning to _UV. ???? Ann Arbor.

Transcription of a page from the diary of Newton Persons, Clarence's
uncle, referring to his nephew's shipment of "mixed paint" to Ann Arbor.
Original diary in the possession of the Northfield Historical Society
Archives and printed by their courtesy.

to demand whatever was left of their outlaw relative. Miller has
another ending in *The Outlaw Youngers*. Brant says that a "pro-
moter" got his hands on Miller's corpse, had him embalmed and
pickled in alcohol, and then put him on display "throughout the
Northwest" until Miller's family succeeded in retrieving what was
left of him for burial.[5]

In time, neither outlaw was much use as a cadaver, most of them
having been used up in the interest of medical education. Wheeler
asked about disposing of Chadwell's remains, now reduced to
bones, and his cohort Persons said, "You shot him, Henry, I guess
he's yours." And thus came Bill Chadwell/Stiles to his final resting
place in Dr. Wheeler's Grand Forks office, where he apparently

remained throughout Dr. Wheeler's long practice in that city. One account says his skeleton was finally consumed in a fire, but more reliable evidence indicates it was simply passed on to another doctor. Bill may be on the move yet.

There is a story that many years after the Northfield fight an elderly man called on Dr. Wheeler and asked to see the skeleton. And when he had, the old man thanked Wheeler and said, "I'm glad you let me see it, doctor. That's my son." Or, in Homer Croy's variation on the story, the old man said yes, that was his son, and added, "Ma—that's the boy's mother—said, 'I believe that's our boy. Now you go an' make sure.' . . . Now I'll have to go back and tell her it is our boy hangin' here in your office."[6] Although the tale is touching, it is unclear how even a devoted father could distinguish his son's bones from anybody else's.

Charlie Pitts also found a new career in medicine. He started out on public display in Northfield, where schoolchildren were ordered to view the remains, perhaps to discourage them from a life of crime. One writer says Charlie was then shipped to St. Paul "packed in ice" and for a couple of days presented an "unpleasant and disgusting spectacle" laid out on a table in the state capitol for the curious to see.[7] In time Charlie was turned over to Dr. J. H. Murphy, the surgeon-general of the state, and he had Pitts embalmed and preserved for use in medical school dissection. Murphy passed Charlie on to his nephew, Henry Hoyt, of St. Paul, then a medical student at Rush Medical College in Chicago. Young Hoyt had need of a skeleton, and as Pitts had not yet progressed to skeletal form he was put in a box, which was then sunk among the water lilies in St. Paul's Lake Como, to remain until Charlie should be reduced to a useful set of bones.

Meanwhile, young Dr. Hoyt went west adventuring, to Deadwood and Tascosa among other places. In early 1878 in Las Vegas, New Mexico, Hoyt finally got letters from home. He was mortified to learn that the box had been spotted by ice cutters the previous winter, pulled up from the lake, and opened. Considerable horror and excitement ensued, followed by a full-scale inquest. Hoyt's brother sought out Dr. Murphy, who "quickly burst the murder bubble and took charge of the bones." In time, when Hoyt did not return to Minnesota on schedule, Dr. Murphy gave Pitts's bones to "a Chicago doctor." In the end all young Dr. Hoyt got out of the episode was an unsigned hate letter from Missouri condemning him for his "brutal treatment of 'pore charley pitts.'"

Bunker confirmed this version of Pitts's later history. The outlaw ended up in Dr. Murphy's St. Paul office, Bunker says, and Bunker saw it when he went to St. Paul to identify Pitts as the one who shot him. Dr. Murphy accommodatingly asked Bunker whether he would like to take home with him "the finger that pulled the trigger as a keepsake." If he wanted a digital souvenir, the doctor told Bunker, "Murphy would cut it off and fix it up for me. I declined the kind offer, thinking I would remember the incident without such a memento."[8]

One of Pitts's ears and a chunk of scalp were severed from his head. This gruesome souvenir, duly marked in ink with Pitts's name, ended up the property of Bill Schilling, longtime columnist for the Northfield *News,* and found a home in Schilling's Hobby House museum. The ear remains in the possession of the Northfield Historical Society to this day, the society having made the decision to retire it from public display.

A California lawyer, writing to Schilling, stated that another Michigan medical student had sliced away the flesh surrounding the entry wound in Clel Miller's chest and carried away the spoil as his own souvenir. The lawyer told Schilling that his father was a Michigan medical student in 1876. A medical school classmate, one Sayles, "had access to the corpse [Clel Miller's] and sliced off a pie-shaped-piece of flesh thru which the bullet reached the heart."

Sayles shoved this messy memento into his pocket and took it home, where he exhibited it as a slice of history and told the story of carving it off.[9] Otherwise sober law-abiding people did things like that in those days, the same period that produced hundreds of photos of smiling citizens posing with the propped-up bodies of assorted dead criminals. In 1892, for example, when the Dalton gang bit the dust in Coffeyville, Kansas, souvenir hunters grabbed everything from snippets of the outlaws' clothing to hair from their horses' tails to handkerchiefs well soaked in Dalton blood.

One last Charlie Pitts tale—grisly and probably apocryphal—deserves to be told. Charlie, the story goes, was resting in a barrel of brine in the back room of Dr. Murphy's office. The doctor asked a visitor named Gibbs whether he would like to see Charlie Pitts. When Gibbs said he would, the doctor took him to the back room, took the cover off the barrel, reached down, and seized the cadaver by the hair. "Come up, Charlie, you have company." Although he would visit the doctor thereafter, Gibbs never again tried to see Charlie.[10]

So much for the history of the dead. As to the survivors, Frank James lived long enough to see the beginning of World War I. He died in 1915. After Jesse was killed in 1882, there was some speculation that Frank would hunt down the Fords and revenge his brother's death. But nothing of the sort happened. For whatever reasons, Frank had had enough of life on the owlhoot trail. From 1877 to 1881 he seems to have lived with his family near Nashville, in a settlement called White's Creek. He had a son now, and responsibility, and his wife, Ann, had never approved of his life of crime.

And so, at last, Frank decided to come in from the cold. At first there was some preliminary negotiation, an attempt to get Frank a full pardon from the governor. The attempt quickly foundered on the rock of public fury. Even in Missouri there was an outcry, and Kansans were outraged: "It would be disgraceful and cowardly to pardon this fellow," said the Great Bend *Inland Tribune*. The Atchison *Champion* waxed angrier still:

> Jesse James was hunted and killed just as he should have been hunted and killed, and if his scarcely less vicious and criminal brother wants to escape the just penalty of his many cruel deeds, let him go to Mexico, or South America, or anywhere else out of this country, in which he has no right to live.[11]

After Frank wrote Gov. Thomas Crittenden a long, verbose letter seeking amnesty, the governor responded directly, telling Frank
he could guarantee nothing but a fair trial. And so, early in October, Frank arrived in Jefferson City, Missouri, accompanied by
none other than the ubiquitous Major Edwards and made his way
to the gubernatorial mansion. Frank turned himself in to Crittenden that afternoon, apparently delivering his pistols personally. "I
surrender my arms to you," Frank is supposed to have said. "I
deliver myself to you and the law."[12]

Frank ended up in the Jackson County jail in Independence. The
jail was an historic place, built in 1859 during the border troubles.
Its walls were two feet thick, constructed of massive limestone
blocks, some as heavy as three thousand pounds. The year after it
was finished it had held Quantrill while he awaited disposition of
charges relating to an attack on a Blue Springs farmhouse, apparently the same incident in which he sold out his Quaker friends to
establish his pro-slavery credentials.

The Jackson County jail could be a pretty grim place, but not for
Frank. He seems have lived pretty well, his cell furnished with a
"Brussels carpet" and various pieces of good furniture. His food
was prepared by the cook at a "nearby hashery" and brought in to
the jail. Frank apparently could move about as he wished and had
the use of a rocking chair in the hallway outside his cell.[13] He was
plainly a celebrity.

Frank spent his days hobnobbing with various friends and playing to the public while his lawyers prepared for trial. Two charges
against him were dismissed—one concerning the murder of
Pinkerton agent Whicher and one arising from the robbery of a
bank in 1867. One charge remained: an 1881 robbery at Blue Cut,
Missouri. At about the same time, in response to rumors that Minnesota would try to extradite Frank to try him for the Northfield
robbery, Governor Crittenden said flatly that he would not honor
a request from Minnesota. In fact, Crittenden would refuse to
honor such a request made two years later, based on a complaint
filed before a magistrate in Northfield.

Meanwhile, the Blue Cut charge still pending, Frank was moved to the Daviess County jail in Gallatin, after 112 days in Independence. In Gallatin he went to trial for the 1881 Winston train robbery in which conductor Westfall and a passenger had been murdered. Frank was defended by a galaxy of prominent attorneys, who presented an alibi defense. They put on many witnesses, including the Confederate general Jo Shelby, who showed up drunk, made an ass of himself, and got fined $10 for contempt of court. Shelby crowned his pathetic performance by asking the judge's permission to shake hands with Frank, only to be rebuffed by the court's tart reply: "You can call on him some other time."[14] After three days of argument by battalions of lawyers, because of General Shelby or in spite of him, Frank was acquitted.

Thereafter, both a second charge in Daviess County and the remaining charge in Jackson County were dismissed, and Frank was whisked off to Huntsville, Alabama, to stand trial for the robbery of a federal paymaster in spring 1881. Once again the defense was alibi, and once more Frank was acquitted. In the next instant he was arrested by the sheriff of Cooper County, Missouri, on still another charge, the 1876 Otterville robbery that had bankrolled the strike on Northfield. This arrest was widely seen as something of a sham, however, a ruse to keep Frank from being arrested by policemen from Minnesota, if any were lurking outside the federal courthouse in Huntsville.

Sure enough, in due course the Otterville indictment was also dismissed, the reason given being that the principal witness had died, and Frank James walked free at last. In later years he worked as a burlesque house doorman, a county fair race starter, a shoe salesman in Missouri and Texas, and a bit player in traveling stock company shows. At other times he went on the road to sell a new coaloil burner or ran a cigar store in St. Joseph, Missouri. For a time he lived on an Oklahoma farm, and in 1903 he and Cole Younger, finally out of prison, became partners in a traveling Wild West show.

He and Cole were growing gray, the last of the old, bold outlaws. Most of their foes and pursuers were gone by now, and much of the venom and fury had gone out of the whole business of robbery, alarm, and flight. The fires of controversy had burned down to embers, and even old enemies could come to terms. In the fullness of time, William Pinkerton, son of the gang's most implacable pursuer, met Frank James in the office of the St. Louis police chief. For a moment there was silence, and then Frank said, "If he'll shake hands with me, I will with him." And so it was. And in later years Pinkerton told a St. Louis newsman,

> I rather like Frank James. It is my impression that his brother Jesse was the vindictive and cruel one of the two. If it hadn't been for Jesse, I am inclined to think Frank would have become a good citizen long before he did.[15]

Frank attended and helped to organize reunions of the survivors of Quantrill's guerrilla band. They were warm, sentimental occasions. In the fall of 1898 the Independence *Jackson Examiner* reported that "Frank James stood near the center of the line and was the center of interest with his old comrades as well as with others at the picnic. . . . He was called on for a speech and in response said that in his life he had done many foolish things but had never yet made a public speech."[16]

As the years went by, the reunions continued, but at each one the ranks of the old fighters became thinner. The fire was gone now, and the rage. As the *Jackson Examiner* put it, "They prefer to tell of the happy incidents, of the occasional jokes of the war, or the good times they have had since and of the future. Many talk of religion quicker than of war."[17] In 1906 the same paper reported, "signatures on rolls are more trembly and the old stories are told with less bitterness and less feeling." In that year one of the old guerrillas present at the reunion was regular attendee John Noland of Blue Springs, whom the others called "a good companion, . . . a man among men," although Noland was black. When he died two years later, his pallbearers were old Confederate soldiers.

At last Frank James settled on the family farm in Kearney, charging visitors four bits to tour the old home place. There he died with his boots off, of a stroke, on February 18, 1915. His funeral was quite a happening and featured a long, passionate oration by Judge John F. Phillips, who had appeared as counsel for Frank at his Daviess County trial. The judge waxed eloquent over Frank's simplicity and decency, from the days of childhood when he was "just a plain, simple hearted farmer boy" to the latter days, when the judge had warned Frank of "pharisees who would be delighted should he fall down."

"Oh, be his failings covered by the tomb," said the judge, winding up his speech, "may guardian laurels o'er his ashes bloom." Which, if the meter wasn't quite right, surely fit this solemn occasion. And if in life Frank had been a good deal more scoundrel than simple-hearted farm boy, he still left friends and kin behind, and the occasion called for something warm and soothing.

The mythmakers made one last try to embellish the story of Frank James. The "real" Frank James lived on, said Columbus Vaughn and Frank Snow in their incredible *This Was Frank James*, as one Joe Vaughn, in Newton County, Arkansas. Somebody called Sam Collins settled in at the James homestead in Kearney masquerading as Frank James. He was paid well by the James brothers—oh yes, Jesse was still living; now as J. Frank Dalton. The same amazing book invents a number of nonexistent relatives, calls Quantrill "Quantral," and recites a blood oath supposed to have been administered to the bushwhackers in a lurid nighttime ceremony.

The Younger boys paid dearly for their part in the Northfield raid. All three were sent to Minnesota's Stillwater prison for life. Even here, however, the James-Younger mythology offers an alternative story: a wildly unreliable book about the Jesse James imposter J. Frank Dalton asserts that the Youngers "never served a day in Stillwater Prison." Instead, according to Dalton, the three "Dodson brothers" stood in for the Youngers for $300 a month apiece.[18] In fact, there is no question that it was the Younger boys who served years of grindingly slow hard time, and served it apparently without complaint.

Bob Younger was a model prisoner who applied himself to the study of medicine while he was behind bars. With his brothers, he hoped against hope for parole as the years crawled by, but Bob's prison term was a life sentence indeed. In the autumn of 1889 he died of tuberculosis, still inside the walls of the Stillwater prison. Only in death could he come home again, to the family burial plot in Lee's Summit.

Faithful Warren Bronaugh never wavered in his crusade to see the Youngers freed, and he spent enormous amounts of time rounding up support from dozens of prominent citizens in and out of Minnesota, including most of the Missouri legislature. At first his efforts were directed at obtaining a pardon, but that effort was frustrated by the abiding anger of many Minnesotans over the wanton killing of Heywood, whose memory remained green. In 1897, for example, Bronaugh's efforts failed when Northfield sent the governor a citizens' petition in opposition.

The Rice County attorney and the mayor of Faribault weighed in with three simple questions they thought the Youngers ought to answer. Was Frank James at Northfield? Who was the last man out of the bank? Who was the man on the buckskin horse? These were precisely the questions the Youngers would not answer, and the mayor and county attorney commented trenchantly, "These men come here and ask for a pardon on the ground that they have reformed in mind and morals. . . . It is not an element of good citizenship to conceal a murderer."[19]

Jim Younger was not much luckier than Bob. In the summer of 1901 both he and Cole were paroled, and Bronaugh was there for the great event. He celebrated the boys' freedom by giving Cole "a Methodist handshake," whatever that may be. But there was a condition to the parole. The brothers were released only on condition that they remain in Minnesota. With a certain irony, both men found work as tombstone salesmen, but Jim had to leave the job after he was injured. He tried selling insurance, but before long he discovered that policies written by convicted felons had no validity. To make matters worse, he fell deeply in love with a newspaperwoman named Alix Miller, only to discover that parolees were not allowed to marry. For Jim Younger, it was the final straw. He had been in poor health ever since Northfield, and although a prison doctor had removed the slug from his jaw he remained in pain and could eat little beyond a sort of gruel.

There would be no modification of Jim's parole conditions, in spite of his own pleas and a heartrending letter from gentle Alix: "It is within your power to make Jim and myself happy, and feeling that, kind as you have been, your sympathy must go out to us in our great desire to have a home and to live for one another."[20] In October 1902, chronically ill and deeply depressed, Jim Younger returned to his room at St. Paul's Reardon Hotel and blew his brains out. He, too, rests in the family plot in Lee's Summit. According to one version of the story, Alix wrote a heartbroken letter to a newspaper after Jim's death: "I am his wife, understand, spiritually. . . . [B]efore God he is mine and mine alone."[21]

The year after Jim died Cole received a full pardon, one condition being that he never breathe Minnesota air again. Cole was free to go anyplace else he wanted, and he teamed up with Frank James in something called the Cole Younger and Frank James Historical Wild West Show, which rumor said was funded in part by a "Chicago brewer." The show would, Cole said, "give the people the worth of their money and . . . show the frontiersman of my early manhood."[22] He wrote the Stillwater warden, Henry Wolfer, who had helped with his parole, asking for his help in removing the condition that Cole was not to "exhibit himself in public in any way," presumably to free himself up to lecture and take part in the "reenactments" that were part of such shows in those days.

Wolfer was furious and replied in what a newspaper story called "one of the warmest roasts that ever went through the mails." Wolfer wrote to Cole that he was a coward and would be back behind bars if he ever appeared again in Minnesota. "You have not only violated the spirit of your pardon but you have, by your conduct, outraged every principle of manhood."[23] There would be no unconditional pardon, then or later.

The anger of Wolfer and other Minnesotans did not stop Cole. When the Wild West show stopped in Kansas City, some old Quantrill guerrillas attended as the guests of Cole and Frank. But the show seems not to have been an unqualified success. Cole's old friend Todd George later wrote that Cole "was persuaded by irresponsible individuals to take such part in a wild west show as his partial pardon would permit. . . . His relatives and close friends suffered a total financial loss which fell bitterly on Cole."[24]

Perhaps because the grass was a little short, the old outlaws were sometimes not above some small-time skullduggery. In fall 1903, the Studebaker Brothers, carriage and wagon makers, wrote a plaintive letter to the prison seeking an address for Cole Younger. It seems that the show owed "a small bill." The prison sicced the Studebakers on long-suffering Younger champion Bronaugh, a poor recompense for all the years of Bronaugh's devoted service.

After Frank had finally had his fill of life on the road, Cole combined his show with the Greater Lew Nichols Show and kept right on. Cole's enterprise was now a sort of something-for-everybody show, with acrobats, bands, sideshows, a lady parachutist who dropped from a balloon, and "General" Younger's "Big Roman Coliseum." When Cole's show stopped in Richmond, Missouri, in 1908, he discovered that the bushwhacker Bloody Bill Anderson was buried there in potter's field. Cole organized a happening in Bloody Bill's honor, providing a brass band from his traveling show, some scripture reading, a eulogy by a local orator, and even a speech by Cole himself. The event was a good deal more honor than Anderson deserved, but maybe it served to further dilute whatever remained of the old hatreds, and maybe it helped attendance at the show, too.

Over time Cole developed a pretty fair repentance speech. He used it a lot, too, touring the country to talk earnestly about the evils of crime and the dangers to young people of "a certain class of moving-picture shows." Cole's oration was called "What My Life Has Taught Me," and he worked the crowd as smoothly as he had charmed the credulous in Faribault so many years before. "I am getting old now," he told his rapt listeners, and perhaps I cannot expect to accomplish much, but as long as God grants me life I shall do what I can in what is now my sole remaining object in life. If the unvarnished story of my life, and of my incarceration for twenty-five years in a prison cell will keep only one boy from suffering as I have suffered, I shall feel I have not labored in vain. . . . It all looks so easy and heroic to the impressionable young fellow down in front. And then comes temptation, as it came to me.[25]

Which may even have been, for once, the unvarnished truth.

In any case, Cole made quite a thing of his crime-does-not-pay speech, often delivered to his young audiences in churches. He was probably effective, too, for he salted his talks with choice bits of James-Younger legend. During his talks around Atoka, Indian Territory, he enchanted his young listeners with tales of the cave in the Booger Boo country nearby. In this secret refuge, he said, he and the James boys had lived for six months, scrounging their food at night from a confederate in Atoka, watching the animals who played in the glade in front of the cave.[26] Cole also managed to make the silver screen, appearing in something called *The Younger Brothers*, filmed by a little Tulsa movie company.

In his last years Cole Younger lived with his niece, Nora Hall, in a house in Lee's Summit, Missouri. He spent a good deal of time at his "headquarters," the Lee's Summit real estate and insurance office of his old friend Todd George. Cole joined the Lee's Summit Christian Church in 1914, at the culmination of a six-week revival by a spellbinding preacher. As Todd George told the story,

> On the last Sunday night of this revival Cole and his niece were sitting somewhat toward the rear of the tent, and, when the very last invitation was offered to anyone to come forward, Cole arose slowly and walked down the aisle. All eyes were turned upon him as he went forward and gave his hand to the minister and his heart to Christ.[27]

Converted or not, Cole still relived the wild old days for those who craved to hear about them. His old friend Frank James was gone, his brothers were, too, his own health had broken, and all that remained to him now were memories of a bloody past. He still talked about the Northfield raid, insisting that the robbery had failed because the inside men at the bank had filled up on firewater that long-ago afternoon. As he told Todd George, "Had it not been for a big jug of whiskey in his group the day and night before the North-field episode at the bank, the cashier would not have lost his life."[28]

Cole also continued to insist that he had not approved of rob-bing a bank so far from home and said that the gang planned on Northfield being their last robbery. And now, heavy with years, he added to his repertoire of stories the amazing assertion that the 1863 raid on Lawrence, Kansas, had succeeded in spite of six hun-dred Union troops waiting in town for Quantrill's men. If that fig-ment of his imagination fed his ego, it also went a little way toward wishing wanton murder into lawful warfare, at least in Cole's aging mind.

In March 1916 Cole Younger died of uremia and nephritis, with cirrhosis of the liver as a contributing cause. He died only two days after giving his statement to Harry Hoffman and Jesse's son. It was only a little more than a year after Frank James's death on the fam-ily farm in Kearney.

With Cole's passing ended the saga of the old James-Younger gang in the real world, but the memories lingered and began to grow. The gang and their exploits continued to hold a peculiar attraction for all sorts of people who had never laid eyes on any of the outlaws. After the brothers' release, Stillwater Prison was deluged with requests for information on the Youngers' whereabouts and pleas for photo-graphs of them. In 1918, for example, the prison got a letter request-ing photos from one Hubert "Gun Boat" Kittle, who billed himself as an "Expert Balloon Pilot and Parachute Jumper" and the "World's Renowned Professional Motorcyclist." His "people," he wrote, "knew the boys very well, and have told me so much of them that I would like very much to hang their pictures in my home."[29]

So the public fascination continued, just as it does to this day. It even spawned a ghastly play called "The Northfield Bank Robbery," a turgid 1903 epic by somebody named Ernest Stout. The play is another reprise of the deathless good-boys-driven-to-crime theme, in which, sure enough, the Youngers are framed by the real outlaws. The leader of these scoundrels turns out to be none other than Jim Lane, the notorious Kansas redleg, conveniently ignoring the fact that Lane had been dead for a decade at the time of the Northfield raid. In the play Cole kills Lane, then surrenders to the townspeople, as his true love promises to wait for him as long as she lives. "Your face," replies Cole, "shall always be before me to comfort me."

Not everybody harbored warm thoughts for the brothers, even long years after they were all dead and gone. In 1924 the Mankato *Free Press* bitterly recalled the people who campaigned to obtain a pardon for Cole Younger. They would not, said the paper, "shed a tear at the bier of a victim of merciless bandits like the Youngers. . . . No good reason was ever advanced for the pardon of the Youngers." Even so, the Myth of the Noble Outlaw continued to flourish; as late as 1971 a representative of Colt's Fire Arms Company wrote the prison seeking facsimiles of the signatures of both Jim and Cole. The firm wished, said the writer, to produce a "deluxe pistol" and to "include the signatures of Cole and Jim Younger on the revolver."[30]

So the legends gained a life of their own, even though all the brothers were gone. And now the gang's career on paper and in film was about to begin. Starting in 1908 there have been a number of attempts to write serious histories of the James and Younger brothers. Some of them are excellent, such as Brant's *The Outlaw Youngers*, the eminently readable result of long research. There has also been, however, an astonishing amount of claptrap produced about the gang's exploits, and a lot of the worst of it has appeared at the Bijou. The silver screen has produced no fewer than thirty-five films about the outlaw brothers, mostly about the James boys. They starred a number of famous names, from Roy Rogers and Clayton Moore (better known as the Lone Ranger) to Audie Murphy and Robert Duvall. The Hollywood epics range all the way from serious attempts—*The Return of Frank James*—to the absolutely nauseating—*Jesse James Meets Frankenstein's Daughter.*

At the beginning Jesse and Frank were all unalloyed good: chivalrous cavaliers, faithful lovers, all-around decent guys. Tyrone Power played Jesse, all gleaming teeth and well-cut clothing, and established the model for Jesse the superhero. Why, Jesse and Frank were druv to it, when the nasty railroad tried to steal Mrs. James's land and the boys fought back. By the time we get down to later films like *The Great Northfield, Minnesota, Raid*, Jesse (played by Robert Duvall) is pure evil, without a single redeeming virtue. No film has paid much attention to historical fact, and neither 1939's *Jesse James* nor *The Great Northfield, Minnesota, Raid* is an exception to the rule.

The latter movie is well produced, with a fine cast, but mostly inaccurate. To begin with, it describes the citizens of Northfield as cruel, cowardly, and ineffective. The film introduces characters who didn't exist: there's the Village Idiot, for instance, a man who lost his son in the Civil War and his own sanity afterward and now wanders about babbling, convinced that every young man he encounters is his son come back to see him. Then there's the steam calliope man, who sets up his machine outside the bank for no apparent reason, giving Cole Younger an opportunity to make it work right. Probably silliest of all, there's the kid with terrible eyesight, for whom Cole rigs a special rifle sight. Guess who shoots straight during the raid. Finally there's the weird notion that the raid is being staged to "counterbribe" the Missouri legislature, which has granted amnesty to these poor boys and then reneged on it. The legislature did so, it appears, because it was bribed by the Pinkerton detective agency.

Using these people who never were, acting out events that never happened, the movie tries very hard to portray Northfield's citizens as a pack of inept, sadistic fools and the bank men as dishonest schemers. For example, the Northfield banker is portrayed as a swindler who hoodwinks his fellow citizens. One of the bandits is shut into the vault during the raid, and when the door is later opened he is butchered in an attempt to hide the bank's fraud. Citizen posses are shown firing into one another and raiding a country whorehouse and hanging a number of customers, mostly because the possemen don't know who the hapless customers are and don't like their looks.

In fact, the defenders of Northfield put on a first-class show, taking on the most feared and famous killers of the day and driving them off in wild retreat—that is, those who did not die on the streets of Northfield. Northfield citizens and men from neighboring communities joined in the massive manhunt and showed courage, fighting ability, and compassion of a high order. It is hard to find a more extraordinary demonstration of cold courage than the valor of Murphy and his men wading straight ahead into dense cover, facing the guns of criminals with nothing much to lose. Both on Division Street and at Hanska Slough, the citizens outshot professional gunmen hands down. The Northfield bank men were anything but venal or scheming. They were nothing short of heroic. The loyalty and courage of one of them cost him his life.

Why Hollywood has made such a fetish of sneering at hardworking citizens and glorifying America's worst criminals is not at all clear. The real heroes of the Northfield raid were the ordinary folks who laid their lives on the line to fight off the Jameses and Youngers. The town's defenders were everyday citizens, without any motive to fight back save hard-nosed anger at a bunch of hoodlums trying to buffalo their quiet town. The Northfield fight was a good-versus-evil contest, a sort of nineteenth-century morality play. The angels won.

If the James and Younger brothers left behind a sort of mythic legend, Joseph Heywood left a legacy that abides to this day. His courage was widely admired, so much so that the Grand Army of the Republic (GAR) post in Northfield was named for him. His portrait hung in the GAR meeting hall, and another portrait was placed in the Carleton College library, along with a plaque commemorating his heroism. The Congregational church installed a window in his memory, a window inscribed *Fidelitas*, faithfulness.

The Northfield bank gave $5,000 to a fund for Heywood's family, and bankers all over the United States increased the fund to more than $12,000, a circumstance that enabled his daughter to graduate from the Carleton College School of Music.

Heywood was buried on the Sunday following the raid. The day began with religious services in the school hall, which was jammed with between eight hundred and a thousand people. That afternoon much of the town attended Heywood's funeral, which was held at his home. The house was packed with mourners. The big yard in front was full of people, too, in spite of the dreary day, and the street was crowded with the rigs of people who could not find a closer place. A long procession followed his casket to the cemetery afterward, and three of his pallbearers, appropriately, were J. S. Allen, A. R. Manning, and postmaster French.

Encomiums poured in to newspapers all over the country. Heywood's sacrifice even inspired a poem printed in the *New York Times,* a florid but admiring work called "On a Faithful Bank Cashier":

> If he betrayed not, death was sure;
> Before him stood the murderous thief;
> He did not flinch . . . of one life fewer
> The angels turned the blood-sealed leaf
> That night, and said: 'The page is pure.

There was a good deal more as well, all about the "iron crown of virtue." If it was stilted and stuffy by today's standards, in 1876 the poem was the acme of praise and respect, and it reflected the enormous admiration felt by every law-abiding citizen in the country. The Minnesota governor, John S. Pillsbury, responded in the same vein in a speech to the state legislature. "Without the pomp and emblazonment," he said, "which so much impel to deeds of daring, Mr. Heywood opposed gentle firmness to brutal diabolism, and calmly made choice of death in preference to life purchased at the cost of its severest fidelity."

Newspapers all over the country hastened to eulogize Heywood and to urge contributions to the fund for his family. Their words were flowery, after the fashion of the day, but sincere for all of that. "Whoever lays down his life at the call of duty," one said, "dies a hero—whether he falls behind the counter of a bank or the ramparts of a fort." "He died," wrote another paper, "rather than betray his trust." And the Boston *Advertiser* summed it all up:

> His name will live in honor. He fell at the post of duty as gallantly as any knight of any age. . . . He belonged to the high order of manhood which yields to no threat, and calmly confronts all the odds of fate.[31]

Which is about as fine an epitaph as any man could want.

For the other heroes of the raid, the future would be a happier one. Wheeler went back to Ann Arbor to finish up his senior year, accompanied by what remained of Bill Chadwell. He continued his medical studies at Chicago's College of Physicians and at Columbia University, and in 1878 he married Adeline Murray, who was the patient in Dr. Whiting's dentist's chair when the raiders began to shoot up Northfield. Wheeler lost his wife and a tiny daughter three years later. Haunted by his grief, he almost immediately left the town where he had lived since he was two years old and moved to Grand Forks, North Dakota. Devastated by the death of his wife and child and determined to help others avoid the same horror, Wheeler specialized in obstetrics and gynocology in the years afterward.

Wheeler married again and became a pillar of Grand Forks. One of the first doctors in that area, he served for many years as surgeon for the Great Northern Railway and the Northern Pacific, as the first dean of the University of North Dakota Medical School, and as mayor. Through all the years, Bill Chadwell graced the doctor's Grand Forks office. One story says that when Dr. Wheeler was in his seventies, both Chadwell and the office were consumed by fire.[32] Or maybe the bones of the outlaw were passed onto another doctor, as more recent evidence indicates. Late in life the doctor married a third time, and at the age of seventy he had a son, Henry Jr., who still lives in Minnesota.

The doctor died suddenly of a heart attack in Grand Forks on April 14, 1930, only two weeks after he had visited Northfield to see an ailing relative. In Grand Forks city offices closed in mourning, and hundreds of people attended a Masonic service in his honor. Wheeler's heart was still in Northfield, however, in the town for which he had fought so well. His body was returned from Grand Forks to Northfield, and there another service was held. When he died Wheeler was still carrying the gold watch awarded him in gratitude by the Northfield bank.

By the time Dr. Wheeler passed to his reward, most of the rest of the defenders were also gone. After the fight, after the capture, after the excitement and adulation died away, these modest men went back to their peaceful, productive lives. The redoubtable Captain Murphy stayed on at Madelia and returned to farming and stock raising. A retiring man, he did not talk much about the fight at Hanska Slough. He died in the summer of 1904, of heart failure. He was only sixty-five, but perhaps he was feeling the ravages of his Civil War bullet wound and the saber slashes from that long-ago day at Piedmont, Virginia. And maybe he still felt the unforgiving aftermath of the many months he had languished in the appalling conditions of infamous Andersonville prison.

Sheriff Glispin left Madelia four years after his triumph at Hanska. He went off to California, the promised land, as so many others did, and in Santa Rosa he ran a dry goods business. He then moved on to Spokane, Washington, where he served as chief of police, put in two terms as county sheriff, and afterward worked in real estate. He died in 1890. His Spokane obituary called him "a conscientious, painstaking man and the soul of integrity, honor and worth." Not a bad epitaph.

Ben Rice, the "southern gentleman," very quickly heeded the call of the South. He moved back and settled in Murfreesboro, Tennessee. He married there but within a few years moved on to Lake Weir, Florida. He died in 1889. Dr. Overholt, the sharpshooter who cut Cole Younger's stick out of his hand, stayed on in Minnesota and died in Kenyon at the age of eighty-seven.

Col. Tom Vought harbored no grudge against the Youngers. In fact, he admired their grit enough to say in later years that he would not fear them if they were freed from prison. Rather, he said, "I have not a friend that would throw themselves between me and danger any quicker than would the Youngers." And if Vought's admiration seems a little eccentric, the sentiments certainly do him credit. At the same time, however, he opposed a pardon for the outlaws: "I been taught from my earliest recollections that to be a loyal man I must help to enforce the laws." He would defend the prisoners with his life, but their future was a matter for the law.[33]

Vought and his wife left Minnesota, too, living over the years in Dakota Territory, New York, and Wisconsin and finally settling in La Crosse, where Vought died in 1889. Like most of the others who brought down the James-Younger gang, Vought did not like to talk about his part in it. In fact, however, his Northfield *News* obituary was probably correct when it said "that it was to his advice and courageous action when the bandits were at bay that the end of the outlaws' careers was largely due." It was he who listened to the eager young Oscar Sorbel; had he not paid attention to the lad, the fugitives might have gotten clear of the Madelia area. Had they done so, they might well have escaped entirely.

George Bradford married not long after the Hanska fight and went back to the mercantile business. He became clerk of the court and moved to nearby St. James. After eight years in that post, in 1910 he moved his family to Grants Pass, Oregon, and ultimately to Portland. He died there in 1935, survived by six children, a whole company of grandchildren and great-grandchildren, and his wife of fifty-seven years.

Young Asle "Oscar" Sorbel, who rode his father's farm horse to Madelia to give the alarm, was deliberately called "Suborn" in accounts of the raid, to protect him from possible retaliation from vengeful outlaws. In fact, it would be a very long time before any-body discovered who the young man was. In time the boy became a man and the man became a veterinarian. He practiced for many years in Webster, South Dakota. He died in the summer of 1930, by then recognized as one of the heroes of the Northfield raid. One story, probably apocryphal, relates that twice in later years Oscar was found in Montana by "friends of the Youngers," who asked him if he was the one who rode to Madelia. "Sensing the danger," says this tale, "Oscar told the men it had been his brother."

Charles Pomeroy married three years after the fight at Hanska Slough. He and his wife raised seven children on the Pomeroy farm east of Madelia on a small stream that came to be called Pomeroy Creek. The family moved to Cleveland, North Dakota, in 1898, but Pomeroy kept in touch with his relatives in Madelia. He was the last of the Northfield heroes to pass away. Almost ninety, he died in his daughter's home in Cleveland in the summer of 1941. In the end he returned to his roots, for he was buried in Madelia.

Manning, the sharpshooting hardware merchant, did not like to talk about his part in the robbery. He simply picked up his steady, industrious life where he had left it on that memorable September morning. Manning spent the rest of his days selling tools and ploughs and stoves, peddling ice to Northfield's housewives, wheat farming at Devil's Lake, and living quietly with his wife and family in Northfield. In 1882 he became the foreman of the Acme Hose Company Fire Department, an important and respected post. Three years later he was elected second assistant fire chief of the town. He was, as his Northfield *News* obituary said, one of the town's "loved and respected citizens." Manning's luck held to the last: walking to his barn of a January morning, he simply collapsed, dead of a heart attack before his hired man could get him back inside. He was seventy-five.

Like Manning, bank man Wilcox did not talk much about the raid. He stayed on with the bank, in time rising to be its assistant cashier. Son of a Massachusetts Baptist preacher, he had lived in Northfield since he was ten years old, with a little time off to attend the University of Chicago. His modest history says only that he was "prominently connected with other business enterprises in the city, and . . . held various official positions, educational and municipal."

He married three years after the raid, and he and his wife became pillars of the Northfield Baptist Church.

After the capture and conviction of the Youngers, Northfield was a long year in returning to its placid ways. There was a worrisome succession of anonymous letters threatening the town and its citizens. And for a time there was a good deal of visitation by tourists eager to see the scene of the great raid. Some of the visitors came into the bank to gawk at the place where Heywood was mortally wounded, and the bank personnel eyed these people with some unease. Bunker, back on the job, found himself suspicious of such visitors, especially when

> one would enter, and without introducing himself or asking questions would proceed to look about the room. At such times I often stood watching the visitor, with my hand on a double action revolver underneath the counter, and had the caller made a quick move, I am sure I would have shot through the counter at him.[34]

Northfield was not the only community alarmed by the raid. There was a considerable boom in firearms sales all across the country, and "rifle companies" were organized here and there. Banks everywhere stocked up on weaponry and took steps to fortify their working areas. Captain Ames of the First National even devised a system to close off everything inside the counter with an "iron cell" at the "touch of a secret spring." Sadly, as Bunker dryly commented, Ames "had not perfected his device so far as to get the bankers out of the cell again, hence no patent is yet issued."[35] Which was a shame, for in the climate of alarm after the raid, the iron cell would have sold like hotcakes.

Afterword

Long after the smoke blew away from Division Street, long after Captain Murphy's men had pushed their way into thick brush at Hanska to end the long chase, long after no man lived who was part of the raid, the legend of the Northfield raid grew and prospered. And something else remained for those with eyes to see. Leaving aside Hollywood and the bumper crop of books and stories about the raid, there is something lasting and important to be learned from the Northfield story.

It is simply this. Good men can band together to destroy evil, if they have the heart and the will and if they are willing to unselfishly lay their lives on the line for something worth fighting for. Bad men seldom have causes, and never good ones. Besides the satisfaction of their own ego, they are driven mostly by greed, and greed is a puny weapon against righteous anger. Good men have much to lose in life, but this may be what makes them fight the harder and hate evil the more.

The men of Northfield, Murphy's posse, and all the others who hurt and harried the outlaws also had much to lose, but they were willing to risk it all. Theirs was the same generation that flocked to join the army when Fort Sumter was fired on, the same generation who believed enough in the Union to march into harm's way without anybody ordering them to. The outlaws who struck Northfield were just another enemy who came to kill and rob and desecrate the industrious peace of their town. The outlaws had to be stopped, and the citizens did not wait for somebody else to do the job.

Fifty years on, a Northfield *News* editorial took a long look back and drew all the right conclusions. The perceptive editor's words sum up the lesson of the raid as well as anybody can:

> When circumstances arose in Northfield necessitating the utmost fidelity, courage and quick-thinking, the ordinary townsmen of a quiet Minnesota community were found ready-made for heroic stature. Quiet, cultured Joseph Lee Heywood chose death rather than betray his trust to the institution employing him and the public it served. It never occurred to young collegian Wheeler or merchants Manning and Allen and their comrades that stopping the robbers was somebody else's business. They made it theirs—with telling results. And the captors at Madelia—not to mention countless other ordinary folks who did their share on the side of good citizenship—did not stop to weigh the fine points of duty, but in support of the common interest faced death to bring to justice those who had plundered and murdered their neighbors.[1]

Which says it all.

NOTES

INTRODUCTION

1. Edwards, obituary for Jesse James, April 1882, reprinted in Fellman, *Inside War*, 261.
2. Fellman, 262.
3. Statement, Dan W. Holt, March 1938, Indian-Pioneer Papers.

CHAPTER 1

1. James, *In the Shadow of Jesse James*, 128. Another niece became the mother of the much-touted (and overrated) gunfighter John Ringo of Tombstone fame.
2. Schraeder, *Jesse James*.
3. Ibid.
4. Richardson, *Some Portions of His Narrative Concerning Kansas*, n.p.
5. Starr, *Jennison's Jayhawkers*, 8.
6. Zornow, *Kansas, a History of the Jayhawk State*, 78.
7. Starr, *Jennison's Jayhawkers*, 31.
8. Leslie, *The Devil Knows How to Ride*, 358.
9. Catton, *This Hallowed Ground*, 6.
10. Ibid., 5.
11. Monaghan, *The Civil War on the Western Border*, 116.
12. Richardson, *Some Portions of His Narrative Concerning Kansas*, n.p.
13. Paxton, *Annals of Platte County, Missouri*, 336.
14. Fellman, *Inside War*, 32.
15. Ibid., 99.

16. Cited in *History of Platte County*, 708.

17. Fellman, *Inside War*, 77.

18. Ibid.

19. Paperback mentioned in Love, *The Rise and Fall of Jesse James*, 48–49.

20. Fellman, *Inside War*, 259.

21. Ibid., 260.

22. Bidlack, "Erastus D. Ladd's Description of the Lawrence Massacre," 120.

23. Triplett, *The Life, Times and Treacherous Death of Jesse James*, 8.

24. Love, *The Rise and Fall of Jesse James*, 47.

25. Edwards, *Noted Guerillas*.

26. Ibid., quoting a ms. of the Kansas State Historical Society.

27. Time-Life, *The Gunfighters*.

28. Edwards, "A Terrible Quintette," 14.

29. Russell, "Jesse James, Postwar Bandit."

30. Love, *The Rise and Fall of Jesse James*, 24.

31. Triplett, *The Life, Times and Treacherous Death of Jesse James*, 5.

32. Settle, *Jesse James Was His Name*, 53.

33. Letter, Harry Hoffman to B. J. George, n.d., "Statement of Cole Younger." University of Missouri Western Historical Manuscript Collection.

34. Brant, *The Outlaw Youngers*, 31.

35. Croy, "Last of the Great Outlaws," *America's Frontier West*, 44.

36. *History of Clay and Platte County*, 259–60.

37. Brant, *The Outlaw Youngers*, 76, quoting Cole's statement to Harry Hoffman.

38. Time-Life, *The Gunfighters*, 61.

39. Dalton, *Under the Black Flag*, 143 ff.

40. Croy, "Last of the Great Outlaws," 35.

41. Letter, Harry Hoffman to Homer Croy, 26 August 1955, University of Missouri Western Historical Manuscript Collection.

42. Petrone, *Judgment at Gallatin*, 8.

43. Paxton, *Annals of Platte County, Missouri*, 485.

44. Brant, *The Outlaw Youngers*, 107.

45. Settle, *Jesse James Was His Name*, 46.

46. Statement of W. B. Morrison, August 1937, Indian-Pioneer Papers.

47. Schraeder, *Jesse James Was One of His Names*.

48. Settle, *Jesse James Was His Name*, 72.

49. Statement of Ethel B. Tackitt, Indian-Pioneer Papers.

50. Statement of William Boas McAlpin, Indian-Pioneer Papers.

51. Brant, *The Outlaw Youngers*, 153.

52. Brant, *Outlaws*, 110.

53. Horan, *Desperate Men*, 92.

54. Stevens, "Notes on the Jameses and Youngers," 21.

55. *St. Louis Dispatch*, 27 January 1875.

56. Stevens, "Notes on the Jameses and Youngers," 20.

57. Petrone, *Judgment at Gallatin*, 10. But this book also calls bank employee Bunker "Brinker" and has Frank entering the Northfield bank "knife in hand."

58. *Northfield News*, 3 May 1915.

59. Croy, *Jesse James Was My Neighbor*, 106.

60. George, *The Conversion of Cole Younger*, 13.

61. Statement of Carrie Marshall Pitman, April 1938, Indian-Pioneer Papers.

62. Cantrell, *The Youngers' Fatal Blunder*, 9.

63. *The Story of Cole Younger, by Himself*, 76.

64. Ron Hunt of Mantorville, Minnesota, Northfield *News*, centennial edition.

65. Bunker, "Recollections of the Northfield Raid," 1.

66. Statement of Jennie Lamar, September 1937, Indian-Pioneer Papers.

67. Schraeder, *Jesse James Was One of His Names*, 93.

CHAPTER 2

1. This was Perry Samuels, who worked for Harry Hoffman in later years. *See* Hoffman, "The Younger Boys' Last Stand."

2. Cantrell, *The Youngers' Fatal Blunder*, 10.

3. Love, *The Rise and Fall of Jesse James*.

4. Northfield *Independent, Kansas City Star*; summarized in the *Northfield News*, 9 September 1971.

5. *Northfield News*, 9 September 1976.

6. Brant, *The Outlaw Youngers*, 171.

7. Trenarry, *Murder in Minnesota*, 87.

8. Trenarry, *Murder in Minnesota*, 86–87.

9. Cantrell, *The Youngers' Fatal Blunder*, 16.

10. Brant, *The Outlaw Youngers*, 172.

11. *Rice County Journal*, 14 September 1876; *Northfield News*, 31 August 1907.

12. *Rice County Journal*, 14 September 1876.

13. Hoffman, "The Younger Boys' Last Stand," 6.

14. B. J. George, parenthetical comments in Hoffman, "The Youngers' Last Stand."

15. Hanson, *The Northfield Tragedy*, 5.

16. Horan, *Desperate Men*, 108.

17. Cole Younger Account of the Raid, Stillwater, 1897, Minnesota Historical Society, 1.

18. Letter, First National Bank to Folwell, June 1921, Folwell Papers, Minnesota Historical Society.

19. Garrison, *A Treasury of Minnesota Tales*, 137–38.

20. *History of Clay County*, 12.

21. The whole episode was recorded in the *Northfield News*, 8 July 1947.

22. Brant, *The Outlaw Youngers*, 176.

23. Bertha Germann Thomforde Narrative, Minnesota Historical Society.

24. *Rice County Journal*, 14 September 1876.

25. Cole Younger Account of the Raid, Stillwater, 1897, Minnesota Historical Society, 1–2.

26. Ibid.

CHAPTER 3

1. Letter, Francis Butler to Walter Trenarry, Minnesota Historical Society.

2. Curtiss-Wedge, *History of Rice and Steele Counties*, 196 ff.

3. *Continuum*, 41.

4. Ibid., 42

5. "The Northfield Bank Robbery," *Northfield News*, 12 November 1947.

6. Younger, *The Story of Cole Younger, by Himself*, 77.

7. Letter, 1921, First National Bank of Northfield to W. W. Folwell, Minnesota Historical Society.

8. Horace Goodhue, Jr., quoted in Headley and Jarchow, *Carleton, the First Century*, 14.

9. *Continuum*, 36.

10. Huntington, *Robber and Hero*, 46.

11. Museum personnel advise that the clock was taken to Yakima, Washington, by Wilcox. It remained in his family for years, until his widow donated it to the Northfield museum.

CHAPTER 4

1. Trenarry, *Murder in Minnesota*, 88.

2. Huntington, *Robber and Hero*, 13.

3. Drago, *Outlaws on Horseback*, 70.

4. Brant, *The Outlaw Youngers*, 127.

5. For example, see Stevens, "Notes on the Jameses and Youngers," University of Missouri Western Historical Manuscript Collection.

6. Drago, *Outlaws on Horseback*, 72.

7. *Northfield News*, 9 September 1976.

8. Huntington, *Robber and Hero*, 13 .

9. Cantrell, *The Youngers' Fatal Blunder*, 30.

10. Drago, *Outlaws on Horseback*, 71.

11. *Northfield Magazine* 6, no. 2 (1992): 9.

12. *Rice County Journal*, 14 September 1876.

13. Cole Younger Account of the Raid, Stillwater, 1897, 3.

14. *Northfield News*, 10 July 1897.

15. *Northfield News*, week of September 7, 1976.

16. Northfield *Independent*, 28 August 1947, 4.

17. *Northfield News*, 9 September 1976.

18. McKinney, "The Northfield Raid and Its Ann Arbor Sequel," 39.

19. Rice County *Journal*, 14 September 1876.

20. *Northfield News*, 10 July 1897.

21. Younger, *The Story of Cole Younger, by Himself*; Northfield *News*, 18 April 1930.

22. *Cole Younger Account of the Raid*, Stillwater, 1897, 4.

23. *Northfield News*, 9 September 1976.

24. Huntington, *Robber and Hero*, 18.

25. Bunker, "Recollections of the Northfield Raid," 4.

26. *Northfield News*, 10 July 1897.

27. Garrison, *A Treasury of Minnesota Tales*, 55. This account also contains a good deal of dialogue that appears nowhere else.

28. *Rice County Journal*, 14 September 1876.

29. *Northfield News*, 10 July 1897.

30. Bunker, "Recollections of the Northfield Raid," 5.

31. Huntington, *Robber and Hero*, 22.

32. Ibid.

33. *Northfield News*, 10 July 1897.

34. Vaughn, *This Was Frank James*, 116.

35. Younger, *The Story of Cole Younger, by Himself*, 85.

36. *Northfield News*, 26 November 1916.

37. Bunker, "Recollections of the Northfield Raid," 8.

38. Cantrell, *Youngers' Fatal Blunder*, 36–37.

39. Hoffman, "The Youngers' Last Stand," 7.

40. Drago, *Outlaws on Horseback*, 73.

41. Triplett, *The Life, Times and Treacherous Death of Jesse James*, 140.

42. A 1897 *Northfield News* interview, quoted in the *News* of 9 September 1976.

43. Letter, B. J. George to Homer Croy, 4 July 1955, University of Missouri Western Historical Manuscript Collection.

44. Letter, Hoffman to Crow, 6 September 1955.

45. *Northfield News*, 9 March 1970.

46. McKinney, "The Northfield Raid and Its Ann Arbor Sequel," 42.

47. Northfield *News*, 10 July 1897.

48. Northfield *Independent*, 28 August 1947.

49. Younger, *The Story of Cole Younger, by Himself*, 80.

50. *Northfield News*, 26 November 1915.

51. Ibid.

52. Hoffman, "The Younger Boys' Last Stand," 7.

53. Brant, *The Outlaw Youngers*, 185–86.

54. William Ebel, quoted in the Northfield *News*, 9 September 1976.

55. Breihan, "The Northfield Raid," *The West* (November 1966): 11.

56. Giffen, "Charlie Pitts—R.I.P." *True West* (April 1963): 42.

57. *Northfield News*, 9 September 1976, from a 1929 letter written by the general to the editor.

58. *Northfield News*, 10 July 1897.

59. Ibid.

60. McKinney, "The Northfield Raid and Its Ann Arbor Sequel," 43; and see the *Northfield News*, 2 August 1890.

61. Hanson, *The Northfield Tragedy*, 15.

62. Ibid.

63. *Northfield News*, week of September 7, 1976.

64. Huntington, *Robber and Hero*, 30.

65. Hanson, *The Northfield Tragedy*, 8.

66. *Northfield News*, 10 July 1897.

67. *Rice County Journal*, 14 September 1876.

68. B. J. George Collection, an unidentified St. Paul newspaper, 13 June 1897, University of Missouri Western Historical Manuscript Collection.

69. Hoffman, "The Younger Boys' Last Stand," 8.

70. Ibid.

71. *Northfield News*, 10 July 1897.

72. Ibid.

73. Trenarry, *Murder in Minnesota*, 91.

74. Susan Garwood-DeLong, Executive Director, Northfield Historical Society.

75. *Northfield News*, 10 July 1897.

76. Ibid.

77. Younger account, Folwell Papers.

78. *Northfield News*, 10 July 1897.

79. J. A. Hunt, quoted in the Northfield *News*, 10 July 1897.

80. *Northfield News*, 10 July 1897.

81. Letter, Lillie LeVesconte to Jacob Hodnefield, 19 February 1945, University of Missouri Western Historical Manuscript Collection.

82. 14 September 1876.

83 *Rice County Journal*, 14 September 1876.

84. Michigan Historical Collection, quoted in the *News* centennial edition, 18.

85. Schraeder, *Jesse James Was One of His Names*.

86. Trenarry, *Murder in Minnesota*, 91.

87. *Northfield News*, 3 September 1970.

88. *Northfield News*, centennial edition, 18.

CHAPTER 5

1. Archives, First National Bank of Northfield, reproduced by the Northfield Historical Society, commemorative calendar, 1997.

2. Hoffman, "The Younger Boys' Last Stand," 8.

3. Drago, *Outlaws on Horseback*, 73.

4. Folwell notes, 10. Minnesota Historical Society.

5. Huntington, *Robber and Hero*, 52.

6. Trenarry, *Murder in Minnesota*, 92.

7. Folwell "Northfield Robbery," notes, 3.

8. Hanson, *The Northfield Tragedy*, 27.

9. Letter, Charles Armstrong, "Recollections of a nine-year-old-boy concerning events following the Northfield Bank Robbery," Minnesota Historical Society.

10. *Northfield News*, centennial edition, 9 September 1876.

11. Cole Younger Account of the Raid, Stillwater, 1897, 8.

12. Huntington, *Robber and Hero*, 58.

13. Account of L. M. Demarary, quoted in Brant, *The Outlaw Youngers*, 192.

14. Letter, Harry Hoffman to Homer Croy, n.d., University of Missouri Western Historical Manuscript Collection.

15. Croy, *Last of the Great Outlaws*, 124.

16. Unidentified St. Paul newspaper, 13 June 1897. University of Missouri Western Historical Manuscript Collection.

17. Breihan, "The Northfield Raid," *The West* (November 1966): 13.

18. Hoffman, "The Fog around the Rumors Cleared Away," 2, University of Missouri Western Historical Manuscript Collection.

19. A. E. Bunker, quoted in the Northfield *News*, centennial edition, 9 September 1976.

20. Hanson, *The Northfield Tragedy*, 41.

21. Hoffman, "The Younger Boys' Last Stand," 8.

22. Croy, *Jesse James Was My Neighbor*, 123.

23. Homer Croy, interview with Mosher's son, Northfield *News*, centennial edition, 9 September 1976.

24. *Northfield News*, 21 September 1898.

25. Drago, *Outlaws on Horseback*, 75.

26. Time-Life, *The Gunfighters*, 80. But note that this source makes other statements about the raid that are clearly inaccurate, such as the assertion that "another Northfield man discharged a load of buckshot that shattered Bob's right elbow."

27. *Northfield News*, 21 September 1898.

28. Breihan, *The Escapades of Frank and Jesse James*, 183.

29. Cantrell, *The Youngers' Fatal Blunder*, 47.

30. George, *Just Memories and Twelve Years with Cole Younger*, 86.

31. Horan, *Desperate Men*, 5. It's possible to wonder more than usual about the veracity of this one, because Horan calls Uncle Dick "Henderton" at 5 but "Herndon" at 130.

32. *Rice County Journal*, 11 February 1876.

33. Rice County *Journal*, 2 November 1976.

34. Hawes, "Frank and Jesse James in Review for the Missouri Society," 5.

35. *Northfield News*, centennial edition, 9 September 1976.

CHAPTER 6

1. Letter, Oscar Sorbel to Carl Weicht, 19 August 1929, Minnesota Historical Society.

2. Croy, *Jesse James Was My Neighbor*, 119.

3. *Northfield News*, 9 September 1971.

4. MacBeth, "The Minnesota Magnificent Seven," 8.

5. Ibid.

6. Madelia *Times-Messenger*, 15 September 1998.

7. Younger, *The Story of Cole Younger, by Himself.*

8. Unidentified St. Paul newspaper, 13 June 1897, Minnesota Historical Society.

9. Triplett, *The Life, Times and Treacherous Death of Jesse James,* 146.

10. Hanson, *The Northfield Tragedy,* 51.

11. Ibid.

12. Croy, *Last of the Great Outlaws,* 127.

13. Hanson, *The Northfield Tragedy,* 52.

14. A. E. Bunker, Northfield *News,* centennial edition, 9 September 1976.

15. Armstrong, "Recollections of a nine-year-old boy concerning events following the Northfield Bank Robbery," 5.

16. Glispin expense statement, Minnesota Historical Society.

17. Letter, A. W. Heath (?) to "cousin Wm."—stationery of T. H. Loghed Hardware, Faribault, 29 September 1876, Minnesota Historical Society.

18. Trenarry, *Murder in Minnesota,* 96.

19. Croy, *Last of the Great Outlaws,* 128.

20. Appler, *The Younger Brothers,* 238.

21. Hanson, *The Northfield Tragedy,* 66.

22. Huntington, *Robber and Hero,* 74.

23. Trenarry, *Murder in Minnesota,* 95.

24. 27 September 1876, quoted in Trenarry, *Murder in Minnesota,* 98.

25. Adelbert Ames to his wife, Northfield *News,* centennial edition, 9 September 1976. The egregious Appler has the capture reported by "Sheriff McDonald, of Sioux City."

26. *Northfield News,* 21 September 1898.

27. Letter, Eunice E. Hall to "Editor Minn. Histories," 31 October 1954, Minnesota Historical Society.

28. *Northfield News,* 7 September 1976.

29. Hoffman, "The Younger Boys' Last Stand," 10.

30. Bunker, "Recollections of the Northfield Raid," 17.

31. Younger, *The Story of Cole Younger, by Himself,* 97.

32. Quoted in Trenarry, *Murder in Minnesota,* 102.

33. Letter, Minnesota parole agent to J. A. Lawrence, 18 June 1924, Minnesota Historical Society.

34. Croy, *Last of the Great Outlaws,* 133 ff., 228.

35. *Northfield News,* 31 August 1907.

36. Quoted in the Northfield *News,* centennial edition, 9 September 1976.

CHAPTER 7

1. Younger, *The Story of Cole Younger, by Himself*, 98.
2. Northfield *Independent*, 25 November 1948.
3. *Northfield News*, 9 May 1924.
4. Hoffman, "The Younger Boys' Last Stand," 1.
5. Breihan, *The Complete and Authentic Life of Jesse James*, 150 ff.
6. Ibid., 148–49.
7. See, for example, Ramon F. Adams, *Burs under the Saddle*, 47 ff ("full of errors"), and especially *Northfield Magazine*, final edition, 15 ("Unreliable Publications. . . . Any book by Carl W. Breihan [contains] totally fictitious stories, [with] no standard of accuracy").
8. Bunker, "Recollections of the Northfield Raid," 15.
9. Letter to J. A. Lawrence, Northfield, 18 June 1924, Minnesota Historical Society.
10. Letter from Warden, Stillwater Prison, to I. H. Marmon, Superintendent, State Bureau of Identification, 14 February 1930, Minnesota Historical Society.
11. Brant, *Outlaws*, 128–29; and *The Outlaw Youngers*, 179.
12. "The Northfield Bank Raid," Northfield *News*, 24.
13. Milton F. Perry, Superintendent of Historic Sites, Clay County, Kearney, Mo. Northfield *News*, 25 September 1980.
14. *Northfield News*, 25 September 1980.

CHAPTER 8

1. *History of Clay County*, 272.
2. McKinney, "The Northfield Raid and Its Ann Arbor Sequel," 45.
3. *Northfield News*, 7 September 1976.
4. Northfield Historical Society.
5. Brant, *The Outlaw Youngers*, 251.
6. Croy, *Jesse James Was My Neighbor*, 131.
7. Trenarry, *Murder in Minnesota*, 97.
8. Bunker, "Recollections of the Northfield Raid," 16.
9. Northfield *News*, 15 April 1948.
10. "Charlie Pitts—R.I.P," *True West* (April 1963).
11. Cited in Petrone, *Judgment at Gallatin*, 27.
12. Ibid., 35.
13. Ibid., 44–45.
14. Ibid., 128.
15. Stevens, "Notes on the Jameses and Youngers," 19.

16. Enclosures to letter, B. J. George to Homer Croy, 20 November 1948, University of Missouri Western Historical Manuscript Collection.

17. Letter, B. J. George to Homer Croy, 30 November 1948, University of Missouri Western Historical Manuscript Collection.

18. Schraeder, *Jesse James Was One of His Names*, 32. This book is more fun than a barrel of monkeys. In addition to the fanciful notions related here, it also tells its bemused readers that Grat Dalton didn't die at Coffeyville in 1892 but in 1909 appeared in Bolivia as the Sundance Kid and died in Montana in 1965. Bob Dalton wasn't killed at Coffeyville either but settled in northeastern Oklahoma as "Bob McWhorter." And so on.

19. *Northfield News*, 17 July 1897.

20. Letter, Alix Miller to Governor Van Sant, 8 January 1902, Minnesota Historical Society.

21. Knowles, "The Lost Love of Jim Younger," *Old West* (Spring, 1967): 36.

22. Folwell notes, 20, Minnesota Historical Society.

23. Brant, *The Outlaw Youngers*, 306.

24. George, *The Conversion of Cole Younger*, 15.

25. Newspaper story, date and paper unknown, Minnesota Historical Society.

26. Statement of Mrs. W. H. Reynolds, August 1937, Indian-Pioneer Papers.

27. George, *The Conversion of Cole Younger*, 19.

28. Ibid., 15.

29. Letter, Kittle to Warden, Stillwater Prison, 25 November 1918, Minnesota Historical Society.

30. Letter, R. L. Wilson to Records Clerk, 22 October 1971, Minnesota State Prison.

31. Rice County *Journal*, 21 September 1876.

32. Holz, "Bankrobbers, Burkers and Bodysnatchers," 97. This author suggests that the skeleton residing so long in Dr. Wheeler's office was that of Clel Miller.

33. *Northfield News*, 10 July 1897.

34. *Northfield News*, 12 October 1895.

35. Ibid.

AFTERWORD

1. *Northfield News*, 10 September 1926.

BIBLIOGRAPHY

BOOKS

Adams, Raman F. *Burs under the Saddle*. Norman: University of Oklahoma Press, 1989.

Appler, Augustus. *The Younger Brothers: The Life, Character and Daring Exploits of the Youngers, the Notorious Bandits Who Rode with Jesse James and William Clarke Quantrell [sic]*. New York: Fell, 1955.

Baldwin, Margaret. *Wanted, Frank and Jesse James: The Real Story*. New York: Messner, 1981.

Berg, Lillie Clara. *Early Pioneers and Indians of Minnesota and Rice County*. San Leandro, Calif.: Berg, 1959.

Brant, Marley. *The Outlaw Youngers: A Confederate Brotherhood*. Lanham, Md.: Madison Books, 1992.

———. *Outlaws: The Illustrated History of the James-Younger Gang*. Montgomery, Ala.: Elliott & Clark, 1997.

Breihan, Carl W. *The Complete and Authentic Life of Jesse James*. New York: Fell, 1954.

———. *The Escapades of Frank and Jesse James*. New York: Fell, 1974.

Bronaugh, Warren C. *The Youngers' Fight for Freedom*. Columbia, Mo.: E. W. Stephens, 1906.

Butler, Laura. *Western Movies*. Albuquerque: University of New Mexico Press, 1979.

Cantrell, Dallas. *The Youngers' Fatal Blunder*. San Antonio: Naylor, 1973.

Catton, Bruce. *This Hallowed Ground*. New York: Doubleday, 1955.

Continuum: Threads in the Community Fabric of Northfield, Minnesota. Northfield: Northfield Printing, 1976.

Croy, Homer. *Jesse James Was My Neighbor*. New York: Duell, Sloan and Pearce, 1949.

———. *Last of the Great Outlaws: The Story of Cole Younger*. New York: Duell, Sloan and Pearce, 1956.

Cummins, Jim. *Jim Cummins' Book*. Denver: Reed Publishing, 1903.

Curtiss-Wedge, Franklyn. *History of Rice and Steele Counties*. Chicago: H. C. Cooper Jr. & Co., 1910.

Dalton, Kit. *Under the Black Flag*. Memphis: Lockart, 1914.

Donald, Jay. *Outlaws of the Border*. Philadelphia: Douglas Brothers, 1882.

Drago, Harry. *Outlaws on Horseback*. New York: Dodd Mead, 1964.

Edwards, John N. *Noted Guerrillas*. St. Louis: Bryan, Brand, & Co., 1877.

Fellman, Michael. *Inside War*. New York: Oxford University Press, 1989.

Garrison, Webb. *A Treasury of Minnesota Tales*. Nashville: Rutledge Hill Press, 1998.

Garwood, Darrell. *Crossroads of America: The Story of Kansas City*. New York: Norton, 1948.

George, Todd Menzies. *The Conversion of Cole Younger and the Battle of Lone Jack: Early Day Stories*. Kansas City, Mo.: Lowell Press, 1963.

———. *Just Memories and Twelve Years with Cole Younger*. N.p., 1959.

Goodrich, Thomas. *Bloody Dawn: The Story of the Lawrence Massacre*. Kent, Ohio: Kent State University Press, 1991.

Griswold, William B. *Mankato and Blue Earth County*. Mankato: Griswold & Neff, 1867.

Hanson, Joseph H. (John Jay Lemon). *The Northfield Tragedy, or, The Robber's Raid*. Northfield: John Jay Lemon, 1876.

Hathaway, Herman, and Archer Jones. *How the North Won*. Urbana: University of Illinois Press, 1991.

Headley, L., and M. Jarchow. *Carleton, the First Century*. Northfield: Carleton College, 1966.

History of Clay and Platte County. St. Louis: National Historical Co., 1885.

Horan, James D. *Desperate Men*. New York: Bonanza Books, 1949.

Hoyt, Henry F. *A Frontier Doctor*. Boston: Houghton Mifflin, 1929.

Huntington, George. *Robber and Hero: The Story of the Northfield Bank Raid*. Northfield: Northfield Historical Society Press, 1994.

James, Jesse E. *Jesse James, My Father*. Cleveland: A. Westbrook Co., 1906.

James, Stella Frances, *In the Shadow of Jesse James*. Thousand Oaks, Calif.: Revolver Press, 1989.

Leslie, Edward E. *The Devil Knows How to Ride*. New York: Random House, 1996.

Lomax, John A., and Alan Lomax. *Cowboy Songs and Other Frontier Ballads*. New York: Macmillan, 1955.

Love, Robertus. *The Rise and Fall of Jesse James*. New York: Putnam, 1926.

Markham, George. *Guns of the Wild West*. London: Arms and Armour Press, 1991.

Marshall, James. *Santa Fe: The Railroad That Built an Empire*. New York: Random House, 1945.

Monaghan, Jay. *The Civil War on the Western Border, 1954–1865*. Boston: Little, Brown, 1955.

Neill, Edward D. *History of Rice County*. Minneapolis: Minnesota Historical Co., 1882.

Patterson, Richard M. *The Train Robbery Era*. Boulder, Colo.: Pruett, 1991.

———. *Train Robbery: The Birth, Flowering and Decline of a Notorious Western Enterprise*. Boulder, Colo.: Johnson Books, 1981.

Paxton, W. M. *Annals of Platte County, Missouri*. Kansas City, Mo.: Hudson-Kimberley, 1897 (8th reprint, Platte County Historical Society, 1990).

Petrone, Gerard S. *Judgment at Gallatin*. Lubbock: Texas Tech University Press, 1998.

Pilkington, William T., and Don Graham, eds. *Western Movies*. Albuquerque: University of New Mexico Press, 1979.

Richardson, Albert D. *Some Portions of His Narrative concerning Kansas*. Coffeyville, Kan.: Zauberberg Press, 1958.

Richmond, Robert W. *Kansas, a Land of Contrasts*. St. Charles, Mo.: Forum Press, 1974.

Rosa, Joseph G. *The Age of the Gunfighter*. New York: Smithmark Publishers, 1993.

———. *The Gunfighters, Man or Myth*. Norman: University of Oklahoma Press, 1969.

Schraeder, Del. *Jesse James Was One of His Names*. Arcadia, Calif.: Santa Anita Press, 1975.

Schultz, Duane. *Quantrill's War*. New York: St. Martin's Press, 1996.

Settle, William A. *Jesse James Was His Name*. Columbia: University of Missouri Press, 1966.

Shackleford, William Yancey. *Gun-Fighters of the Old West*. Girard, Kan.: Haldeman-Julius Publications, 1943.

Shirley, Glenn. *Belle Starr and Her Times*. Norman: University of Oklahoma Press, 1982.

———. *West of Hell's Fringe*. Norman: University of Oklahoma Press, 1990.

Smith, Robert Barr. *Daltons! The Raid On Coffeyville, Kansas.* Norman: University of Oklahoma Press, 1996.

Starr, Stephen Z. *Jennison's Jayhawkers: A Civil War Cavalry Regiment and Its Commander.* Baton Rouge: Louisiana State University Press, 1973.

Steele, Phillip W. *Jesse and Frank James: The Family History.* Gretna, La.: Pelican, 1987.

Swanberg, L. E. *Then and Now: A History of Rice County, Faribault, and Communities.* Minneapolis: Rice County Bi-Centennial Commission, 1976.

Time-Life. *The Gunfighters.* New York: Time-Life Books, 1974.

Trenarry, Walter. *Murder in Minnesota.* St. Paul: Minnesota Historical Society, 1962.

Triplett, Frank. *The Life, Times and Treacherous Death of Jesse James.* Chicago: Swallow Press, 1970.

Vaughn, Columbus, and Frank Snow. *This Was Frank James.* Philadelphia: Dorrance & Co., 1969.

Wellman, Paul I. *A Dynasty of Western Outlaws.* Lincoln: University of Nebraska Press, 1986.

Williams, R. H. *With the Border Ruffians.* Lincoln: University of Nebraska Press, 1982.

Younger, Cole. *The Story of Cole Younger, by Himself.* Houston: Frontier Press, 1955.

Zornow, William Frank. *Kansas, a History of the Jayhawk State.* Norman: University of Oklahoma Press, 1957.

PERIODICALS AND PAMPHLETS

Bidlack, Russell E. "Erastus D. Ladd's Description of the Lawrence Massacre." *Kansas Historical Quarterly* 29, no. 166 (1963):

Brant, Marley. "Jesse James Defender John Newman Edwards." *Wild West* (December 1998):

Breihan, Carl W. "The Northfield Raid." *The West* (November 1966):

Conway, Alan. "The Sacking of Lawrence." *Kansas Historical Quarterly* 24, no. 144 (1958):

Croy, Homer. "Last of the Great Outlaws." *Saga* (September 1956):

Giffen, Guy, "Charlie Pitts—R.I.P." *True West* (April 1963):

Haws, Harry B. "Frank and Jesse James in Review for the Missouri Society. Washington, D.C., 1930.

Holz, William V., "Bankrobbers, Burkers and Bodysnatchers." *Michigan Quarterly Review* (Spring 1967): 97.

Howard, William F. "George Benson Fox's Letter to His Father." *Military History* (December 1998):

Johannsen, "A Footnote to the Pottawatomie Massacre, 1856." *Kansas Historical Quarterly* 22, no. 236 (1956):

Knowles, Edward. "The Lost Love of Jim Younger." *Old West* (Spring 1967):

MacBeth, Rex. "The Minnesota Magnificent Seven." Pamphlet, Madelia, Minn., 1998.

McKinney, Francis. "The Northfield Raid and Its Ann Arbor Sequel." *Michigan Alumnus Quarterly Review* 61, no. 38 (Autumn 1954):

Northfield Magazine 6, no. 2 (1992):

"The Northfield Bank Raid." Northfield *News*, n.d.

"The Northfield Raid." Northfield *News*, 1933.

Russell, Don. "Jesse James, Postwar Bandit." *Chicago Westerners Brand Book*. Chicago: Chicago Westerners, 1944.

Smith, Nathan, ed. "Letters of a Free-State Man in Kansas, 1856." *Kansas Historical Quarterly* 21, no. 166 (1954):

Watonwan County Historical Society. *Captured at Madelia*. Watonwan County Historical Society, Madelia, Minn., 1976.

MANUSCRIPTS

Armstrong, Charles. "Recollections of a nine-year-old boy concerning events following the Northfield Bank Robbery." N.d. Minnesota Historical Society.

Bunker, A. E. "Recollections of the Northfield Raid." Minnesota Historical Society.

Edwards, John Newman. "A Terrible Quintette" (ca. 1874). University of Missouri Western Historical Manuscript Collection.

Folwell, William Watts. "Northfield Robbery" (1921). Notes and enclosures for Folwell's 4-volume history of Minnesota. Minnesota Historical Society.

Hoffman, Harry. "The Fog around the Rumors Cleared Away." University of Missouri Western Historical Manuscript Collection

———. "Statement of Cole Younger." University of Missouri Western Historical Manuscript Collection.

———. Untitled manuscript concerning the James-Younger gang, 7 September 1959, with attachments. University of Missouri Western Historical Manuscript Collection.

———. "The Younger Boys' Last Stand" (1936). University of Missouri Western Historical Manuscript Collection.

Pye, William F. "The Northfield Robbery." Fall 1947. Rice County Historical Society, Faribault, Minn.

Stevens, Walter B. "Notes on the Jameses and Youngers" (ca. 1924). University of Missouri Western Historical Manuscript Collection.

Thomforde, Bertha. "An Incident in the Career of the James Brothers." Minnesota Historical Society.

Younger, Cole, Account of the Raid. Written in Stillwater Prison, 1887. Folwell Collection, Minnesota Historical Society.

NEWSPAPERS

Rice County Journal
New York *American*
Northfield News
St. *Paul Pioneer Press*
St. Paul *Globe*
Northfield *Independent*
Independence *Examiner*
Mankato *Free Press*

LETTERS

First National Bank of Northfield to Folwell, June 1921. Minnesota Historical Society.

William Folwell to W. C. Bronaugh, 1 July 1921. Minnesota Historical Society.

B. J. George to Homer Croy, 4 July 1955. University of Missouri Historical Manuscript Collection.

B. J. George to Homer Croy, 13 January 1956. University of Missouri Historical Manuscript Collection.

B. J. George to Homer Croy, 30 November 1948. University of Missouri Historical Manuscript Collection.

Todd George to Homer Croy, 31 October 1956. University of Missouri Historical Manuscript Collection.

Eunice E. Hall to "Editor Minn. Histories," 31 October 1954. Minnesota Historical Society.

A. W. Heath, Faribault, to "cousin Wm.," 29 September 1876. Minnesota Historical Society.

Harry Hoffman to B. J. George, n.d. University of Missouri Historical Manuscript Collection.

Harry Hoffman to Homer Croy, 26 August 1955. University of Missouri Historical Manuscript Collection.

Harry Hoffman to Homer Croy, n.d. University of Missouri Western Historical Manuscript Collection.
Hubert "Gun Boat" Kittle to Warden, Stillwater Prison, November 1918. Minnesota Historical Society.
To J. A. Lawrence, Northfield, 18 June 1924. Minnesota Historical Society.
Lillie LeVesconte to Jacob Hodenfield, 19 February 1945. Minnesota Historical Society.
Alix Miller to Governor Van Sant, 8 January 1902. Minnesota Historical Society.
Oscar Sorbel to Carl Weicht, 19 August 1929. Minnesota Historical Society.
Warden, Stillwater Prison, to I. H. Marmon, 14 February 1930. Minnesota Historical Society.

OTHER SOURCES

Glispin, James. Expense statement. Minnesota Historical Society.
Indian-Pioneer Papers, Western History Collection, University of Oklahoma. Interviews with:
    Travis Carrol Ely
    W. B. Morrison
    Judge Michael O. Ghormley
    Ethel B. Tackitt
    Fannie Blythe Marks
    William Boas McAlpin
    Carrie Marshall Pitman
    Mike German
    Will R. Robison
    Jennie Lamar
MacBeth, Rex. "The Minnesota Magnificent Seven," *Commemorative Booklet*, Madelia, Minn., 1998.

INDEX